Global Feminism

Global Feminism

*Transnational Women's Activism,
Organizing, and Human Rights*

EDITED BY

Myra Marx Ferree and Aili Mari Tripp

New York University Press

NEW YORK AND LONDON

2006

NEW YORK UNIVERSITY PRESS
New York and London

Library of Congress Cataloging-in-Publication Data
Global feminism : transnational women's activism, organizing, and
human rights / edited by Myra Marx Ferree and Aili Mari Tripp.
p. cm.
Includes bibliographical references and index.
ISBN–13: 978–0–8147–2735–5 (cloth)
ISBN–10: 0–8147–2735–2 (cloth)
ISBN–13: 978–0–8147–2736–2 (pbk.)
ISBN–10: 0–8147–2736–0 (pbk.)
1. Feminism. 2. Feminism—International cooperation.
3. Transnationalism. I. Ferree, Myra Marx. II. Tripp, Aili Mari.
HQ1111.G56   2006
305.42—dc22   2006004307

Manufactured in the United States of America

c 10 9 8 7 6 5 4 3 2 1
p 10 9 8 7 6 5 4 3 2 1

Contents

Preface

Myra Marx Ferree and Aili Mari Tripp

Feminism in the twenty-first century has unmistakably global dimensions but is also ever less obviously one, single movement. Diversity and differences, not only by race and class but also in national culture and policy, shape the interests that women define as their own. The demands that feminists raise are increasingly being articulated in transnational forums and with the support of international organizations.

In this book we define "feminism" as the broad goal of challenging and changing gender relations that subordinate women to men and that thereby also differentially advantage some women and men relative to others. We assume that there are many different strategies and practices that are consistent with this goal. We do not assume that feminism can be or ever should be the only or primary goal of feminists, but instead gather under this banner all who include a commitment to more equal and fair gender relations as one of their goals. We know that the historic connotations of the term "feminism" in specific locales may make some people who are struggling to change women's subordination unwilling to use this label, but we also believe that, whether or not individuals or groups choose to call themselves feminists, their goal of empowering women should be considered feminist.

We also recognize that women (and some men) practice feminism in a variety of institutional contexts, from grassroots social movements to international organizations, both governmental and nongovernmental, and with a variety of specific strategies. Transnational contexts are increasingly important venues for feminist work. The transnational arena is the intersection of the international and the local. Transnational activism brings feminists out of their local contexts to work across national borders, and feminist discourses, such as the definition of women's rights as human rights, travel from the international level where they were first formulated to offer new leverage to local activists. International organizations institutionalize new political mechanisms and provide new material resources for confronting gender inequality on a global basis.

The transnational arena is thus obviously a place of great opportunity for feminists. Since the United Nations World Conference on Women in Beijing (and its associated NGO Forum) in 1995, there has been a tremendous expansion not only of feminist activities at the transnational level but also in awareness of the significance of transnational resources and networks for feminism. Building on organizational frameworks that in some cases date back to the previous century, and drawing on an understanding of human rights as transcending the boundaries of nation-states, feminists have campaigned with increasing success for recognition of women's full personhood. Feminism today, with all its local variation, is best understood to be a truly global phenomenon: a product of transnational dialogues and disagreements, coalitions and networks. In spite of the common perception that feminism originated in the West and diffused to the rest of the world, the contributors show how the influences have historically been multidirectional and a product of transnational mutual learning and sharing.

In this book we gather together a number of case studies that explore the opportunities and obstacles that the transnational arena presents for feminist activism. We think of the webs of organizations, treaties, and discourses that circle the globe as an opportunity structure, and we use specific cases to illustrate what is being done within the constraints and with the possibilities that such a transnational opportunity structure provides. We divide these cases into two broad types: those that consider national, regional, or local uses of the transnational opportunity structure for feminism and those that examine the construction or operation of the transnational opportunity structure itself. Feminism is a product not only of transnational influences of ideas and norms; it also has taken root in local contexts and emerged as a consequence of varying and independent local objectives, dynamics, and trajectories.

This book owes its existence, as all books do, to a network of supporters who have contributed in many ways to making it possible. The Havens Center for the Study of Social Change at the University of Wisconsin–Madison provided initial funding for an interdisciplinary seminar on transnational women's movements that we taught together in spring 2002.

Most of the papers in this volume originate with this seminar, which provided us with the opportunity to focus closely on a rather specific subject with the wealth of perspectives from around the world. Through the Transnational Feminism Research Circle, the University of Wisconsin's International Institute and Women's Studies Research Center have also helped to financially and intellectually support the wider project of studying gender, state, and society of which this book is a part. The European Union itself has underwritten the university's EU Center as part of a network of European Union Centers of Excellence. The UW European Union Center has played an important role in supporting the study of transnational gender politics and brought to campus some of the speakers for the seminar whose work is included here. The university's support for our participation in the 2002 Women's Worlds conference in Kampala, Uganda, also provided us with a forum for reflecting on and learning about these themes.

We especially thank the authors of the chapters included here for going well beyond their initial commitments, writing original and thoughtful papers that incorporate many issues raised in discussion, and rewriting their chapters extensively with reference to other draft chapters. They have been outstandingly patient as we tried to bring all the contributions together. We appreciate the difficulties of writing in a language that is not one's native tongue, of producing an academic paper when one is more engaged in activism than scholarship, of taking scholarly work and presenting it in terms that a student or activist can also understand. Overcoming these and many other challenges, personal and professional, is a great accomplishment, and we are grateful for the commitment and effort that our authors were willing to give to this project.

Last but not least, we thank our patient editor, Ilene Kalish, for the faith in this project she showed from the start. Her questions have ever been constructive and her suggestions valuable. Her high expectations for the book have been a spur to our sometimes flagging energies. Wendy Christensen and Hae Yeon Choo have been vital helpers in the last stages of finalizing the manuscripts and getting this book out the door. For all the support we have received of these many kinds, we will always be grateful.

Part I

Recognizing Transnational Feminism

Globalization and Feminism
Opportunities and Obstacles for Activism in the Global Arena

Myra Marx Ferree

Globalization is the word of the decade. In newspapers as well as scientific journals, globalization is invoked in relation to everything from moviemaking to unemployment. Much of this discussion implies that globalization is a wholly new phenomenon, that this is only a top-down phenomenon that is happening to people rather than also a grassroots process in which individuals and groups are actively engaged, and that there is nothing particularly gendered about it. This book arises from our conviction that none of these three assumptions are true.

A variety of sociological statistics at the macro level suggest the extent of global integration of the early twenty-first century is more like that of the 1910s than of the 1950s. For example, in 1910 levels of global trade measured by imports and exports and of human interconnection in the form of immigration and transnational organizations were at levels very similar to those we experience today. Two violent world wars and a long cold war reduced these international ties to their low point in the 1950s and 1960s. It may be more accurate to see the end of the cold war as allowing the tide to turn back toward greater global interaction in 2000–2010.

To be sure, many linkages between states and across national boundaries have been created only relatively recently. The European Union is one of the most spectacular of these current experiments in reshaping the meaning of sovereignty, but the African Union (as Melinda Adams shows here) is also an important regional form of integration. These pacts follow in the footsteps of other, older links such as the World Council of

Feminism and Women's Movements:
A Difference That Makes a Difference

Although some scholars use the terms "feminism" and "women's movement" interchangeably, this usage creates certain problems. In some contexts, it makes it seem doubtful that men can be feminists, since how can they be members of a "woman's movement"? In other contexts it can seem problematic to apply the label "feminist" to activist women, whether because they refuse to use this term for themselves or because the women's movement in which they are engaged has other goals, even ones in opposition to any change toward greater gender equality. When women mobilize, as they do, to pursue a wide variety of interests, are all such "women's movements" automatically to be considered feminist?

To make clearer just what kinds of activism are feminist, it is helpful to separate this concept from that of a women's movement. Organizing women explicitly as women to make social change is what makes a "women's movement." It is defined as such because of the *constituency* being organized, not the specific targets of the activists' change efforts at any particular time. The movement, as an organizational strategy, addresses its constituents as women, mothers, sisters, daughters. By using the language of gender, it constructs women as a distinctive interest group, even when it may define the interests that this group shares as diverse and not necessarily centered on gender. Naming "women" as a constituency to be mobilized and building a strategy, organization, and politics around issues defined as being particularly "women's" concerns are the two factors that make a women's movement, not a statistical head count of the gender of the membership, though typically women are the activists in such movements. This definition of "women's movement" explicitly recognizes that many mobilizations of women as women start out with a non-gender-directed goal, such as peace, antiracism, or social justice, and only later develop an interest in changing gender relations.

Activism for the purpose of challenging and changing women's subordination to men is what defines "feminism." Feminism is a *goal*, a target for social change, a purpose informing activism, not a constituency or a strategy. Feminist mobilizations are informed by feminist theory, beliefs, and practices, but they may take place in a variety of organizational contexts, from women's movements to positions within governments. Feminism as a goal often informs all or part of the agenda of mixed-gender organizations such as socialist, pacifist, and democratization movements.

Globalization and Feminism
Opportunities and Obstacles for Activism in the Global Arena

Myra Marx Ferree

Globalization is the word of the decade. In newspapers as well as scientific journals, globalization is invoked in relation to everything from moviemaking to unemployment. Much of this discussion implies that globalization is a wholly new phenomenon, that this is only a top-down phenomenon that is happening to people rather than also a grassroots process in which individuals and groups are actively engaged, and that there is nothing particularly gendered about it. This book arises from our conviction that none of these three assumptions are true.

A variety of sociological statistics at the macro level suggest the extent of global integration of the early twenty-first century is more like that of the 1910s than of the 1950s. For example, in 1910 levels of global trade measured by imports and exports and of human interconnection in the form of immigration and transnational organizations were at levels very similar to those we experience today. Two violent world wars and a long cold war reduced these international ties to their low point in the 1950s and 1960s. It may be more accurate to see the end of the cold war as allowing the tide to turn back toward greater global interaction in 2000–2010.

To be sure, many linkages between states and across national boundaries have been created only relatively recently. The European Union is one of the most spectacular of these current experiments in reshaping the meaning of sovereignty, but the African Union (as Melinda Adams shows here) is also an important regional form of integration. These pacts follow in the footsteps of other, older links such as the World Council of

Churches and the United Nations that continue to be important. Such continuing global associations should be understood in the context of other, now-obsolete efforts to integrate political and economic life across national borders, be it the Warsaw Pact or the British colonial system. The commitments, perspectives, and processes that connect the globe today are different in interesting ways from what has gone before, but they are not unprecedented in their scope or consequences, including their facilitation of feminist organization. Comparing 2005 to 1955 and 1905 suggests that feminist mobilization has always been increased by greater globalization.

One way in which global integration today does differ from that of the past is the extent to which it involves ordinary citizens and social movements, not merely governments and elites. Despite the typical assumption that globalization is a massive force bearing down on helpless populations, to look at the actual process is to see a great variety of social actors—including many who are not educational or political elites—engaging in diverse types of integrative work. Social movements of many kinds are finding a voice, alongside more privileged actors such as states and corporations. Certainly there are structures and processes at work here that are far larger than any one individual, group, or even state can control, but this has always been characteristic of the world since the age of global navigation and the emergence of industrialization. What is more striking in the present moment is the intersection of the global with the local, and the expansion of popular, decentralized, and democratic forms of interpreting and responding to the top-down challenges posed by a world economy.

Moreover, rather than a hierarchical colonial world system or the dueling blocs of the cold war, the reconfiguration of the world order is arising today from multiple locations and pulling in diverse directions. Because "the West" is no longer held together by its anticommunist mobilization, Europe and the United States are discovering new tensions and differences in their relationship. The "third world" is no longer merely defined by its history of colonization but by its own diversity, regionally, economically, and politically. Democratic India and authoritarian Pakistan, prosperous Singapore and economically ravaged Zimbabwe all came into the twentieth century as part of the British Empire, but they enter the twenty-first century with very different concerns. World bodies such as the UN are faced with new conflicts that include citizens challenging their national governments for democratic participation, ethnic conflicts within states, and gender conflicts fed by religious fundamentalisms, as well as the more familiar tensions among national and class interests. Globalization is today as much about the multiplicity of centers of power as it is about increases in their interrelationship.

From these diverse local centers, a variety of nongovernmental groups are engaging in the complex process of political renegotiation that hides under the label of globalization. Social movements like Attac, an international mobilization for democratic control of financial markets and their institutions that was founded in France in 1998, raise questions about the justice of international debt management and call for a "Tobin tax" (a fee placed on economic transactions to help defray the costs of development). Such groups are listened to by governments from Iceland to South Africa, although they are less well known in the United States. The World Social Forum connects social justice activists globally, allowing for a sharing of tactics and resources. Democracy movements in Ukraine, China, and Syria have used both mass media and Internet connectivity to draw popular support from abroad in struggles with their own governments. Globalization is also a form of political mobilization, and this grassroots involvement is also growing in scope and significance in many parts of the world.

Among the social actors most mobilized in the context of global opportunity structures are women's movements worldwide. We emphasize that women's global mobilization is neither something wholly new and unprecedented nor unconnected to the variety of local and regional conflicts that are part of the process of reshaping the world system. Gender is very much a part of the structure of the social order globally. Gender is therefore also part of what is being remade in the current reconfiguration of power relations. As with other aspects of this global reorganization, this restructuring involves women and men in a variety of local and transnational settings. Some of these women's movements are feminist, but others are not.

This book looks at this diverse and contested process called globalization from the vantage point of feminism and women's movements. This chapter has three specific goals and sections. First, I offer a conceptual definition of both feminism and women's movements, and an argument about why it is important to distinguish between them. Second, I discuss the transnational opportunity structure that affects how even local feminists act, and I raise some questions about what its most promising and most dangerous features may be. Third, I present an overview of the chapters that follow and discuss why they offer important and complementary insights into how the process of globalization matters for feminism.

Feminism and Women's Movements:
A Difference That Makes a Difference

Although some scholars use the terms "feminism" and "women's movement" interchangeably, this usage creates certain problems. In some contexts, it makes it seem doubtful that men can be feminists, since how can they be members of a "woman's movement"? In other contexts it can seem problematic to apply the label "feminist" to activist women, whether because they refuse to use this term for themselves or because the women's movement in which they are engaged has other goals, even ones in opposition to any change toward greater gender equality. When women mobilize, as they do, to pursue a wide variety of interests, are all such "women's movements" automatically to be considered feminist?

To make clearer just what kinds of activism are feminist, it is helpful to separate this concept from that of a women's movement. Organizing women explicitly as women to make social change is what makes a "women's movement." It is defined as such because of the *constituency* being organized, not the specific targets of the activists' change efforts at any particular time. The movement, as an organizational strategy, addresses its constituents as women, mothers, sisters, daughters. By using the language of gender, it constructs women as a distinctive interest group, even when it may define the interests that this group shares as diverse and not necessarily centered on gender. Naming "women" as a constituency to be mobilized and building a strategy, organization, and politics around issues defined as being particularly "women's" concerns are the two factors that make a women's movement, not a statistical head count of the gender of the membership, though typically women are the activists in such movements. This definition of "women's movement" explicitly recognizes that many mobilizations of women as women start out with a non-gender-directed goal, such as peace, antiracism, or social justice, and only later develop an interest in changing gender relations.

Activism for the purpose of challenging and changing women's subordination to men is what defines "feminism." Feminism is a *goal*, a target for social change, a purpose informing activism, not a constituency or a strategy. Feminist mobilizations are informed by feminist theory, beliefs, and practices, but they may take place in a variety of organizational contexts, from women's movements to positions within governments. Feminism as a goal often informs all or part of the agenda of mixed-gender organizations such as socialist, pacifist, and democratization movements.

Because feminism challenges all of gender relations, it also addresses those norms and processes of gender construction and oppression that differentially advantage some women and men relative to others, such as devaluing "sissy" men or the women who do care work for others. There is no claim being made that one or another particular aspect of gender relations, be it paid work or sexuality, motherhood or militarization, is the best, most "radical," or most authentic feminism. Feminism as a goal can be adopted by individuals of any gender, as well as by groups with any degree of institutionalization, from informal, face-to-face, temporary associations to a legally constituted national or transnational governing body.

Feminist activists and activism typically are embedded in organizations and institutions with multiple goals. To have a feminist goal is in no way inconsistent with having other political and social goals as well. The question of where feminism stands on the list of priorities of any individual or group is an empirical one. It is not true by definition that a person or group that calls itself feminist necessarily puts this particular goal in first place, since in practice it could be discovered to be displaced by other values (such as achieving or redistributing power or wealth, defending racial privilege, or fighting racial discrimination). Nor is it true by definition that a person or group that does not call itself feminist does not have feminist goals, since the identity can carry other connotations in a local setting (whether of radicalism or exclusivity or cultural difference) that an activist may seek to avoid by choosing another label.

These two definitions together generate a dynamic picture of both feminism and women's movements. On the one hand, women's movements are mobilizations understood to be in a process of flux in which feminism may be becoming more or less of a priority issue for them. Regardless of their goals, mobilizations that use gender to mobilize women are likely to bring their constituents into more explicitly political activities, empower women to challenge limitations on their roles and lives, and create networks among women that enhance their ability to recognize existing gender relations as oppressive and in need of change. Thus the question of when and how women's movements contribute to increases in feminism is a meaningful one.

On the other hand, feminism circulates within and among movements, takes more or less priority among their goals, and may generate new social movements, including women's movements. Successful feminist mobilization creates more places and spaces for feminism to accomplish its aims, within movements and within institutional power structures. Thus, for example, feminism can percolate into organized medicine, where activists may then construct women's movement associations of doctors, nurses, or patients, develop new tools to recognize and treat illnesses that affect women and men differently, and make institutions deliver services more appropriately to women in their communities. Feminist mobilizations often intersect with other forms of transformative struggles. Activists originally inspired by feminism may expand their goals to challenge racism, colonialism, and other oppressions, and activists with other primary agendas may be persuaded to adopt feminism as one of their objectives, especially as feminist activists show them how mutually supportive all these goals may be. Thus, it is also a meaningful question to ask how feminism contributes to creating and expanding social movements, including women's movements.

As a consequence of both these processes, feminism and women's movements dynamically affect each other. In this set of changing relations, to restrict analysis to only those temporary phases in which women's movements have chosen to focus exclusively on challenging gender subordination or seeking equality with men of their own group marginalizes the ongoing intersectional elements of both. Distinguishing between feminism and women's movements, and then relating them empirically, moves the multiplicity of constituencies and dynamic changes in goals among activists "from margin to center" among the questions for analysis. When and why do women's movements embrace feminist goals—and when not? When and why do feminists choose to work in women's movements rather than in mixed-gendered ones or policymaking institutions—and when not? When and why do democratization, peace, or economic justice movements make feminism part of their agenda—and when not? These are important questions that can only be asked, let alone answered, if there is a clear definitional distinction between feminism and women's movements. The scope of feminist theory and its overall social critique is also obscured if the difference between feminism and women's movements is not made explicit. For some feminists, feminism means simultaneously combating other forms of political and social subordination, since for many women, embracing the goal of equality with the men of their class, race, or nation would mean accepting a still-oppressed status. For some feminists, feminism means recognizing ways in which male-dominated institutions have promoted values fundamentally destructive for all people, such as militarism, environmental exploitation, or competitive global capitalism, and associating the alternative values and social relations with women and women-led groups. To define feminism in a way that limits its applicability only to those mobilizations that *exclusively* focus on challenging women's subordination to men would exclude both these types of feminism.

When analysts do this, they discover that the groups that are left to study are typically mobilizations of relatively privileged women who are seeking access to the opportunities provided by social, political, and economic institutions to men of their nationality, class, race, ethnicity, and religion.[1] The middle-class, white, Western bias observed in studies of "feminism" is at least in part a result of such an inappropriately narrow and static definition of the object of study ("feminism"). Defining feminism should not be confounded with other criteria such as the preferred constituency addressed (women or both genders), the organizational form preferred (social movement, community group, state or transnational authority), the strategy pursued (working inside or outside institutions, more or less collectively, with transgressive or demonstrative protest activities or not), or the priority feminism takes in relation to other goals (antiracism, environmentalism, pacifism, neoliberalism, etc.). Feminists do many different things in real political contexts in order to accomplish their goals, and working in and through women's movements can be very important strategically. But especially when trying to see just how feminism as a goal is being advanced in and through a variety of transnational strategies, it becomes self-defeating to presuppose that only women's movements can be the carriers of feminism.

Moreover, by stressing how feminism as a goal is characteristically combined with other goals and making its relative priority a question open to empirical examination, this approach more readily looks at the influence of the transnational opportunity structure upon both feminism and women's movements. "Political opportunity structure" (POS) is the preferred term among scholars interested in the positive opportunities and the obstacles provided by a specific political and social structure. Globalization is made concretely meaningful by seeing it as a process that increases the importance and level of integration of transnational political structures. At this transnational level, the POS can vary substantially from that provided at the local level alone. Thus Zapatista rebels reach out through the Internet for support from people and groups spread around the world to counter the repressive power exercised locally by the Mexican government.

The transnational opportunity structure is a political context that seems open to feminism, particularly as it takes up the discourses of human rights and development, as Pietilä argues in her chapter. What other goals are combined with feminism in which local contexts, and how does that help or hinder these ideas to travel transnationally? For example, if feminism is connected to the defense of class privilege, and upper-middle-class women's ability to enter the paid labor market is given priority over migrant women's ability to earn a living wage by their domestic work, then feminism is not going to be an appealing identity for those who do not already enjoy economic advantages.

The *intersectionality* of social movements characterizes them and shapes how they position themselves in the transnational arena in which they operate. Intersectionality means that privilege and oppression, and movements to defend and combat these relations, are not in fact singular. No one has a gender but not a race, a nationality but not a gender, an education but not an age. The location of people and groups within relations of production, reproduction, and representation (relations that are organized worldwide in terms of gender inequality) is inherently multiple. These multiple social locations are often—not, as is often assumed, atypically—contradictory. Organizations as well as individuals hold multiple positions in regard to social relations of power and injustice, and typically enjoy privilege on some dimensions even while they struggle with oppression on another. This multiplicity and the contradictions to which it gives rise are rarely acknowledged theoretically. As Ferree and Roth (1998) argue, scholars of social movements have instead tended to construct ideal-typical movements, envisioning these as composed of ideal-typical constituents: thus "worker's" movements are imagined as organizations of and for white men, "nationalist" movements as of and for indigenous men, "feminist" movements as of and for white, middle-class women.[2] The reality is of course, much more complex, but it only emerges clearly when the goals and constituents of movements are acknowledged as distinct.

In sum, this book approaches feminism as one important goal of social change. It asks the question of how feminism is being related to women's movements and other organizational strategies that are being pursued locally and in transnational spaces, as well as to the various other goals that specific women and men have when they engage in social and political activities. And it looks especially at globalization as a process that is potentially empowering as well as disempowering women as they look for effective strategies to make feminist social change, including sometimes building women's movements.

Transnational Opportunity Structures: Looking for Levers to Move the World

Women's movements are far from the only tools that feminists have taken up to try to challenge and change male domination. Globalization in the sense of integration means speedy flows of ideas across great distances. This has contributed to the sharing of strategies that also reach beyond classic women's movements, protest demonstrations, and projects. Three groups of strategies for making feminist change have spread like wildfire through the world system: developing a "women's policy machinery" within state institutions, building an issue advocacy network outside of formal institutions, and developing women's movement practices that are knowledge-creating, many of which link policy machineries with advocacy networks to multiply political effectiveness. None of these is without its problematic aspects in the transnational system.

First, women's policy machinery has now been put in place in most countries of the world, nearly all of which has come into existence since the first UN Conference on Women in Mexico City in 1975. Such policy machinery includes specific national, local, or regional administrative structures that are targeted to women as a politically relevant group. Women's policy machinery includes ministries of women's affairs, agencies charged with "mainstreaming" gender perspectives into policy and/or bringing women into administrative positions, and programs designed to ensure that women receive a certain share of seats in elected and/or appointed bodies, from parliaments to corporate boards of directors. Women's policy machinery, unlike a women's movement, is formally embedded in state or transnational structures that have institutionalized authority. Policy machineries differ widely in their form and effectiveness, from the old but weak and bureaucratically low-level Women's Bureau in the U.S. Department of Labor to the Ministry for Women's Affairs in France.[3]

Women's policy machinery is a mechanism by which gender inequality can be addressed, but it offers no guarantee that this is how it will be used. The competing goals of those who occupy the positions that this machinery creates as well as the different interests of those to whom they are accountable—typically authorities above them as well as constituents below—make for a mixed picture of what the machinery could produce. The term "policy machinery" itself is one that arose within administrative elites and diffused among activists, but it is not a bad image to use in considering the consequences of these structural innovations. Rather than achieving feminist goals by the very fact of their existence, they are tools, like levers, that require active use—there needs to be pressure put on the lever for it to budge anything within the system of male power. Paradoxically, sometimes the creation of women's policy machinery seems to be mistaken for an end in itself or a substitution for active mobilization to exert pressure for change, and thus in practice can lead to demobilization by the women's movements that helped to create them. Chapters in this book focus attention on the emergence and use of women's policy machinery in the UN (Snyder) and in the nation-states of Europe (McBride and Mazur) and of Africa (Adams).

Second, globalization has facilitated the emergence of feminism as a goal in a wide variety of issue advocacy networks active at the transnational level. Overtly feminist discourse is heard in a variety of nongovernmental organizations that operate across national borders, working on a huge variety of issues from HIV/AIDS to literacy to economic restructuring, and in contexts as different as the World Bank and the World Social Forum. Gender equity as a principle has been taken up in networks concerned with health, peace, and social justice, as well as in networks organized directly to deal with issues seen as especially affecting women, such as trafficking in human beings, prostitution and other forms of sex work, and the use of genetic and reproductive technologies.

Many of these issues cut across national boundaries, and the networks constructed to deal with them are not organized as much on the basis of nationality as was true of their predecessors in the early twentieth century. A typical organization of a hundred years ago was "inter-national" in the sense of multiple national organizations belonging to a coordinating umbrella organization to which each national member group sent representatives. By contrast, in a world today characterized by Internet linkages, cheap airfares, and widespread telephone service, more fluid networks made up of individuals and organizations from many parts of the world actually interacting with each other more routinely can supplement or even supplant the conventional, hierarchical styles of international nongovernmental organizing. NGOs are ever more diverse in their form and can be transnational in membership (individuals and groups not representing nations but belonging regardless of nationality).

NGOs are also linked in wider transnational networks around certain issues and values, as Keck and Sikkink (1998) pointed out, and coordinate the pressure the groups bring on national governments, as Swider shows here in the case of migrant and labor groups in Hong Kong and Bagić shows with regard to NGOs operating in the former Yugoslavia. Such networks are thus becoming potentially powerful transnational actors in their own right. Rather than one unitary principle of feminism being the basis for networking, as the International Council of Women adopted at the beginning of the last century, the actual political work of such NGOs and networks is differentiated and issue-specific. The flexibility and issue focus of networks on specific problems, from the access of women to scientific professions to the work conditions of migrant domestic workers or female genital cutting, makes them politically able to span a wider range of activist groups. Paradoxically, while feminism has entered a great many of these networks, the very variety of their goals fragments feminist attention and makes women's movements as such seem exclusionary, overly broad, and less attractive forms of mobilization. Networks instead tend to combine paid professionals and unpaid local activists, men and women, inside and outside of government, and in many countries.

Global terrorism and "national security" are also increasingly recognized as being intertwined and gendered issues. This feminist concern can take the form of considering how religious fundamentalism, control over women's bodies, national identity, and male pride and privilege are being negotiated and renegotiated in diverse transnational as well as national settings. Both fundamentalists (Christian, Islamic, Jewish, and Hindu) and those who challenge them are linked in networks that may include state as well as nonstate actors. Among the interesting questions that this increasingly global conflict raises is how and when feminist principles become co-opted in the national interests of either liberal modernist states or religious fundamentalism.

In the cold war era, the communist states co-opted the idea of women's liberation as an accomplishment of state socialism, which allowed the communist countries to divert attention from the ways in which women in fact were far from liberated under their regimes, on the one hand, and on the other hand placed Western countries in the position of resisting feminism as godless, antifamily, and a threat to (Western) civilization.

Interestingly enough, in the current global "war on terror" rhetoric it is the Western democracies that attempt to co-opt feminism as one of their greatest accomplishments. The oppression of women is framed as religious, family-based, and a threat to (Western) civilization, which is now defined as the champion of secular modernity and the value of equal rights for all. Diverting attention from the way that women continue to be far from liberated in Western capitalist democracies is one discursive accomplishment of this strategy, and if it succeeds, it could be a demobilizing factor for feminist women's movements.

Thus the strategic use of transnational networks has both a material side in the flow of resources and support for issues they spread globally across national borders and a discursive side in the way that issues are framed and conflicts organized on a global level. The concrete work of building and supporting networks as a way of working on feminist interests is explored in this book by looking at issue-based networks bring resources to women's movements in the former Yugoslavia (Bagić) and labor organizers in Hong Kong (Swider). The relationship of feminism to issues of religion, identity, social justice, and economic development is also examined in both Turkey (Ertürk) and Finland (Pietilä), as women's movements attempt to deal with the challenges of fundamentalism, neoliberalism, and ethnic conflict on a global scale.

The third lever with which feminists have tried to change the world is with knowledge-creation strategies. Women's movements have been prolific producers of "new words" to name old problems from sexual harassment, acquaintance rape, wife beating, the double day/shift, and the nanny chain. Women's movements have been important places for the development of transnational feminist theory and identity, creating the free spaces that foster ideological innovation and strategic inventions, like the women's policy machinery of the 1990s and the shelters for battered women of the 1980s. Creating the space to produce new feminist analyses of gender and of gender systems' effects on both women and men, the many national women's movements and the journals, magazines, and women's studies programs to which they gave rise have developed feminist theory. As McBride and Mazur indicate for Europe, and Ferree and Pudrovska show for the World Wide Web, these new ideas are now moving in a transnational space.

Conferences share this knowledge, none more spectacularly than the 1995 Beijing Fourth Women's World Conference and NGO Forum. Ideas such as "gender mainstreaming" and "gender budgeting" become developed through the active participation of feminists engaged in knowledge production work in their own countries and transnationally. These ideas then become part of the shared language and competences that women's movements and women's policy machineries in many countries adopt and use. Conferences organized on a transnational basis in and across many disciplines offer social support to women to keep them actively pursuing feminist goals in their scholarship and carrying their theory out into practice with activist groups and transnational networks. Knowledge and its creation become a sustaining aspect of the work of making feminist change, and this work especially blurs the distinctions among those in policy machinery, in movements, in social service, and in academia. Evaluation research accompanies social change projects, and feminist theory informs statistical data collection.

All over the world, women's associations fund and conduct studies, disseminate reports, encourage discussion, and train researchers and policymakers to develop greater awareness of gender inequities and greater commitment to redressing them. Lobbying, monitoring, funding demonstration projects, assessing best practices, and encouraging new networks are all activities in which feminist women's movements are increasingly engaged as they become more institutionalized as policy relevant actors in their own right.

Knowledge work links policymakers and social movements, serving as a powerful strategy for spreading feminism. But feminist ideas can spread without any accompanying feminist identity. Feminist women's movements struggle to create and sustain feminist identities that women will find meaningful for themselves, and through such identities, movements give meaning to even the losing battles that they fight. As crucibles of identity, community, and commitment for feminists, women's movements can play a critical role in sustaining activism across time (generations) and space (geography). However, feminist women's movements do not just provide the sometimes-comfortable homes where valiant feminists can return and refresh themselves but are themselves at times sites of tremendous diversity and conflict.

Thus the decline in popular mobilization in the form of autonomous feminist women's movement organizations and mass demonstrations can be partly attributed to the crucible for conflict that they can offer. Feminist identity is a highly charged and much-debated concept, and for some networks and organizations it may be more convenient and effective to simply avoid the issue. But the heat of conflict in feminist women's movements has also been accompanied by the light of developing feminist theory and the warmth of a feminist community in times of struggle. If feminism becomes so diffused in networks and policy institutions that women's movements themselves fade out as an active part of the picture, there paradoxically might emerge a time in which we have feminism without feminists. In this book, feminist identity is considered both as a transversal, linking strategy (Yuval-Davis) and as a contested and much-avoided term (Ferree and Pudrovska). The specific knowledge and frames for issues that women's movements have developed have spread, often from the "bottom up" from local movements in the global South to transnational networks and state institutions in the affluent countries of the North, raising issues of control for those still in local settings (Tripp) and highlighting the danger of not taking differences seriously into account (Yuval-Davis).

Global Feminism, Situated Activism: Perspectives on Power and Social Change

Although the present wave of globalization is different than the one that crested in the early twentieth century, some questions about the relationships among feminism, women's movements, and globalization persist. How can women's movements manage the challenges of diversity, of generational succession, and of organizational institutionalization that are posed by becoming a more fragmented field of special interest groups that share a concern with women's equal rights but differ in so many other regards? How can the inequality of resources around the world be used to create constructive flows of support? What conditions foster democratic participation transnationally and build solidarity for addressing problems not one's own? These are the types of issues that the chapters of this book address as they situate feminism in its current transnational context.

Just as this chapter offers a theoretical orientation to the issues facing feminists and women's movements globally, Margaret (Peg) Snyder offers an empirical perspective on how the UN facilitated the emergence of both feminism and women's movements worldwide. As the longtime director of the United Nations Development Fund for Women (UNIFEM), Snyder has a perspective on networking that comes from inside the policy machinery, specifically from her decades of work inside the UN. Her view of how feminist NGOs gradually changed and were changed through their transnational cooperation over issues of development highlights the important role that the UN itself played in creating the venues (from conferences to committees) where fruitful interaction could occur. Unlike McBride and Mazur, who see movements as the actors and political institutions as their targets, Snyder highlights the way the programs and priorities of the UN affected women's movements, and in some ways even could be said to have created the transnational movement that we now observe. Because the UN's structures give political voice to otherwise weak states and perspectives, the concerns of women from the global South could be brought to the attention of more privileged women and raise their consciousness. Similar to what Sarah Swider shows at a local level in Hong Kong, the structure of representation makes an enormous difference in just whose concerns are heard and how the overall agenda is set at this global level. Peg Snyder argues that the UN structures were suitable to be actively used to create empowerment opportunities for women, a clear case of co-opting and changing the UN as an institution, as well as making it a "godmother" to a variety of local feminist initiatives. Tripp then takes up this theme to spell out the ways that local women's movements seized the chances thus created. She argues that the UN forums and resources offered more than a "boomerang" to influence gender politics at the national level, instead creating a truly transnational opportunity structure. One of the key contributions of this transnational POS was in allowing local activists of the global South the opportunity to challenge and change the perspectives and priorities of the North.

The next part of the book addresses the concrete ways in which feminist challenges are met in specific movements and networks that operate on this modern transnational terrain. The purpose of these chapters collectively is to indicate how the world-traveling concept of feminism meets the needs of local women's movements—or, as is often the case, does not. As Tripp's contribution here suggests, in these chapters the transnational level is taken as an opportunity structure that allows for but does not insist on positive uses of transnational resources in local settings and creates spaces for locally based ideas to be taken up by other actors.

Yakin Ertürk has a particularly valuable perspective to offer on this question, bringing together her years at the Division for the Advancement of Women at the UN and her teaching and administrative experience in higher education in largely secular and democratic Turkey and in fundamentalist, authoritarian Saudi Arabia to consider the various meanings that transnational Islamicist mobilization can have for women. Focusing on the experiences of women in relation to the changing fortunes of the Islamicist political party in Turkey, she argues that both (un)veiling as a symbol and women's movements as a form of politics need to be seen in a historical context to understand their feminist implications. Rather than forcing them into universalist categories, Ertürk indicates the open-ended negotiations of identity conducted by women through a diversity of women's movement organizations. But she also places these in the context of a global mobilization of fundamentalist Islam that has put pressure on politicians and movements in Turkey and the equally transnational pressures arising from Turkey's desire to enter the European Union, where gender equality is treated as a test of human rights.

Sarah Swider then takes up the way that transnational support can matter for women's practical organizing by looking at the innovative multilevel association that migrant domestic workers formed in Hong Kong. Using resources drawn from transnational NGOs concerned with migrant rights and local resources that support union organizing, the Filipina majority among domestic workers and the more disadvantaged Indonesian and Thai women migrant workers built a network of associations that gave nationalities representation and offered grassroots-level support services for each ethnic/national community. Unlike the conventional labor union structure that collapsed based on differences in interests among the women, this multilevel "women's economic association" had the structural ability to accommodate minority perspectives. It mobilized the migrant domestic workers to protect themselves from state cutbacks in maternity benefits and to fight for equal pay across divisive lines of nationality, thus striking the balance between universal rights and specific needs that Nira Yuval-Davis later associates with successful transversal politics.

Aida Bagić also focuses on the question of how transnational support and national differences in a locality can aid or interfere with women's movement organizing. Looking at the support that transnational donors channeled to women's NGOs in the late 1990s, she shows how donor preferences followed media attention to what were defined as the characteristic problems of Croatia, Bosnia and Herzegovina, Macedonia, Serbia, and Montenegro. The women's NGOs in these post-Yugoslav states responded to donor preferences as well as local needs in setting their own priorities, thus developing sometimes stereotypical national profiles for organizations. Although the women's NGO scene flourished in the western Balkans, her case study provides more of a cautionary tale about the limits of feminist politics in practice than a shining example of transnational understanding and organizing.

Hilkka Pietilä takes advantage of her years of experience in women's development politics in the UN and in transnational bodies coordinating women's international agenda setting to raise some questions about the nature of these transnational agendas in an era of militarization and neoliberal economics. She uses the example of Finland as a state that was relatively rural, poor, and "underdeveloped" until a few decades ago to suggest what a constructive agenda for development would be. In her view, gender and development are strongly intertwined, and women's movements have a key role to play in directing this development toward peace and social justice. The UN, rather than the EU, provides a model in her view for how women's policy machinery and knowledge-production work can be directed in fruitful lines. Economic and social development for the nation-state becomes a process of building capabilities among the poor rather than competition among the rich. As Pietilä conceptualizes it, this sort of national development and women's rights are dual engines for women's empowerment. She argues the two women's movements in Finland complemented each other successfully because each chose one such agenda to emphasize, and suggests that women's mobilizations globally might be wise to create a similar division of labor today.

In the next part, the book moves from the organizations that pursue feminist goals to the contexts in which they now operate. Rather than looking at specific local groups that have been more or less successful on the terrain created by global connectivity, these chapters focus on where and how new political opportunities are being created and used. In different parts of the world, diverse transnational mechanisms are emerging as important.

The African Union as a source for transnational standards for gender equality is the focus of Melinda Adams's chapter. Adams focuses on the regional level, one that is often overlooked and undervalued in discussions of global integration. Her model makes clear that women's movements in Africa have built up their own NGO networking, similar to that found in Latin America, and these movements drew on transnational resources to lay a groundwork for a transnational policy machinery in the African Union. At the regional level, the African Union, the NGO feminist policy networks, and the universities and research institutes producing feminist knowledge are clearly active and effective. Autonomous, rather than state-led, women's organizations were the real motors for change in this part of the world, and their lobbying of AU politicians has produced regional-level political commitment to feminist policymaking. How well these aspirations translate into national policy or local women's lives remains to be seen, especially as local-level political policymaking can be more corrupt or conflict-ridden than the AU itself.

Dorothy McBride and Amy Mazur ask how women's movements and women's policy machineries are faring in Western Europe, where they are confronting a new transnational space created by the formation of the European Union. The notion of institutionalizing feminist policy machinery is itself novel, but while this is a strategy that is widespread in Europe (unlike the United States) today, the type and degree of institutionalization achieved varies between countries. By tracking policy outputs that can be defined as feminist, and associating them with variations in the level of mobilization of different types of groups and strategies for working in and outside of the state structure, McBride and Mazur lay a framework for understanding what makes feminist politics effective. As leading figures in the transnational feminist research group Research Network on Gender Politics and the State (RNGS), they have helped to develop the kind of feminist knowledge-producing strategy that can directly inform not only policy makers but also activists. Their view of the political opportunity structure for feminists highlights the way that policy issues and strategies for addressing them spread because of the actions of specific women's movements.

Myra Marx Ferree and Tetyana Pudrovska look at the tool that is most seen as characterizing the new phase of globalization, the Internet, to see how transnational women's organizations make use of Web pages to publicly define themselves and their agenda. As part of the global opportunity structure, the World Wide Web allows groups to connect without direct physical presence, on the one hand, or the intervention of the media and its priorities, on the other. Thus group Web pages offer a public but unmediated look at the group identities. Using Web sites from groups based in different parts of the world, Ferree and Pudrovska argue that these identities are still regionally specific as well as transnationally connected. The North-South connections that Snyder discusses as so effective at the level of organizational development and face-to-face contacts in the UN setting appear to be similarly important in the virtual world of Web-based identities. The transnational women's organizations of Europe stand somewhat aside from this North-South axis of dialogue and seem concerned with the problems and policies stemming directly from the enormous expansion of the European Union. How well they either do outreach into other parts of the world or draw global attention to the feminist political experiments done in and through the EU as a new type of transnational body remains to be seen. But it is striking, as Pietilä suggests, that the UN-sponsored agenda seems to diverge from the EU-sponsored one among nongovernmental women's groups in different parts of the world.

In the final part of the book, the chapters address the continuing problems facing activists who are attempting to work on the transnational level and begin to suggest strategies for constructively dealing with them. Nira Yuval-Davis traces the historical movement of feminism from an exclusionary version of "identity politics" that privileged the definitions of the most powerful to a "transversal" version of feminist identity that is dialogical and reflexive. Based on her work in Britain, in Israel/Palestine, and among transnational feminist groups that are mobilizing against religious fundamentalists, she highlights the potential for transversal feminist identity to contribute to building awareness and support for human rights across ethnic and political lines of conflict. She argues that both the universalism claimed by the left and the identity politics of feminists and others have hardened lines of conflict that can be softened by dialogue that crosses borders both horizontally and vertically (transversally). "Rooting" arguments in one's own experience while "shifting" to encompass the views of the other is crucial to this transversal process, but in this chapter, Yuval-Davis draws out the specific obstacles that stand in the way of achieving this. She uses the discourse around "human rights" to illustrate some of the less than ideal ways that feminist identities and goals enter into dialogue across borders.

Finally, Aili Mari Tripp's chapter concludes by reframing the themes of human rights discourse and transversal strategy that Yuval-Davis lays out theoretically as being issues of practical interrelationships among feminists in and outside of women's movements around the world. How can feminist networks really work more fairly and effectively to incorporate the voices of the most affected women? What strategies of organization and representation allow for the most democratic ways of shaping a feminist agenda inside and across transnational organizations? When are women's movements from privileged settings using too much of their financial and logistical power to shape the agenda of policymakers and women's organizations in developing countries, and when are they valuable allies in pressing for human rights and social justice? Using concrete cases of difficult—and sometimes failed—feminist efforts to cooperate, Tripp presents practical politics as an arena needing more than good intentions from participants to make effective cooperation possible. Although Tripp points to the serious problems that have arisen in specific cases, she argues that the overall trajectory has been one of greater inclusion, responsiveness, and respect for others.

In Tripp's accounting, as well as in many of the specific case studies in the previous parts, the issue of representation for the least advantaged emerges as a critical feminist issue. From a structural position of empowerment inside the UN, as Tripp, Pietilä, and Snyder all argue, the representation of voices from the global South has reoriented the entire women's movement. The presence (or absence) of organizational empowerment plays a crucial role for women in the local case studies of Swider, Bagić, and Ertürk as well, indicating that the way that the local and the transnational intersect to give women the opportunity to represent themselves politically is critical. The new frameworks of the African Union, the EU, and the Web are resources that may complement or contradict the political opportunities provided historically by the UN and its agencies for women and for development, as Adams, Pietilä, McBride and Mazur, and Ferree and Pudrovska suggest. When and how women achieve a greater degree of self-representation at the transnational as well as at regional, national, and local levels is thus the question for feminist organizing. Women's movements will surely play a role in this self-representation, but other tools are important too.

Globalization can work to women's advantage—as especially seen in the UN—but also unleash forces of inequality that will further disadvantage women. Just what feminism means and what women's movements do for women are therefore questions not merely for theory but for the practice of the next decades to determine.

Notes

1. See, for example, studies using such a mixed and static definition as Margolis 1993; Chafetz and Dworkin 1986; and the critiques in Gluck 1998 and Buechler 2000.

2. This approach also offers an alternative to Molyneux's model of women's pragmatic and strategic gender interests, and does not presume that movements, constituencies to which they strategically appeal, and the interests of these con-

stituents can be theoretically known by analysts with access to the "correct" understanding of the social structure, but instead works from the idea that interests,
constituents, and movements all need to be socially constructed. See Ferree and
Mueller 2004 for a more developed discussion of this point.

3. See the discussion of this process especially in Europe in McBride Stetson
and Mazur's *Comparative State Feminism* (1995).

Bibliography

Buechler, Steven. 2000. *Social Movements in Advanced Capitalism.* New York:
Oxford University Press.

Chafetz, Janet S., and Anthony G. Dworkin. 1986. *Female Revolt: Women's Movement in World and Historical Perspective.* Totawa, N.J.: Rowman and Allanheld.

Ferree, Myra Marx, and Silke Roth. 1998. "Kollektive Identität und Organizations-
kulturen: Theorien neuer sozialer Bewegungen aus amerikanischer Perspektive
(Collective identity and organizational culture: An American perspective on
the new social movements)." *Forschungsjournal Neue Soziale Bewegungen* 11:
80–91.

Ferree, Myra Marx, and Carol McClurg Mueller. 2004. "Feminism and the
Women's Movement: A Global Perspective." In D. A. Snow, S. A. Soule, and H.
Kriesi, eds., *The Blackwell Companion to Social Movements.* Malden, Mass.:
Blackwell.

Gluck, Sherna Berger. 1998. "Whose Feminism, Whose History." In N. A. Naples,
ed., *Community Activism and Feminist Politics: Organizing across Race, Class,
and Gender,* 31–56. New York: Routledge.

Keck, Margaret E., and Kathryn Sikkink. 1998. *Activists beyond Borders: Advocacy
Networks in International Politics.* Ithaca, N.Y.: Cornell University Press.

Margolis, Diane R. 1993. "Women's Movements around the World: Cross-Cultural
Comparisons." *Gender and Society* 7:379–399.

McBride Stetson, Dorothy, and Amy Mazur. 1995. *Comparative State Feminism.*
Thousand Oaks, Calif.: Sage.

2

Unlikely Godmother
The UN and the Global Women's Movement

Margaret Snyder

The year was 1975. Thousands of women were in Mexico City at the United Nations' first-ever women's conference—the celebration of International Women's Year. Women from throughout the world agreed on many issues, such as the need for an international convention on women that would be signed by all governments. Yet there were North-South differences: women from industrial countries emphasized gender equality in the workplace and in the home, whereas women from developing countries of the South asked: How can women achieve equality when most of a nation's people—women and men both—are repressed under an apartheid system? How can women advance when their nations are subjected to global economic inequalities? A great deal has been written with differing interpretations of those discussions at the UN Conference on Women in Mexico City (Pietilä and Vickers 1990; Winslow 1995; Fraser and Tinker 2004).

This chapter discusses how women worldwide faced those and other issues, and how their actions nudged and pushed communities, countries, and global organizations. Within this discussion, I shall show how the global feminist movement is deeply rooted in women's movements around the world, not solely in Western nations, and how the UN in its turn became women's guardian and advocate, the "unlikely godmother" on whom women have depended to put forward legislation for adoption by all countries, to offer us chances to meet across national and regional borders, to open doors for us to join discussions of issues that impact our lives as farmers, independent workers, and employees, as mothers and wives, as victims of war and agents of peace. This chapter reaches beyond the unifying definition of feminism as "the broad goal of challenging and changing women's subordination to men," to embrace women's search for social and economic justice wherever injustice is found, because women's subordination is often an element of larger subordinations such as colonialism, apartheid, and economic domination. My concept of feminism thus of necessity involves the search for justice: women's empowerment cannot be complete in an unjust society, and a just society cannot be achieved without empowering women. The ultimate goal is freedom and well-being for everyone.

The chapter traces interactions between United Nations organizations at field level and at headquarters through examples of women's tripartite coalitions of diplomats, representatives of nongovernmental organizations (NGOs), and international civil servants. It describes how women's issues have been intertwined with global development issues and how, through the UN, women become knowledgeable about global issues and the stances taken on them by governments. It shows that, while the voices of individual women are sometimes heard, a critical mass is vital to sustainable change, and it illustrates how influential men help to make or break women's concerns. Women had to contest men's assumptions that governed their nations in order to get their voices heard. The policy connections they forged between women's actual lives and development issues created a profound transformation—from seeing women as objects of services to seeing them as agents of change. Thus women reframed the debate, then revised their own strategies and influenced government actions as their movement broadened and deepened. They created a revolution.

Present at the Creation

The creation of the United Nations opened opportunities for women to promote justice for themselves and their societies, and women seized them. They had learned from experiences such as ending slavery and influencing the League of Nations that they must get a "foot in the door" of a new organization. At San Francisco in 1945, four women—representing Brazil, China, the Dominican Republic, and the United States—were among the 160 delegates who signed the United Nations Charter and demanded that its preamble speak explicitly of "equal rights among men and women" rather than "equal rights among men." With support from forty-two NGOs present as observers, they made sure that respect for human rights and fundamental freedoms was without discrimination by "race, sex, condition or creed."

That was an auspicious start. Next there was an agenda item on women's rights at the inaugural meeting of the UN General Assembly in London, and U.S. delegate Eleanor Roosevelt read an "Open Letter to the Women of the World" on behalf of the seventeen women delegates, urging involvement in the work of the organization. When the Commission on Human Rights was created under the Economic and Social Council (ECOSOC, the General Assembly committee assigned to prioritize and discuss economic and social matters), women were immediately given a subcommission on the status of women. That was not enough. They wanted a commission of their own, and they got it in 1947 even though, it is said, they had to convince the initially unwilling Roosevelt to separate it from the Commission on Human Rights that she chaired. The mandate of the Commission on the Status of Women (CSW) was to promote women's rights and equality by setting standards and formulating international conventions that would change national discriminatory legislation and foster global awareness of women's issues. Legal and political equality—the priorities of the dominant Western group—were its early emphasis.

Four Factors Interface to Create "Women and Development"

In the 1960s and 1970s, four factors interfaced to create the concept and the movement "women and development" that soon was flourishing: first, the multiplication of the numbers of newly independent UN member states, which made poverty a priority; second, the search for alternative development models to the modernization theory that had proved unsuccessful; third, mounting evidence, produced mostly by researchers, that women are central to their nations' economic life; and, fourth, the reemergence of the women's movement in industrial countries that led to pressure on Western governments to include women in their foreign assistance, as Sweden legislated in 1964 and the United States would do in 1973. Western women popularized the acronym WID for "women in development," but, rich with communications technologies, they also unwittingly often overlay on developing countries inappropriate gender stereotypes of their own societies.

A turning point for women at the UN was provoked by their participation in their countries' independence movements. When fifty-four former colonies that were home to 28 percent of the world's people joined the UN in the 1950s and 1960s, their emergence from poverty took center stage.

As a result of that overall growth of UN membership, CSW went from six members representing developing countries in 1960, to nineteen in 1969. Many of the new delegates were lawyers, but they came out of the experience of being colonized: they were from countries where education was reserved for elites and where the Victorian ideal of women as dutiful—and silent—had taken hold. For those reasons women from the new countries brought "development" to the agenda of CSW just as their brothers and sisters brought it to other UN agendas. The CSW was soon transformed.

A revolution was stirring. Women as actors and their institutions contested men's assumptions that were embedded in governments—of both North and South—to get their voices heard and their needs recognized. Toward this goal, momentum was building for women to have a fund of their own, and the flood of requests for support when the United Nations Development Fund for Women (UNIFEM), initially called the Voluntary Fund for the UN Decade for Women (VFDW), was established a few years later confirmed beyond a doubt that women received far from an appropriate amount of development resources.

What was the intellectual setting for this revolution? In the early days of development cooperation in newly independent countries, UNICEF—established to help child victims of World War II—provided maternal and child health services to women in developing countries. When asked to name their needs, however, women in Kenya in the early 1960s often said to visitors like me: "We need a small but regular income for ourselves and our children." Those needs could finally be recognized when an economic development focus followed the independence movements of the new countries. In that context, the fledgling women and development movement promoted the point that women be seen not solely as objects of maternal and child health care but also, based on mounting research, as active agents of economic productivity on farms and in markets, and of social and political change—in other words, of development.

The research about women's work became accepted when, for example, it was written by the widely respected agricultural economist Esther Boserup, whose landmark book *Women's Role in Economic Development* was published in 1970, and by the United Nations Economic Commission for Africa (ECA), whose article "Women: The Neglected Human Resources for African Development" (UNECA 1972) included the findings of research presented to African regional conferences in the previous decade. The latter made use of studies and seminar reports in Africa over the previous decade. Its opening statements were startling at the time:

> The traditional role of African women in economic development is "neither evident nor even acknowledged in the modern sectors of agriculture, industry, commerce and government." The persistence of this situation seriously impedes the realization of the expressed intentions of African governments to make full use of all human resources available for purposes of development, and to place primary emphasis on rural transformation as a means of raising the levels of living of the majority of their peoples ... women's economic role in the production and distribution of goods, while often observed, is seldom articulated or acknowledged by development planners. (UNECA 1972, 359)

Another factor contributed to the transformation from seeing women solely as objects of services to seeing them as agents of change. Gradually, the UN's community development approach—involving communities in their own development—opened many eyes to women's work: when the development experts visited farms and markets, they saw women, sometimes *only* women. The UN Economic Commission for Africa, quoted earlier, was the first UN organization to fully recognize and act on that reality. ECA held five Africa-wide seminars for women—asking their advice—and published a multicountry study of what today is called "microcredit." By the end of the 1960s "the role and participation of women in national development" was an item in its overall program.

Early in the 1960s a Swedish parliamentarian, Inga Thorsson, traveled through postcolonial Africa. She decided on the spot that Swedish foreign aid should always include programs for women and persuaded her parliament of this when she returned home in 1964. She had visited the newly established ECA and went back to persuade the Swedish International Development Authority (SIDA) to finance posts for women UN officers to be selected by the ECA, who would devise programs to implement the resolutions women had made at their Africa-wide seminars.

A hint of what was to come and how opportunities for women would be opened can be found in the UN's international development strategy for the second development decade—the 1970s—that stressed improvement in the quality of life for all people. That emphasis replaced the idea that new countries would easily industrialize and that benefits would "trickle down" to all, a perspective typically part of "modernization" theory. For the first time, the strategy contained the phrase "the integration of women in development," inserted on the suggestion of UN staff person Gloria Scott of Jamaica, one of a small network of committed and competent women—the midwives—with whom I worked., These women were scattered throughout the United Nations organizations and would help make the UN the guardian and advocate of the global women's movement—its "unlikely godmother." Scott saw an opening and took it in 1969. Her phrase "the integration of women in development" echoed around the world and, like Boserup's book and the ECA documents, helped the movement coalesce and gain strength.

For countries long subject to colonial rule (and for socialist feminists and many African Americans in the United States), "development" was about social and economic justice. Women, previously viewed mainly as wives and mothers, needed to be recognized by development planners for what they actually were: active agents of economic productivity—farmers, merchants, and entrepreneurs. The policy connections forged between women's lives and development issues created a profound transformation that was the seed of the fledgling women and development movement. In my view, that massive transformation needs far greater recognition and celebration in women's history than it has received. For women, the economy was the entry point to broad development concerns: development became a women's issue, and women became a development issue; the first steps had been taken to give an institutional base to the concept. Those of us who were working for women and development did not realize at the time that women and the UN were creating a revolution.

Reframing the Debate

The 1960s and 1970s were decades of ideas about development proposed by the industrialized countries, the Group of 77 developing countries, and the world's women. Even in the milieu of economic turbulence over skyrocketing oil prices, debt, and subsequent economic control over the new countries by the international financial institutions—the World Bank and the International Monetary Fund (IMF)—the East-West conflict framed development assistance. As explained earlier, several factors strengthened the transformation that connected women and development, including the creation of posts in the UN system, the growth of the global women's movement in civil society and the scholarship it promoted, and changing concepts of what "development" implied. The latter would open doors for women.

The relative handful of women working for women within the United Nations and its agencies gained strength through solidarity. The posts proposed by Sweden's Inga Thorsson were filled in 1971 (I filled the first one, and Daria Tesha of Tanzania the second), and the support of senior men made possible ECA's pioneering women's program, later called the African Training and Research Center for Women (ATRCW), that soon became a model for the world's regions as the first UN-sponsored institution dedicated to women and development (Snyder and Tadesse 1995). ECA's *Data Base for Discussion of the Interrelations between the Integration of Women in Development, Their Situation, and Population Factors* (1974) was the first country-by-country presentation of statistical and qualitative information on women in a world region.

Another step toward reframing the debate was the first-ever, trailblazing global meeting about women and development, held at the UN in 1972, which spread the new movement through participation of the UN regional commissions and agencies, together with government representatives. The Expert Group Meeting on Women in Economic Development attracted as its key figures the renowned Caribbean economist and Nobel laureate Sir Arthur Lewis and the respected agriculture economist and author Esther Boserup, whose book helped to create a strong constituency in donor countries (Boserup 1970).

Two new ideas soon took hold in the larger development community: (1) "basic needs" (food, housing, clothing, public transport, aided by employment and participation in decision making) and (2) overcoming "relative and absolute poverty." A World Employment Program (WEP) launched by the International Labor Organization "brought employment—and people and human needs—back to the center of development strategy" (Emmerij, Jolly, and Weiss 2001, 67). It stressed the informal economy—later called the "peoples' economy" or "off-the-books economy"—as a key source of growth in poor countries and called for the introduction of "appropriate" technologies, and education as investment in people, among other means.

Where people's basic needs and their survival strategies in agriculture and in the informal economy began to dominate both conceptual and field-level development practice, the fledgling women and development movement seized the new emphasis: it was a near-perfect match with its grassroots concerns. Development theory and practice finally focused directly on what constituted women's work, and planners would have to close their eyes to miss the fact. Some did, of course.

Rural development soon became a major theme for women, balanced at the macro level by "national machineries"—women's bureaus and ministries, and commissions on the advancement of women; such institutions would promote and monitor at policy level the collection and interpretation of national data by sex and the flow of national resources to women. Because of their location in governments, the commissions and bureaus were believed to help give the women's movement permanence. Thanks to Swedish foresight, UNECA was ready to promote them, following their approval at an Africa regional conference (Snyder and Tadesse 1995). While those government-sponsored units would not always meet women's high and rising expectations, as UNIFEM evaluator F. Joka-Bangura says, "One gets the feeling that if they had not taken up the question of projects for women, no one else would have" (Snyder 1995, 196). The grassroots to government, micro to macro connections had begun, though that terminology was not yet in use. At UNECA, the staff of the women's program adopted those priorities because African women had set them; they sent itinerant rural development training teams to twenty-eight countries for weeklong courses and specialists on national machineries to eighteen countries for three-day workshops.

The debate on development needed more reframing because, although the second development decade strategy and the basic needs concepts of the early 1970s gave new impetus to development assistance, these approaches shared a major weakness: they did not seek to change the structure of the world economy so that its wealth would be more equitable *between* nations as well as *within* them. Devising a strategy to transform the global economy was left to the developing countries, called the Group of 77, in the UN General Assembly, which created a New International Economic Order (NIEO) proposal that was finally adopted in 1974.

UNECA's women's center hastened to weave the women's thread with the global development one, to write and discuss *The New International Economic Order: What Roles for Women?* (UNECA 1977). According to the UN's first female Under Secretary-General, Lucille Mair (Jamaica), that document was the first discussion of the world economy to come from women in a developing region (Snyder and Tadesse 1995). Its initial measurement of women's labor contributions to the agricultural gross domestic product (GDP) was another first for the world's women and was the forerunner of many economic assessments today.

Regrettably, but not surprisingly, the initial Group of 77 proposal, the New International Economic Order, would never be seriously considered by the rich countries, whose new world order was ruled by "market forces." In fact, neither the second decade strategy nor the NIEO had much to say about women. Yet the struggle for ideas and power between the industrial and the newly independent countries surfaced at the UN's first-ever global conference on women, held in Mexico City in 1975 in connection with the International Women's Year. Some 7,000 women and men of varied nationalities, races, and creeds attended the conference, exchanging their views and experiences and articulating their common concerns and differences. They, too, would reframe the debate.

For women steeped in women's liberation—a phrase that had spread widely internationally in the form of the mocking shorthand of "women's lib" and was used, however inaccurately, to label the Western women's movement—what were called "women's issues" were mainly about equality between men and women. For Western women at Mexico City, equality in the home and in employment were major themes, as *The Feminine Mystique* had set out, although these delegates also supported resolutions favoring women in low-income countries, such as those about research, training, credit, and rural development. For women of newly independent countries, male-female issues could not be resolved while oppression of whole societies—both men and women—prevailed. Could women's lives be improved while apartheid kept a whole society in bondage? Or when thousands of people languished in refugee camps? Could women's formal sector employment increase while the global economic order oppressed poor countries? Global issues were women's issues for what was then called the "third world." As a delegate from the global South said: "To be equal in poverty with men is no blessing; we need development."

Institution-Building for Women and Development

Critical to the global movement is that, in effect, delegates at the Mexico City conference designated the Decade for Women, 1976–1985, as an institution-building decade. They were aware that, although networks are important, the long life of a movement will be assured when institutions are created to backstop and promote it. As already noted, national-level women's commissions and bureaus were being established, and at the regional level there was the ECA model. Interregional and global-level institutions remained to be established, and two new UN organizations were proposed. UNIFEM (the UN Development Fund for Women, first called the Voluntary Fund for the UN Decade for Women) was set up to finance women's activities in low-income countries, and the International Research and Training Institute for the Advancement of Women (INSTRAW) was to engage in research and training. Two new global NGOs were also proposed: Women's World Banking for loan guarantees, and the International Women's Tribune Center for grassroots communications. Each of those institutions had its own significant effect for women's self-understanding and for issues impacting development such as poverty, race, class, and gender. In my view, neither scholars nor activists have ever properly applauded the foresight of the women who ensured the longevity of the movement they were creating by giving it that institutional strength.

I use the example of UNIFEM, which I know best, to illustrate the value of institutions. UNIFEM started to thrive as a two-pronged instrument to support women's innovative and experimental activities directly and to influence major UN funds and programs—especially at preinvestment stages—so that both women and men would be considered in all the activities they financed (today the latter is called "gender mainstreaming"). To multiply its capacities, spread its influence, and reach out to local levels, UNIFEM immediately offered to pay for two senior women's officer positions at each of the UN's regional commissions, in Asia, Africa, and Latin America/Caribbean, and, in addition, to provide each commission with $100,000 for activities. "We never would have survived without UNIFEM," Mariam Krawczyk of the commission for Latin America and the Caribbean told us, "It was the first to open the way" (Snyder 1995, 31).

The most appropriate and effective development innovations came from sitting under a tree and listening to rural women, as I had found. Women brought about major changes in the UN development cooperation system in the late 1970s—not without lengthy discussion and debate with the entrenched establishment that focused on men as primary targets of development assistance and as decision makers and advisers on its allocation. Again, men's assumptions were contested so that women's voices were heard and their needs met. Because UNIFEM asked, "What are women doing?" and "Where are they doing it?" before providing assistance, groups such as Women and Development Unit (WAND) in the

Caribbean and grassroots groups worldwide were consulted. Two transformations in development cooperation are exemplary:

- Community-owned loan funds, rather than handouts, were provided to women's groups. While reviewing a training program the UN sponsored in Swaziland, Dumsile, a community development officer was asked: "What do the trained women need most?" Without hesitation she replied: "They need capital to start or strengthen their businesses." At UN headquarters, finance officers said it was simply impossible for the United Nations Development Programme (UNDP) to give a loan fund to a village community: "You can pay for an expert, or a vehicle, because in time you write them off your books," they said. "But you don't want to write off a credit fund that is intended to be self-renewing!"
- Women's nongovernmental organizations were assisted directly rather than through their governments. In Barbados women's voluntary groups that today are called civil society organizations and community-based organizations needed seed money for their activities. Again, there were seemingly endless negotiations with UNDP finance officers. They explained their view that since the UN is an intergovernmental organization, money is given to government activities, not NGOs.

Acceptable formulas were finally found, and both of these strategies were adopted, eventually transforming women's possibilities for participation. Although seldom credited to UNIFEM (in fact, they have been credited to UNDP, which was used by UNIFEM to deliver financial support to countries) they were also exciting breakthroughs and milestones for overall UN development cooperation.

Following the advice of the Mexico City conference, women's long-term goals to transform oppressive laws and distribute national wealth more equitably were advanced with the acceptance in 1979 of the first human rights treaty for women, the UN's Convention on the Elimination of All Forms of Discrimination against Women. Known as CEDAW, it presaged the women's human rights thread of a decade later and has become a most useful tool for women to pressure their governments, despite the fact that "justice is expensive" in a poor country, as a minister pointed out.

In summary, by the end of the 1970s, the agenda had begun to be reframed as women became a development issue; development itself was a full-fledged women's issue; women had made the UN the guardian and advocate of their global movement; and they had transformed parts of the development cooperation system to enable resource flows to women. But tensions remained between those for whom women's issues were largely gender matters and those for whom women's issues must of necessity include national and global injustices.

Consensus at Last

Even as the global movement gained strength, and perhaps because of that, the tension between North and South rocked the young worldwide women and development movement as the divisions first seen at Mexico City resurfaced with a vengeance at the UN's Copenhagen mid-decade women's conference in 1980. The battles were mainly over apartheid and Palestinian women (Winslow 1995). Again the definition of "women's issues" was split, with the North—especially the United States and Israel—holding that the conference was politicized because these societal issues were believed by the South and the Eastern European countries to impede the empowerment of women and thus be critical for women to address.

Power over the policies of poor countries gradually shifted away from them to the international financial institutions, and the UN development cooperation organizations—which focused on human well-being—lost voice. What was known as the Washington Consensus was the agreement between the World Bank, the IMF, and the U.S. Treasury on conditions developing countries must meet to obtain needed credit. Those conditions, which were set out in the structural adjustment programs (SAPs) of the International Monetary Fund and World Bank, gave priority to market economy over equity goals. Among other stringencies demanded by the IMF, spending on health and education was devastated, shifting new burdens onto women who cared for children and the elderly. Employment and basic needs goals were expunged, negating the needs of grassroots women. At this writing, those practices have mostly been reversed, but as one African woman commented to me: "We lost a generation of our young people," for whom health and education were no longer options. The 1980s were widely labeled "the lost decade," although that period was just the culmination of a lengthy process. The IMF and World Bank—technically part of the UN system but actually independent of it—had become not unlikely godmothers but evil stepmothers!

As economic globalization progressed, the playing field became more unequal as the industrial countries—in particular the United States—pursued what became known as neoliberalism, whose advocates firmly opposed public sector growth and government intervention in or control over the economy. Market forces ruled. Following the removal of national and international controls over capital, many developing states' powers were further diminished. The industrial countries now used 4 percent of their GNP for military expenditures—ten times more than they gave as official aid to the "third world." "Issues of poverty, equity, human development, basic needs and the NIEO were shoved off the global agenda" (Snyder 1995, 23). "Development" began its slide from popularity with all but the most committed of the donor countries—such as all of Scandinavia, the Netherlands, and Canada—and the United States moved rapidly down to the bottom of that generosity list.

Redirecting the Action

Despite, or perhaps because of, the earlier conflicts and confrontations, the third global women's conference, convened by the UN in Nairobi in 1985, witnessed a maturing of the global women's movement. At Nairobi, consensus was found when women of the South were at last ready to speak more freely about male-female relationships, and women of the North, having felt the effects of economic downturn due to the sudden rise in oil prices, and having visited Kenyan women's water and tree-planting activities, saw firsthand that women's issues are not limited to gender equality and accepted at last that global factors affect women's conditions. Feminism in practice demanded a just society. New global feminist organizations, such as Development Alternatives with Women for a New Era (DAWN) and Grassroots Women Organizing Together in Sisterhood (GROOTS) were created. DAWN would later underline the significance of race, class, and nation as well as sex and would popularize the term "empowerment" (Sen and Grown 1987). The standoffs of Mexico City and confrontations of Copenhagen over what constituted "women's issues" faded into history (Snyder 1995, 24).

A historical perspective is essential. Remember that *women and development* as a field for research and action had made strong contributions to reframing the debate: women's economic contributions could no longer be overlooked. The institutions women created were charged with practical applications of those concepts—with reframing the action. UNIFEM provides an example. Like other development agencies, it had to be very flexible and seek innovative operational strategies rather than using the traditional "technical assistance" ones. Its first move had been to strengthen regional and national institutions and leadership capacities, then, having listened to women in the villages and countryside, to provide community-owned revolving loan funds and support local nongovernmental organizations.

Those actions brought to light the importance of government plans and budgets to the process of empowering women. With UNIFEM support, the UN Economic Commission for Latin America and the Caribbean (ECLAC) published a UN best-seller, *Women and Development Planning: Guidelines for Program and Project Planning* (Pezzullo 1983), and cooperated with its regional institute for training men and women planners "who would integrate subjects relating to women into government development plans and programs" (Snyder 1995, 192). Asia, the South Pacific, and western Asia also received funds to train national planners. Thoraya Obaid of the UN Economic and Social Commission for Western Asia (ESCWA) explained her commission's goal "to integrate the issues of women, the needs of women, the concerns of women in the overall policies of the governments" (Snyder 1995, 192–193).

Evolving a new programming approach, UNIFEM looked at development cooperation holistically rather than as a collection of "projects"; its policy framework interwove the priorities of governments with those of women. In India, for example, Rajasthran state government selected sericulture (silk production) as appropriate to a drought-prone area to enhance family incomes. UNIFEM supported technical training for mulberry cultivation, bought silkworm-rearing equipment, and gave a revolving fund for purchasing cocoons. Once evaluated, redirected away from the classic trap of replacing food crops with cash crops, and put more firmly into the hands of the women farmers (rather than their husbands), the innovative and experimental sericulture model that had reached 500 women was adopted by the World Bank to reach thousands more. Children went to school, and whole families were better fed (Snyder 1995, 128–135).

UNIFEM's Africa Investment Plan (AIP), adopted in 1984, related the priorities of a whole geographic region with women's issues and linked government policy formation with grassroots action. For example, Africa's top priority, food and agriculture, was set out in that region's Lagos Plan of Action 1980–2000. UNIFEM's policy framework recognized the Lagos plan and with it women's heavy engagement in food chain activities; it had already successfully assisted the transfer of food cycle technologies such as fish smokers and palm oil presses An early focus of AIP was the then nine member countries of the Southern African Development Coordination Conference (SADCC, later renamed the Southern African Development Community [SADC]), where it supported an office, a ministerial-level seminar on food security, and a series of national activities: maize-grinding cooperatives, artisanal fisheries, fruit tree planting.

In summary, within a reframed debate, and thanks in large part to women's partnership with the UN, "women and development" evolved and matured *conceptually* as regards the inclusiveness of women's issues, and *strategically* as regards the relationship between policy and action, between civil society and government, between grassroots and national levels.

Simultaneously with those evolutionary steps in reframing the debate and the action, the term "gender" emerged from Western scholars to denote that the sexual division of labor is a human construct and therefore can be changed. "Gender" clarified the social nature of many inequities between men and women, implying that the desired change in relationships was possible. It was a useful concept. Actually, *women and development* had made *gender and development* (GAD) possible, and the greater individualism of GAD would soon make *women's human rights* possible. Yet the *women and development* image was quickly tarnished by accusations from the newly minted GAD community: WID addressed women exclusively, they said, and it fostered "all those small projects" that were mainly "income generating"; it was not speaking directly to power issues. Staff of UNIFEM heard quite a bit of that and were curious that the abundant research on the gendered division of labor was overlooked and that such criticism was seldom leveled at microfinance projects valued as low as $100 or at their male sponsors.

Analysis of the WID/GAD controversy suggests that new concepts, such as gender in this instance, can cause setbacks rather than progress unless their theoretical and practical foundations are acknowledged and made use of. Here it is also a warning signal that power struggles are part and parcel of institutional development, among feminists as others. For WID advocates, emphasis on the economy was both a giant step from maternal and child health programs to the larger realities of women's lives, and a pragmatic political strategy. Since economic growth was the primary concern of newly independent countries, women seized the chance to be recognized as economic actors. For GAD advocates, an economic emphasis overlooked interpersonal relationships of power that fostered inequalities between men and women. For those men and women in major development organizations who had not understood the concept of WID, GAD sometimes offered a relief from the persistent emphasis on women and an excuse for setting aside women's issues.

Regrettably, the controversy interrupted the momentum of the programming approach. The conceptual shift from WID to GAD ought to have been seen as an evolution, but it captured the energies of many in the academic community, distracting attention from compelling contemporary issues such as economic globalization, poverty, peace, ownership of land and water, and other potential transformations that the women's movement, including its academic wing, is positioned to influence.

The Movement Broadens and Deepens

Economic globalization followed its unremitting course as the twentieth century came to a close and the twenty-first began. It was led by powerful Western governments and by multinational corporations and the international financial institutions, using the "trade, not aid" slogan of the neoliberal revolution—that promoted the market values cherished by the Washington Consensus. As power was wrenched from the borrowing governments by some of the loan conditions they had to meet, AIDS stole lives across the developing world, depleting the numbers of parents and skilled workers who sustain their nations and leaving millions of orphans to cope on their own or be inherited by relatives who already had large families or were themselves grandparents. Vicious civil and subregional wars raged across Eastern Europe, Asia, and Africa: 90 percent of their casualties were said to be civilians, and the majority of them were women and children who were raped, enslaved, killed, or exiled. Yet the democracy movement gained ground, and "civil society" became a buzzword attracting donor support.

As the global women's movement evolved in this environment—often in partnership with the UN—the momentum of Nairobi and preparations for the Fourth World Conference on Women to be held in Beijing energized women worldwide. Books were timed to be published before the celebration (Snyder 2000). The momentum soon carried women to leadership of six important UN agencies—WHO (health), WFP (food), UNHCR (refugees), UNICEF (children), UNFPA (population), and UNIFEM—and a woman would become the first ever UN deputy secretary-general as women's numbers at professional levels in the UN increased. The movement broadened and deepened, opening new areas of concentration: women's human rights, economic globalization, peacemaking and peacekeeping, and grassroots organizing.

Women's Human Rights

A fresh interpretation of twentieth-century women's rights and a new and initially competing framing of the debate appeared when the slogan "women's rights are human rights" took hold, thanks largely to the ideas and hard work of the nongovernmental International Women's Tribune Center with the Center for Women's Global Leadership in preparation for the United Nations world conference on human rights in Vienna, 1993 (Peters and Wolper 1995). The campaign spread like fire as violence against women became a key issue worldwide, with an annual sixteen days of activism and a petition that gained signatures in 123 countries. Once again women selected the UN to globalize their actions. Committed to the rights-based approach earlier, UNIFEM had supported nongovernmental organizations' use of CEDAW by underwriting their capacity to monitor government commitments. Its attractive "women's rights are human rights" lapel pins appeared everywhere. In 1996 UNIFEM established a trust fund to finance actions to eliminate all forms of violence against women, and seventy countries soon benefited from it, with support of activities ranging from training police officers to producing TV sitcoms to legal support for rape survivors.

Women's human rights can easily be viewed as a component of the women/gender and development movement, expressed as "women's rights in development," and the Association for Women's Rights in Development (AWID) proposes that the two—gender/women and development, and women's human rights—converge in order to strengthen the women's movement (Kerr 2001).

Economic Globalization

In the realm of economics, the end of the twentieth century saw abundant new evidence of the devastating effects of structural adjustment programs on people's well-being—especially on education and health services. Little girls were left standing outside school doors, and health clinics had empty medicine shelves across Africa and elsewhere. The unbearable cost of debt service and repayment by poor countries to the rich stimulated movements such as 50 Years Are Enough and Jubilee 2000 in the West and the Women's International Coalition for Economic Justice worldwide. Women formally led some of these organizations and participated in these and other worldwide economic and social justice movements. Along with such collective resistance, women also actively sought new ways to survive and prosper. For example, women producers sought entry to global markets. One needs only to board planes leaving Africa to find women entrepreneurs seeking markets everywhere.

"Another world is possible," women and their male colleagues say as they fight against oil pipelines and dams they judge to be destructive to both people and their environment. Organizations like TANGO (the Tanzanian nongovernmental organization group) educate civil society organizations about the workings of the World Trade Organization, the World Bank, the IMF, the U.S. Treasury, and other external organizations that drastically affect their countries and their lives, right down to the village and farm. They seek to heighten participation of developing countries in intergovernmental decision making and demand accountability from multinational corporations operating worldwide through, for example, the World Social Forum. Marjorie Mbilinyi (2001) observes, "The resistance against corporate-led globalization has been led in Africa by women and gender activists, a dynamic force which challenges the economic reform process associated with globalization and calls for an alternative development strategy" (1). Recall the definition of feminism at the beginning of this chapter, that it "of necessity involves the search for justice: women's empowerment cannot be complete in an unjust society, and a just society cannot be achieved without empowering women."

UNIFEM pioneered studies of the impacts of trade liberalization on women producers at macro and meso levels, whose findings are being used to influence trade treaty organizations such as the Southern Common Market (MERCOSUR) in Latin America's southern cone and the North American Free Trade Agreement (NAFTA) in the Americas (Bakker,

1999). Their goal: to make globalization a force for good rather than for greed. Meanwhile, at country level women are finding new ways to strengthen their indigenous rotating savings and credit associations (ROSCAs), for example, by joining several of them in a federation, thus having a larger capital base to borrow against and avoiding the often high costs of bank loans and microcredit.

Also in the economic realm, the gender budget initiative that is ongoing in some fifty countries (and assisted by UNIFEM in half of them) improves on the earlier described national planning thrust noted in the 1980s. Macro policy as expressed in the allotment of national income is linked with financing of actions at meso and micro level to overcome poverty and its associated gender injustices by encouraging governments to apply gender analysis to the expenditure side of their national budgetary process. Gender budgeting is practiced at local government as well as national levels. It reveals constraints that challenge us to further action: Mbilinyi (2001) points out that the effectiveness of the gender budgeting effort is still constrained because it "lacks a conceptual framework to analyze global capitalism and understand globalization," and needs grounding in a "strong poor peoples' movement" (22).

Peacemaking and Peacekeeping

Global issues and women's issues can be seen again as interwoven in the 1990s' focus on peace. Women are victims of exaggerated violence during wartime. They are also activists for peace, which appears as a near-universal issue for women worldwide. A comment by Etweda Cooper of wartorn Liberia about gendered views during wartime is telling. When rebels came near their village, she said, "men were more prone to say 'Let's go . . . kill them,' and women would say 'Let's go talk to the boys'" (African Women and Peace Support Group 2004).

The turn of the century saw women's peacemaking and peacekeeping initiatives become an international issue as the Women in Black followed in the footsteps of the Mothers of the Plaza de Mayo of Argentina of the late 1970s. UNIFEM helped create African Women in Crisis and supported other peace networks in South Asia, Eastern Europe, and Latin America. Its peace torch was lit by President Nelson Mandela in South Africa and carried across Africa and Asia to the Fourth World Conference on Women at Beijing in 1995. Thanks to a woman judge from South Africa, Navanethem Pillay, rape was declared an international crime of genocide at the UN's Rwanda criminal court.

Then came women's new breakthrough and crowning achievement—penetration of the highest intergovernmental decision-making body, through passage in 2000 of the historic UN Security Council Resolution 1325 on women, peace, and security—another thrust to help women be seen, counted, and engaged in peace processes wherever they take place—in their own countries and internationally.

Grassroots Organizing

Poor people's movements did get stronger in rural areas and in the informal economy of cities and towns in the 1990s. The Self Employed Women's Association (SEWA) grew to more than 600,000 rural and poor urban members, who see India's "second freedom" as the economic empowerment of poor working women. Their prescient trade union leader Ela Bhatt has long understood the need for strong poor people's movements. She says: "Organization is the answer for those who are weak economically or socially. . . . In India we have many political rights, but because the poor are still dependent on others for their livelihood, they cannot exercise those rights" (Snyder 1995, 20). Inspired by Gina Vargas, another woman of vision, the network of Peruvian rural women's organizations named for Flora Tristan (an activist of the early twentieth century) strengthens their capacities to influence local government policy. UNIFEM assisted Flora Tristan in its early years and has also assisted Women in Informal Employment: Globalizing and Organizing (WIEGO) and GROOTS.

In summary, the movement broadened and deepened both intellectually and strategically as the debate was reframed and action followed: women's human rights provided a new conceptual theme, continuing economic globalization called for new strategies, peacemaking and peacekeeping became a new arena for activists, and grassroots organizations allowed peasant voices to be heard—all these with tripartite collaboration between UN, NGOs, and political leaders. But the growth of the movement threatened some traditionalists—religious fundamentalists in particular. They would organize a backlash.

Seeds of Backlash

The centerpiece of the fruitful 1990s was the UN's Fourth World Conference on Women at Beijing, 1995, that marked a new level of solidarity among both government and NGO delegations and attracted some 50,000 participants. Those of us who had participated at Mexico City in 1975, Copenhagen in 1980, and Nairobi in 1985 found the positive evolution palpable: Beijing was the most unified and productive conference of all. As joyful and peaceful as it was, however, the conference revealed seeds of backlash against women's advancement: religious fundamentalists discovered and acknowledged the importance of the UN, then used it as a vehicle to turn back gains made by the world's women over decades. Representatives of the Vatican and of Muslim and Christian fundamentalists joined hands. Women were sharply reminded that they were not exempt from entanglement in global political issues—a fact first discovered in Mexico in 1975 but not previously experienced personally by the new generation who participated at Beijing.

The millennium thus brought new, seemingly insurmountable challenges. Women were paying the price of success: a millennium backlash. The outspoken UN human rights commissioner Mary Robinson was denied a second term, and women's influence waned as they lost power in the UN Secretariat. "It's not the same in the UN as the 1980s when you and I were active," one diplomat explained. Only two women would remain as heads of major organizations in the early 2000s. The "era of women leaders in the UN . . . , if glorious, was also brief" (Crossette 2002).

The New Millennium: The Unfinished Revolution

Viewed from the historic perspective and as a social revolution, the women/gender and development movement, including its recent human rights thread, has made extraordinary progress. A brief four decades ago, developers saw women in their domestic roles only, as objects of services. Today women are seen as farmers, merchants, and entrepreneurs, as sole sustainers of nearly a third of the world's families, and as competent participants in public life as agents of change. Today, some sit at peace tables, redesign national budgets, and propose new international trade regimes. The continuity is clear: one phase of the movement enables the next, and the issues of each are tightly interwoven with global development issues.

Over the decades, *women and development* generated masses of research, information, and sex-disaggregated data (Snyder, 2000), rewrote much of colonial history, raised widespread awareness of women's hefty contribution to economic growth and its distribution, leveraged a flow of major multi- and bilateral development resources to women, helped women strengthen their organizations and build new local and cross-border ones, stimulated moves to elect more women to national and local offices, and helped foster worldwide networks and trade unions among scholars and practitioners. Yes, women and development had—and has— weaknesses (only dishonesty can claim no failures), but there can be no question that it reframed the debate: it made development a women's issue and women a development issue; it made women's issues global issues and global issues women's issues.

This strong growth of the twentieth-century and early twenty-first-century women's movements in different parts of the world was in large part made possible by co-opting the UN as their unlikely godmother, using the power of its blessing to influence the policies and programs of major global and national institutions and to build new institutions to sustain the movement women were creating. UNIFEM, the International Women's Tribune Center, Women's World Banking, programs of the UN regional commissions, and specialized UN agencies all helped create a new multistrand global women's movement, with the UN as its unlikely godmother. What woman leader has not used one or several of these institutions? Through them, activists have been able not only to pursue women-specific goals but also to examine the larger society for evidence of and to take action on institutional racism, sexism, gender, class, war, and other injustices. And, aided by the communications revolution, they have used this infrastructure to forge worldwide networks.

In addition, as Marilyn Porter, scholar and activist, says, "There is no doubt about the importance of activity around the UN in the formation of an entire generation of feminist activists from around the world . . . the conferences and related activity have introduced large numbers of women from around the world to each other and each other's concerns and ideas and to the excitement of working with women from different backgrounds on common issues" (in Porter and Judd 1999, 8). For those working within the UN, the way has not always been smooth. Despite widespread support of our institutions by many male leaders, some powerful ones tried to undermine them. Women had to contest men's assumptions to get their voices heard. I have vivid memories of how both the

African women's center and UNIFEM escaped such victimization and eventual demise only through the creative efforts of their staff, political supporters, and NGOs. One instance stands out: a very senior UNDP officer, after learning of UNIFEM's development of conceptual frameworks such as the Africa Investment Plan in order to base its investments on regional priorities, told astonished UNIFEM managers: "You are not supposed to conceptualize!" We were reminded of colonials trying to suppress intellectual life among the colonized. The words of Ingrid Palmer, whose observations on women's issues internationally are widely respected, still ring true for some mainstream organizations: "There is an evident intellectual inability to cope with women's issues" (United Nations 1980).

Other obstacles arose from women's own pursuits, such as the rush to "engender the mainstream" that was invested with too much promise and led some of us to neglect or even disparage women-specific institutions that have been and still are the font of ideas and innovative actions and a source of our collective strength. Like the 1970s slogan "Integration of women in development," some women saw "the mainstream" as the only important place to be, in effect denying the value of their own organizations.

Political encounters also took their toll: the U.S. government's voluntary contributions to UNIFEM ceased for two years, then resumed at a lower level following the controversial 1980 Copenhagen conference. UNIFEM was scapegoated as guilty by its association with the United Nations and falsely accused of financing the UN-sponsored conference. In fact, as a special fund, UNIFEM's resources were allocated solely to development activities in low-income countries, and the conference was funded by the U.S. Agency for International Development (USAID), among others (Snyder 1995). Since that time, American women have never pressed hard for a government contribution for women globally through UNIFEM commensurate with the needs: as recently as 2001, using population figures together with voluntary, non-earmarked contributions of governments in dollars to UNIFEM, every Dutch person gave twenty-five cents to UNIFEM, every Norwegian gave forty-five cents, and it took two Americans to give just one cent! For well over a decade, the United States gave a miserly $1 million or less a year for the world's poor women through UNIFEM.

Our unfinished revolution also confronts well-organized opposition at the dawn of the millennium: the intransigence of fundamentalists of all beliefs, some of whom have a hold on government votes and UN discussions. Fundamentalists, too, are globalizing. Their power grows and threatens women's hard-won gains; at this writing they remain formidable adversaries.

As women/gender and development evolved, its meaning and the means to attain it have increasingly been defined, broadened, and enriched by its primary stakeholders—women of developing countries, many of whom are young and proficient users of new information and communication technologies and some of whom refuse, for political reasons, to identify themselves as "feminist," although they are fully committed to the women's cause. They illustrate our definition of feminism as the broad goal of challenging and changing women's subordination to men, while simultaneously searching for social and economic justice, because women's empowerment cannot be complete in an unjust society, and a just society cannot be achieved without empowering women.

A number of women's organizations in the North have lost momentum. Perhaps younger women are not fully aware of the struggles undergone in gaining ground, and so just take it for granted; perhaps they are resting on their impressive achievements in the workplace and the home; or perhaps they have not viewed equality for women as the *interim* goal, and justice for all people as the *long-term* one.

In Finland, for example, the women-friendly welfare society has integrated women into male society to the extent that many seem to consider the struggle to be over. Reality reveals otherwise, as economic globalization erodes years of the benefits bestowed by their welfare society (Pietilä 2002). It appears that they failed to foresee the impact that neoliberal practices such as "free trade" would have on people's freedom and well-being, and how such approaches could reverse human security.

This history tells us that Finnish women are not alone in failing to foresee the impact that neoliberal practices would have on people's freedom and well-being and on the vigor of their own organizations. As women and their NGOs put their energies into larger issues such as the environment, population, militarism, and peace, "pure" feminism lost the broad appeal it had earlier. In Europe, by the 1990s it was "impossible to organize large numbers of women" (Harcourt 1994, 194).

In North America, the U.S. women's movement has long hesitated to identify with and support the global women's movement. Why? Women in the United States have "a peculiar set of blinders," says Linda Tarr-Whelan (2003), that separates their interests from those of women worldwide: the U.S. government's failure to ratify the CEDAW and its miserly contribution to UNIFEM express this distance eloquently. "What's in it for us?" these women seem to ask, and many Americans ask of the International Criminal Court, the Kyoto environmental accords, and other multilateral conventions and treaties.

For me, those lessons reinforce the principle set out by southern delegations long ago in Mexico City in 1975, that macropolitical and economic issues must indeed be women's issues. Global issues are women's issues, and the two are interwoven as threads in a fabric. Yesterday there was apartheid; today there are fundamentalism, militarism, and greedy forms of globalization. A feminism that fails to include these broad issues that inhibit the empowerment of both women and men is incomplete and denies its own potential.

In conclusion, despite differences among areas, countries, and regions, a global women's movement does exist, thanks in large part to its unlikely godmother, and to the tripartite coalitions of UN civil servants, NGOs, and diplomats that made its adoption effective. Possessing a rich experience, those in this movement know that gender equality cannot be achieved and maintained separately from other major social, economic, and political issues, and that gender equality is a necessary but not a sufficient condition for people's freedom and well-being—for development. Today, concern with global issues is critical to the relevance and even the survival of the women's movement. Where national feminist goals are mainly gender equity, the movement appears to lose momentum, and social protections erode. Global women's movement activists know that in the North, we must fight injustice in our own societies and governments and in their relationships with poor countries, not just fight for justice in other peoples' societies and governments in the South.

Today, the women's movement is strongest in the global South, but that vitality is threatened by the lagging energies and low mobilization of the women's movement in the global North. Happily, signs of a resurgence of women's leadership in the North are visible, for example, in antiwar and debt-cancellation campaigns; I believe it is needed far more widely and must be representative of a broad spectrum of classes. Feminism is about human beings; we say, it is about justice for everyone.

Our revolution is unfinished, but our effect on the entrenched structures of the privileged and still male-led world can draw sustenance from history and from the actions of poor contemporary women. By protesting multinational companies' destruction of the environment and just one global corporation's failure to share oil earnings with local communities so that their own land can give them food, shelter, jobs, education, and health services, 2,000 Nigerian village women of the oil delta conspired to test the conscience of the rich, corporate-led world and of their own government (IRIN-WA 2002). They are telling us about justice for everyone. Do we dare listen?

Bɪʙʟɪᴏɢʀᴀᴘʜʏ

This chapter is derived in part from the author's article in *Signs,* winter 2004, that traces the interweaving of women's issues with development issues, copyright 2004 by the University of Chicago. All rights reserved.

African Women and Peace Support Group. 2004. *To Be Seen, to Be Heard, to Be Counted: Liberian Women's Pursuit of Peace: 1989–1997.* Trenton, N.J.: Africa World Press.

Bakker, Isabella. 1999. "The New Global Architecture: Gender and Development Practices." In Marilyn Porter and Ellen Judd, eds., *Feminists Doing Development: A Practical Critique,* 206–217. London: Zed Books.

Boserup, Esther. 1970. *Women's Role in Economic Development.* New York: St. Martin's Press.

Crossette, Barbara. 2002. "An Era of Women Leaders Ends at the U.N." Women's eNews.org. September 12.

Development Dialogue. 1982. "Dakar Declaration on Another Development with Women." 1/2:13.

Emmerij, Louis, Richard Jolly, and Thomas G. Weiss. 2001. *Ahead of the Curve? UN Ideas and Global Challenges.* Bloomington: Indiana University Press.

Fraser, Arvonne S., and Irene Tinker, eds. 2004. *Developing Power: How Women Transformed International Development.* New York: Feminist Press.

Geiger, Susan. 1997. *TANU Women: Gender and Culture in the Making of Tanganyikan Nationalism, 1955–1965.* Portsmouth, N.H.: Heinemann.

Grewal, Inderpal. 1999. "Women's Rights as Human Rights: Feminist Practices, Global Feminism and Human Rights Regimes in Transnationality." *Citizenship Studies* 3, no. 3: 337–354.

Harcourt, Wendy, ed. 1994. *Feminist Perspectives on Sustainable Development.* London: Zed Books.

IRIN-West Africa. 2002. "Nigeria: Focus on the Growing Role of Women in Oil Region Crisis." IRIN@irinnews.org (IRIN), August 6.

Jaquette, Jane S. 1995. "Losing the Battle/Winning the War: International Politics, Women's Issues and the 1980 Mid-Decade Conference." In Anne Winslow, ed., *Women, Politics and the United Nations,* 45–60. Westport, Conn.: Greenwood Press.

Kerr, Joanna. 2001. "International Trends in Gender Equality Work." AWID Occasional paper no. 1. Toronto.

Leys, Colin. 1996. *The Rise and Fall of Development Theory.* Bloomington: Indiana University Press.

Mbilinyi, Marjorie. 2001. *Budgets, Debt Relief and Globalisation.* Accra: Third World Network Africa.

Oloka-Onyango, Joseph, and Sylvia Tamale. 1995. "The Personal Is Political or Why Women's Rights Are Indeed Human Rights: An African Perspective on International Feminism." *Human Rights Quarterly* 17:691–731.

Peters, Julie, and Andrea Wolper, eds. 1995. *Women's Rights, Human Rights: International Feminist Perspectives.* London: Routledge.

Pezzullo, Caroline. 1983. *Women and Development Planning: Guidelines for Program and Project Planning.* Santiago, Chile: United Nations.

Pietilä, Hilkka. 2002. *Nordic Welfare Society: A Strategy to Eradicate Poverty and Build Up Equality.* Helsinki: International Household and Family Research Conference.

Pietilä, Hilkka, and Jeanne Vickers. 1990. *Making Women Matter: The Role of the United Nations.* London: Zed Books.

Porter, Marilyn, and Ellen Judd, eds. 1999. *Feminists Doing Development: A Practical Critique.* London: Zed Books.

Sen, Gita, and Caren Grown.1987. *Development, Crises and Alternative Visions: Third World Women's Perspectives.* New York: Monthly Review Press.

Snyder, Margaret. 1995. *Transforming Development: Women, Poverty and Politics.* London: IT Publications.

———. 2000. "Women and African Development." *CHOICE,* February, 2–14.

Snyder, Margaret C., and Mary Tadesse. 1995. *African Women and Development: A History.* London: ZED Books, 1995.

Tarr-Whelan, Linda. 2003. Speech to the International Council for Research on Women. New York, February 27.

United Nations. 1980. A/CONF. 94/19.

United Nations Economic Commission for Africa. 1972. "Women: The Neglected Human Resources for African Development." *Canadian Journal of African Studies: Ottawa* 6. no. 2: 359–370.

———. 1974. *The Data Base for Discussion of Interrelations between the Integration of Women in Development, Their Situation, and Population Factors.* Addis Ababa: United Nations Economic Commission for Africa.

———. 1977. *The New International Economic Order: What Roles for Women?* Addis Ababa: UN Economic Commission for Africa.

Winslow, Anne, ed. 1995. *Women, Politics, and the United Nations.* Westport, Conn.: Greenwood Press.

3

The Evolution of Transnational Feminisms
Consensus, Conflict, and New Dynamics

Aili Mari Tripp

In the past two decades, we have witnessed the evolution of an international consensus around particular norms regarding women's rights. This rights-based consensus combines development and human rights interests, engages advocates within and outside transnational women's groups, and has been very much a product of global dialogue and interaction. Much of this consensus has been reflected in the various international agreements and treaties, including the 1979 Convention on the Elimination of All Forms of Discrimination against Women, the 1995 United Nations Beijing Platform of Action, the 1996 International Labour Organisation Convention on Homeworkers, the 1999 UN Jomtien resolution on Education for All, and the 2000 UN Security Council Resolution 1325 on the participation of women in peace-building. These and other international decisions indicate increasing international recognition of women's rights and interest in changing women's status and removing key impediments to women's advancement in almost every arena.

The impetus in these international forums has been truly transnational, with non-Western and Western countries alike contributing to the growth of this consensus. The consensus represents an important convergence of feminisms and women's rights advocacy worldwide. Regardless of the common perception in the West that ideas regarding the emancipation of women have spread from the West outward into other parts of the world, this chapter argues that, in fact, the influences have always been multidirectional, and that the current consensus is a product of parallel feminist movements globally that have learned from one another but have often had quite independent trajectories and sources of movement.

Today's global consensus is far from absolute. There remains polarization around issues such as lesbian rights, abortion, trafficking in women, and sex work. There is disagreement over the importance of other issues, such as militarization and global economic inequalities. These differences can be found within countries, as well as across various transnational divides. Slowly, however, the debates around these issues are changing even in regions that have been very resistant to incorporating these concerns into a women's rights agenda. In Uganda, where homosexuality is illegal and carries a maximum sentence of life imprisonment, a conference was held in May 2004 to discuss the rights of gays and lesbians in the country, and feminists were visible in discussing how to decriminalize homosexuality. Interestingly, the right to abortion was articulated for the first time in international law when, in July 2003, the African Union adopted the Protocol on the Rights of Women in Africa, a supplementary protocol to the 1981 African Charter on Human and Peoples' Rights. The new protocol, which covers a broad range of human rights issues, explicitly sets forth the right of women to medical abortion when pregnancy results from rape or incest or when the continuation of pregnancy endangers the health or life of the mother. Women from the North actively supported women from the South in getting the UN Security Council Resolution 1325 passed in 2000 to include women in peace negotiations and give them roles in peacekeeping missions around the world. These are small steps as new actors take up issues that have previously been sidelined or shunned. These changes represent a trend that is gaining momentum, especially as global diffusion of norms and ideas continues.

At the same time, there exist very serious challenges to this consensus from the Vatican and Islamic countries such as Saudi Arabia and Iran. The United States under the Bush administration has similarly worked against this consensus through policies like the gag rule and withdrawal of support to the United Nations Population Fund (UNPFA). On January 22, 2001, U.S. president George W. Bush imposed what is known as the "Global Gag Rule," which restricts foreign nongovernmental organizations (NGOs) that receive U.S. family planning funds from using their own, non-U.S. funds to provide legal abortion services, lobby their own governments for abortion law reform, or provide accurate medical counseling or referrals regarding abortion. Then, in July 2002, under pressure from anti–family planning organizations, Bush withdrew all U.S. support from the UNPFA, which has grave repercussions for international family planning efforts and the prospects for women's health around the world. This was money for contraception and sex education, for maternal health care and AIDS education that would have helped prevent millions of unwanted pregnancies and thousands of induced abortions and maternal deaths. Groups fighting AIDS abroad faced new restrictions in 2005 by USAID. They were given a litmus test that required them to pledge opposition to sex trafficking and prostitution in order to obtain funds. They are also required to inform clients of condom failure rates. The Global AIDS Alliance and many others fear that by stigmatizing populations most at risk for AIDS, they will end up creating distrust and undermining the effectiveness of their programs.

Under the Bush administration, the United States has adopted a unilateral approach of undoing multilateral agreements. For example, the United States was the only country out of 179 that refused at a 2004 UNFPA meeting in Chile to endorse the 1994 Cairo consensus (International Conference on Population and Development Programme of Action) affirming the need for reproductive health information and services to improve economic development and slow population growth. The Convention on the Elimination of All Forms of Discrimination against Women (CEDAW) has been ratified by 174 countries with a few holdouts, including the United States, along with Iran, Oman, Qatar, and Sudan.

In the post–Beijing conference period, the United States has generally been uninterested in following up on the goals and gains made at that landmark 1995 gathering. Under the Bush administration, the United States has worked against the agreed-upon goals. At the 2004 meeting of the UN Commission on the Status of Women, the United States openly refused to continue its endorsement of the Platform of Action of the Fourth World Conference on Women at Beijing in 1995. U.S. unilateralism in the CSW has undermined the commission's work overall.

The European Union countries have made considerably more progress than the United States in using the Beijing Platform of Action to shape their women's agenda. The European Union has been engaged in the Beijing Plus Five meetings and in the Beijing Plus Ten discussions. The EU Committee on Women's Rights and Gender Equality has a wide range of gender-related concerns that intersect with the Platform of Action, such as equal opportunities in employment, the gender pay gap, violence against women, child care, and trafficking in human beings, especially women. The Beijing process, in particular, influenced the EU's efforts since 1995 to bring gender mainstreaming into the administrative institutions of the EU and its member states. There has being continuing pressure to continue this process and gain high-level support for it. Drawing on the Platform of Action, the Council of Europe adopted the Community Framework Strategy on gender equality (2001–2005) to foster awareness-raising campaigns regarding gender, improve the collection of data, and implement transnational projects. Other specific concerns coming out of the Beijing process have included an emphasis on reconciling family and working life and improving women's status in decision making (European Parliament Committee on Women's Rights and Gender Equality 2004; European Commission 2002).

Even though the European Union endorses the Beijing Platform of Action, there has been an underlying perception within Europe that it is relevant primarily to developing countries and not to advanced industrialized countries, which are seen as already having largely attained equality. Such complacent attitudes in Europe and the United States have resulted in a situation where the most aggressive changes in attitudes regarding the need to improve women's status have tended to come from outside North America and Europe, especially since 1995.

This chapter offers a framework for understanding how local women's movements around the world responded to broader national political, economic, and cultural trends and events, as well as how they influenced and were influenced by global women's movements over the course of a long history of global development. The national contexts of these movements affected the possibilities for change at any given time, as well as their choice of strategies, timing, and priorities. I suggest that many of the challenges in forging transnational linkages among these movements are a product of a difficulty in fully appreciating these differences, even when the goals have intersected. This has resulted, for example, in Western scholars often defining the global movement with respect to the first and second waves of feminism in the West as though these phases occurred universally and as though Western movements were the precursors to similar movements in other parts of the world. Looking through the prism of the history of transnational feminism, instead one sees national and local trajectories always featured significantly, creating regional waves of feminism with their own dynamics and pace that did not necessarily correspond to Western trends. In more recent years, for example, the momentum for feminist mobilization has picked up in non-Western countries, whereas activism in Western countries has declined relative to them, as well as in absolute terms.

First Wave of Transnational Mobilization (1880–1930)

During the first wave of *international* women's mobilization (1880–1930), many organizations focused on issues of peace, suffrage, temperance, equal access to education and industrial training, equal pay for equal work, and labor legislation, but also on social welfare and religious concerns. The year 1868 marks the formation of the first transnational women's organization, the Association Internationale des Femmes, in Geneva to address issues of suffrage and secular education (Adams 2004). Between the years 1880 and 1900, the global mobilization of women expanded with the formation of new transnational women's organizations around a wide range of issues and in a variety of contexts. For example, although transnational influences were also evident, the suffrage movement in Japan in the 1880s emerged in response to a domestic popular rights movement; in China the suffrage movement of the early 1900s was part of an anti-Qing movement that demanded political rights for women. In both countries, the struggle for the right to vote was coupled with campaigns to get women elected into office. Later in the 1920s in Japan, suffragists like Ichikawa Fusae saw the struggle for the right to vote as more than just a means of getting legislation passed to benefit women and children, as women's suffrage had been framed in the United States. For her and other Japanese feminists, the women's vote would allow women to assert themselves on a wide range of issues affecting society. The 1920s suffrage movements in Japan and India were, according to Ellen DuBois, more feminist and vigorous than any other such movements in that period worldwide (DuBois 2000, 541–549). Similarly, the Chilean Women's Civic Party, formed in 1922, advocated suffrage for women but saw it in a broader context of obtaining civil, political, and economic equality with men (Pernet 2000, 671).

Some of the earliest transnational women's influences were religious in nature, like the Mother's Union, which originated in Britain. In addition to its Protestant Christian message, the organization also promoted education, leadership, and organizational skills among women, which had spillover implications for women's political activism around the world.

Other international women's organizations established in this period included the World Women's Christian Temperance Union (founded in 1883), the International Congress of Women (1888), the International Council of Women (1888), the General Federation of Women's Clubs (1889), which was one of the world's largest and oldest women's volunteer service organizations, the World Young Women's Christian Association (1894), and the International Women's Suffrage Alliance (1904) (Boulding 1977, 188). These particular transnational organizations were based in the West, and their leadership was almost entirely Western, although there were exceptions right from the beginning. The International Congress of Women's founding meeting in 1888 had delegates not only from Europe but also from India. The Women's Christian Temperance Union chapters that were formed in China, Japan, India, Korea, and Burma in the 1880s became an important focal point for the suffrage movement in these countries (DuBois 2000, 547).

One of the first major transnational struggles of women was over the right to vote, which started in the Pacific and Europe and quickly spread worldwide with decolonization. New Zealand and Australia were the first countries that granted women this right, in 1893 and 1902, respectively. Finland was the first country in Europe to grant voting rights to women, in 1906; Canada was the first in North America (1918), with the United States following two years later; Ecuador was the first in Latin America (1928), as were Sri Lanka in Asia (1931) and Senegal in Africa (1945). After World War II, many countries granted women universal suffrage along with men as part of the process of creating newly independent nations, since by then the inclusion of women as voters had been institutionalized within new nations (Ramirez, Soysal, and Shanahan 1997, 736).

Ramirez and coauthors show how suffrage movements were only partially national struggles; they were part of transnational movements drawing on universal aspirations that use the resources of various kinds of international organizations. They appealed to global principles that transcended national boundaries. However, it is important to recognize that transnational influences were being absorbed by local movements in distinctive ways and that the inspiration and form the movements took were shaped by national events and trends. Moreover, the suffrage movement was not the only transnational movement in this period. In 1910 the International Women's Congress in Latin America met in Buenos Aires with delegates from Peru, Paraguay, Uruguay, and Argentina; their focus was on women's education and civil and political rights as well as divorce.

Although early Chilean feminists were influenced by North American and European suffragists whom they encountered while studying abroad, feminists like Amanda Labarca distinguished themselves from English-speaking feminists and their liberal approaches, claiming that they were too individualistic, too hostile to men as the enemy, and not sufficiently concerned with the family (Pernet 2000, 666).

Transnational influences were even stronger in the period following this initial wave of suffrage acquisition, although Europe and North America experienced a downturn in feminist linkages in the 1930s. With the rise of fascism in the 1930s, economic depression in Europe and North America, and the outbreak of World War II, international mobilization was hampered. Communication and meetings became difficult to organize. Some early organizations were torn by nationalist pressures that challenged their internationalist impulses. Other groups found themselves conflicted on principles of pacifism that they had adopted.

Winning the right to vote for women in Europe and North America had taken the momentum out of many women's rights movements in these countries, but for the rest of the world, major women's rights movements were gearing up. Women in Pacific Rim countries, for example, met in 1928 in Honolulu to establish a women's rights network, and out of these early meetings the Pan-Pacific Women's Association was formed in 1930. In 1935 a coalition of women's rights organizations brought the treaty to the League of Nations, which voted to further study the issue.

A series of Pan-American Congresses of Women were held from 1910 onward, and the Pan-American Association for the Advancement of Women (PAAAW) was formed in 1922 to promote women's education, property rights, suffrage, and peace in North and South America. As the North Americans in the PAAAW shifted their efforts to focus on peace issues, the organization dissolved and eventually was replaced by the Inter-American Commission of Women (IACW) of the Pan-American Union (later to be known as the Organization of American States), which was formed in 1928 in Havana. In the 1920s, Latin American feminists had distanced themselves from North American feminists, but by the 1930s these differences had begun to dissolve. Lack of funds prevented extensive travel between North and South America and so international communication largely took the form of correspondence and exchanges within newspapers.

The IACW focused on women's civil and political rights and began monitoring progress on the legal status of women in the region. In the

1930s an initiative of the IACW led by Marta Vergara of Chile and Maria Pizano of Colombia lobbied the League of Nations to allow married women citizenship rights worldwide (DuBois 2000, 550). Although suffrage was clearly a concern, it is important to note that the emphasis of Latin American feminists in this period was much broader than suffrage and focused on women's equality and political rights as the touchstone of democracy. Women's rights in the international rhetoric of the time were about peace, democracy, and progress. In fact, these Latin American activists saw democracy in the Americas as worthy of European emulation, given the fascist tendencies that had emerged by the mid-1930s in Europe (Pernet 2000, 664, 681). During World War II, democracy became even more central to their cause, and after the war their emphasis shifted to peace building.

In the decades under colonial rule in Asia and Africa, transnational activism was characterized by efforts by some Western women to work with colonized women in the areas of education, health, political representation, and legal status. These initiatives were complicated by the fact that they were frequently closely entwined with the colonial project of modernization and the missionary project of promoting Christian beliefs, values, and lifestyle. At times these initiatives were welcomed by local activists and contributed to their own efforts to eradicate various practices. This was the case with the efforts to abolish foot binding in China (1874–1911) and the initiatives to abolish bride wealth in Uganda in the 1950s.

In other instances, as in Kenya in 1920–1931 and later in the 1950s, efforts to abolish female genital cutting strengthened the nationalist cause and gave new salience to the practice, which came to symbolize nationalist opposition to colonialism. In 1930, the Anglican Church in Meru banned female genital cutting and said it would excommunicate African members for practicing it. When the colonial government banned the practice in 1956, girls in Meru went so far as to circumcise themselves in protest. Africans left the church in droves to protest the ban. Similarly, Adams (2004) shows how in both French and British Cameroon, efforts by colonial administrators and missionaries to abolish bride wealth through the education of women were largely ignored by the local population.

Women from the colonial countries themselves varied in orientation, as Kumari Jayawardena (1995) has shown in the case of South Asia. Some colonial feminists thoroughly supported the imperial project and were bent on carrying out their civilizing mission, whereas others were social reformers who did not challenge colonialism but did not actively support it either. Although few in number, there were individual Western women's rights advocates who actively supported the cause of third world independence. Similar variance in colonial women activists was found in Africa (Callaway 1987; Denzer 1992; Jayawardena 1995; Labode 1993; Ranchod-Nilsson 1992; Strobel 1991; Tripp 2002).

Second Wave of Transnational Mobilization (1945–1975)

After World War II, a new wave of international gender-based mobilization took off as women became active in efforts to secure independence for their countries and resist colonialism. Organizations that had a European and North American focus became more international in scope. The membership of the International Council of Women (ICW) jumped from having 78 percent of its affiliate councils based in Europe and the United States in 1938 to having only 47 percent of its membership from these countries by 1963.

Many women's movements worldwide sprang up in this period quite independent of women's movements in the West, contrary to claims that they originated in feminist movements in North America and Europe (e.g., Keck and Sikkink 1998, 168). In Africa, as Margaret C. Snyder (2003) has argued, the African women's movement evolved from its own independent base with its own intrinsic philosophy and distinct goals. It was not a carbon copy of Western movements and in fact predated the second-wave movement in the West. Its beginnings were African, rooted mostly in the fight for independence. DuBois (2000), Jayawardena (1986), Lavrin (1995), Pernet (2000), and others have shown much the same in the case of women's rights movements throughout Asia, Latin America, Africa, and the Middle East. In their local struggles for equal rights, women in these regions developed their own feminisms distinct from Western feminisms.

After World War II, the UN Commission on the Status of Women, established in 1945, became a focal point of international advocacy and for the promotion of women's rights in all spheres. It was largely a product of efforts of Latin American women suffragists. The 1950s was not a period of "doldrums" for feminism in Latin America but rather the decade in which many Latin American countries extended the franchise to women and activists there were energized and internationally engaged. Nonetheless, when the CSW began, its fifteen members came primarily from Western countries. Today it has forty-five members, including thir-teen from African states, eleven from Asian states, four from Eastern Euro-pean states, nine from Latin American and Caribbean states, and eight from Western European and other states. The makeup of the CSW not only reflects global demographics and changes in the structure of the UN that took place after independence but also suggests a geopolitical realign-ment that has resulted from shifting dynamics within transnational women's movements globally, giving more voice and legitimacy to the global South.

Third Wave of Transnational Women's Mobilization (1985–)

Although influences from the global South had always been in evidence throughout the two earlier waves of mobilization (1880–1930 and 1945–1975), it was not until the third wave of transnational women's activism (1985 to present) that the South began to challenge in a concerted fashion the ideological dominance of the North in framing the international women's agenda. This coincided with a major expansion of transnational mobilization.

The 1970s were a period of ferment in the West. Large numbers of organizations formed around feminist principles with the rise of "second-wave feminism" in the United States and Europe. Women's movements and broader social movements increasingly interacted with and influenced one another. New international organizations and networks, such as Women's International Network (WIN), International Feminist Network, and International Women's Information and Communication Service, emerged and were focused on women's health, reproductive rights, peace, human rights, poverty, prostitution, and violence against women. But many of the established international groups in the 1970s were led by white, middle-class women from the North, and the majority of their funding came from North America and the United States (Stienstra 1994, 100–101). This became an increasing source of tension.

Early Challenges to Northern Dominance: Women in Development Agendas

The UN conferences became a venue in which various North-South tensions were played out. Many of the conflicts focused on the objections by women in the South to the northern women's emphasis on the primacy of feminism and on relations between men and women. Many women from the South, for example, accused women from the North of coming to the UN women's conference in Mexico in 1975 presuming that a specific feminist orientation would provide a common framework for action. Gloria Steinem had drawn up a feminist manifesto without any input from women in the South, which seemed to many third world women to be a subtle form of cultural imperialism. Women from the South tended to focus on how women's problems were defined by global inequality, imperialism, and other political concerns that were not seen as gender-specific. At this first UN conference on women, and even more so at the Copenhagen conference (1980) that followed, women from the South challenged Northern women to see development issues as women's concerns.

Similarly, at a conference of academics held at Wellesley College in 1976 to bring together women from the North and South to discuss the concerns of third world women, participants from the South criticized what they perceived as a limited and singular vision of feminism presented at the conference, one that ignored global inequalities and political differences and the ways in which multinational corporations and trade relations were tied to the oppression of women. Rather than just a critique, alternative visions were offered.

Third world networks of activists and scholars, like Development Alternatives with Women for a New Era (DAWN) formed in 1984 in the Caribbean, Latin America, and South Asia, pushed for an agenda that incorporated women's concerns in development strategies, policies, and theories. These concerns became integral to the efforts of the United Nations Development Fund for Women (UNIFEM), which supported women's projects and women's participation in mainstream development programs (Pietilä 2002, 37, 38). The formation of many third world–based international networks—like DAWN and Women Living under Muslim Laws in the mid-1980s and Women in Law and Development in Africa (WILDAF) in 1990—represented the beginning of the shift in the center of gravity in global women's mobilization dynamics. These organizations were not just coexisting alongside organizations based in the North, but claimed a leadership role in transnational women's movements (Bunch 2001, 380).

Shifting Momentum

By 1985 at the UN Nairobi conference, the earlier North-South tensions over agenda priorities had subsided. Feminist activists in the North had come to accept the importance of global development concerns as relevant to women, and women in the South became more willing to focus on gender equality (Snyder and Tadesse 1995). More than 60 percent of the attendees in Nairobi were from the South. It was at this point that the overall feminist center of gravity began to move from the North to the South.

Transnational networks were formed around violence against women as early as 1974, with the creation of Isis. By the 1990s, violence against women had gained in importance as a major issue around which activists forged networks and alliances around the world. By the end of the century, it had become the most important international women's issue and the most dynamic human rights concern globally (Keck and Sikkink 1998, 166).

Women's organizations had been working on issues of state violence against women in the 1970s and 1980s. The 1981 feminist Encounter for Latin America and the Caribbean in Bogotá held a Day to Resist Violence against Women, which led to annual commemorations throughout Latin America and eventually to the global campaign Sixteen Days of Activism against Gender Violence. Transnational networks focused on violence began to emerge at the UN Women's Conference in Copenhagen in 1980 and in Nairobi in 1985. Regional groups formed in Asia, Latin America, and elsewhere, and global networks formed around particular issues such as the trafficking of women. At the UN conference in Nairobi, understandings of violence against women were broadened from domestic violence and rape to violence against women caused by economic deprivation, structural adjustment, environmental degradation, war, and political repression.

The 1993 World Conference on Human Rights in Vienna marked a turning point: it represented a major success in bringing the women's rights agenda into the human rights agenda. Foundations made funding available in this area of women and human rights, and new organizations emerged, like the Global Campaign on Women's Human Rights organized by the Center for Women's Global Leadership (Keck and Sikkink 1998, 181). New international conventions adopted these concerns. The phrase "violence against women" was first used by the Organization of American States when it adopted the Inter-American Convention on the Prevention, Punishment, and Eradication of Violence against Women in 1994. It was the culmination of years of work by women's activists.

There was also a new awareness that emerged around the use of rape in civil war in former Yugoslavia that could then be used to highlight the use of rape in other conflicts as well. In part, as Charlotte Bunch explained, the unities came from a realization that while everyone shared these problems, no one had a monopoly on the solutions, thus laying a better basis for discussion. Violence against women was absorbed into the language of human rights, which already had gained acceptance as a legal norm (Bunch and Fried 1996). Particular experiences of violence, for example, sati, dowry deaths, and female genital cutting, were treated as examples of violence against women rather than as "exotic practices signifying the primitive nature of national cultures," as they had been characterized in UN conferences in Mexico and Copenhagen. The inclusivity of the movement was key to its success, Weldon argues (2004).

By the beginning of the twenty-first century, the two strands within the global women's movements had come together: human rights issues and sustainable development concerns. They merged into what is referred to as the "rights-based approach." Human rights is seen as the central focus of sustainable human development: it offers the means, the ends, and a framework for assessing sustainable development and for guaranteeing a full array of rights that went well beyond those found in legislation and constitutions. This rights-based orientation had a more expansive reach beyond the approaches to development that emphasized donor or NGO assistance and local participation by adding to these concerns another level of action. The rights-based advocacy approach stressed the need for coalitions of NGOs and local activists and other actors to lobby governments, corporations, international financial institutions, and other global and domestic actors to create the necessary political, economic, and human rights conditions for equality, sustainable human development, and social justice.

This new universalism faced challenges when it came into conflict with defenders of cultural practices who regarded women's rights as secondary to ethnic, religious, clan, and other such particularistic practices and beliefs. While theorists became interested in attempting to resolve these issues intellectually (Kymlicka 1995; Okin 1999; Phillips 2002), it was also increasingly clear that these seemingly intractable issues would ultimately need to be struggled through in real-world political battles and accommodations.

By the time of the UN's Fourth World Conference on Women in Beijing in 1995, there was considerable unity around the framing of "women's rights as human rights" and opposition to violence against women, which helped further bridge Northern and Southern interests. The gap between the North and South was closing. Thus, in the third-wave debates around human rights and development, women's movements in the South were especially important in expanding definitions of what women's concerns included and in looking at the broader global political and economic forces that influence women's status. They pointed to changing factors that shaped gender relations, ranging from colonialism during the struggles for independence, to poverty, militarization, and democratization both in newly independent states and in the former colonial powers, to contemporary issues of globalization that institutionalize inequality through international debt, structural adjustment policies, and unequal trade relations.

In sum, the changing global dynamics in women's mobilization can be traced to the initial challenges to Western dominance around the time of the 1975 Mexico conference. The 1985 Nairobi conference marked a major turning point in North-South dynamics as new third world networks emerged. The impetus generated by the 1995 UN Beijing conference produced a new rights-based approach blending sustainable development and human rights concerns in the twenty-first century. Today, the shift in momentum from North to South is evident in three ways: in the types of issues being put on the table; in the kinds of organizations championing these agendas, including informal networks; and in the extent to which women's rights is perceived as a universal goal rather than as a Western feminist project.

Changing Agendas and Actors

In the past decade, many of the specific initiatives pertaining to women's rights have come from the global South. For example, a key demand of many women's movements is equal representation of women in legislative bodies, local government, and other decision-making bodies. In various African countries like South Africa, Namibia, Uganda, Kenya, and Sierra Leone, there are 50/50 movements advocating that women claim half of all parliamentary seats. International and regional bodies, including the Inter-Parliamentary Union, the Beijing conference on women, the Southern African Development Community, the Socialist International, and the Organization of American States, have been debating the use of quotas to promote women's parliamentary representation. More than eighty countries have adopted some form of quotas to improve the selection of female candidates running for office, and another twenty have launched quota debates over the past ten years (Krook 2004). These include legislative or constitutional provisions for the adoption of party quotas or reserved seats or the adoption of quotas on a voluntary basis by parties themselves. Some regional organizations set targets for member states to attain. In the 1990s, new efforts to introduce quotas to improve women's legislative representation were especially common in Latin America and Africa. Drude Dahlerup and Lenita Freidenvall (2003) have argued that the incremental model of increasing women's representation in parliament that led to high rates of female representation in the Nordic countries in the 1970s was replaced by the fast-track model one finds in many developing countries, where dramatic jumps in parliamentary representation are brought about by the introduction of electoral quotas.

Another area that has generated considerable momentum in the South has been the adoption of "gender budgets," or attempts to make the gender implications of national spending priorities more explicit and ultimately more fair. After the UN women's conference in Beijing (1995), many countries adopted women's budgets patterned along the lines of South Africa's 1994 budget exercise and the budgets of federal and state governments in Australia that were adopted as early as 1984. By 2000, gender-sensitive budget initiatives were under way in eighteen countries in four regions. Gender budget initiatives are generally coordinated by the ministry of finance and involve collaboration among NGOs and the legislature. The gender budgeting process involves analysis of existing budgets to determine the differential gender impact on women, men, girls, and boys, and making recommendations for future budgets to improve the way in which funds are allocated (Budlender 2000). Much of the impetus for gender budgeting came through the Commonwealth Secretariat, which explains why most of the countries that first adopted the budget initiatives were formerly part of the British Empire, including Uganda,

Botswana, Zimbabwe, Malawi, Sri Lanka, Barbados, Namibia, and Tanzania, as well as Australia. Gender budgeting has now spread more widely in the West; the European Union has endorsed this as an approach, as have the parliaments of some of its member states such as Germany.

Women's economic activity also gained recognition as new women's entrepreneurial organizations linked economic empowerment and access to credit to social empowerment issues, including access to health care, literacy, and housing, opposing domestic violence and other such issues. Feminist economists and activists struggled to make policymakers understand that key economic indicators like the gross domestic product and gross national product do not account for women's unpaid labor in the home and the community. Such labor includes care work of the family, voluntary work, subsistence agricultural labor, and self-employed or subcontracted labor in informal markets, all of which are important to the economy in many developing countries. Were such labor to be accounted for, they argued, economic reform, welfare, labor, and other such policies would be shaped in fundamentally different ways. Policies should respond not only to the demands of the market, which is only a portion of the economy, but also to the needs and priorities of those involved in unpaid labor, informal labor markets, and other forms of "hidden" labor, they argued. These new understandings of women's labor began to reconfigure the way many policymakers thought of the market, as well as notions of value, efficiency, and productivity.

Another aspect of gendered globalization is the flow of labor across borders. In December 2000, 121 countries signed the UN Convention against Transnational Organized Crime to States, and more than 80 countries signed one of its supplementary protocols—the Protocol to Prevent, Suppress and Punish Trafficking in Persons, Especially Women and Children—which was aimed at undermining international crime networks and fighting the trafficking of people, especially women. Trafficking includes the recruitment, transportation, transfer, holding, and receipt of people through coercion, abduction, fraud, or deception. It also refers to the abuse of power to exploit someone through prostitution, sexual exploitation, forced labor, slavery, servitude, or other such means. The protocol was the result of years of extensive lobbying by coalitions, alliances, and organizations of women's rights, antitrafficking, human rights, and migrants' groups, many of which had very different views on prostitution and its relation to trafficking (Sullivan 2003).

One of the main strategies that has developed to foster women's empowerment in poor countries is the provision of microcredit and the means to a living, generally through self-employment. The Self Employed Women's Association (SEWA), based in Ahmedabad, India, adopts a holistic approach to women's empowerment, serving as a model globally. SEWA was formed in 1972, drawing inspiration from the thinking of the Indian nationalist leader and pacifist Mahatma Gandhi. It is an advocacy organization and at the same time a movement of poor, self-employed women workers themselves. Such women workers are part of the larger sector of nonsalaried unprotected labor that makes up 93 percent of all workers in India. SEWA not only has pressed the Indian government to provide training programs and other services for this sector and lobbied for better legislation for self-employed workers in India but also has taken its campaign onto the global arena. It was a leading force in mobilizing international pressure to get the International Labour Organisation's Home Work Convention (1996) adopted.

Regional Influences on Transnational Women's Activism

Some of the new influences come out of particular regions of the South. African influences, for example, have been numerous, as Peg Snyder argues (2003). Snyder has shown how African women had not merely absorbed a brand of feminism diffused by Western activists. Rather, women's activism in Africa developed from indigenous bases and influenced international women's movements. African women's organizations pressed the UN Economic Commission for Africa to establish a training center for women. The African Training and Research Center for Women, which was formed in Addis Ababa, became the first regional center in the world and soon became a model for the UN system as other such centers were established.

Similarly, Women's World Banking was inspired by women's economic activity in Africa. At a preconference seminar before the 1975 Mexico City UN World Conference on Women, the successful Ghanaian entrepreneur, industrialist, and philanthropist Esther Ocloo pioneered the idea of formalizing local women's credit associations to help women access capital to improve their economic situation. Ocloo worked with Ela Bhatt, founder of the Self Employed Women's Association in India, and Michaela Walsh, a New York investment banker, and together they founded Women's World

Banking in 1979. Ocloo became the first chairperson of its board, serving in that capacity from 1980 to 1985. As of 2005, Women's World Banking operates in forty-five countries around the world.

In the early 1970s, African women pioneered the collection of gender-disaggregated data, and in particular information on the gender division of labor. Scholars of African households like Simi Afonja, Nancy Folbre, Judith Bruce, and Eleanor Fapohunda were among the first to highlight the divided nature of households along gender lines. This led to a dramatic shift in the way many leading economists and development practitioners worldwide thought of household income and labor, challenging previous conventions in economics that assumed a unitary household defined by male preferences.

Coming from a continent that has experienced a great many of the world's civil conflicts, African women also were very proactive in pushing issues of peace and peacemaking in international forums and in confronting various heads of states. Women's marginalization from politics meant that they brought a different set of interests to bear on peace processes and talks. African women, in particular, made peace a central issue at the UN Beijing conference on women in 1995. Their efforts contributed greatly to the passing of the UN Security Council Resolution 1325 on October 31, 2000, to include women in peace negotiations and give them roles in peacekeeping missions around the world. The resolution requires protection of women and girls against sexual assault in civil conflicts and heightened efforts to place women in decision-making positions in international institutions.

Already women had been active in informal peace initiatives in civil conflicts in Colombia, Guatemala, Burundi, Rwanda, Bosnia, Northern Ireland, and elsewhere. In these countries they had formed coalitions of women's organizations across "enemy lines" focused on very practical concerns. In Africa, the equal representation of women in peace negotiations and peace-building initiatives has become a key agenda item in conflict-ridden societies because women believe they have a different approach to conflict and different perspectives to bring to bear. In peace negotiations in Burundi, Democratic Republic of Congo, Sierra Leone, Somalia, and elsewhere, women generally came to the peace table already united as a bloc of women. Unity across ethnic or religious division is their starting point rather than the end point. Their demands were more oriented toward pragmatic solutions to health, education, and other problems, rather than vying for positions of power in a restructured state.

Africa was by no means the only region exerting these types of transnational influences. Women in Latin America forged and expanded some of the strongest regional networks: they took the lead in developing networks among movement activists and state policymakers and in creating models for networking worldwide (Keck and Sikkink 1998, 170). For example, each year since 1981, Latin American and Caribbean feminist *encuentros* (meetings) have brought together thousands of women from across the region to discuss issues of transnational importance to the movement. In some cases activists formed networks around particular themes (reproductive rights, trafficking of women and children, domestic violence). New regional networks in Africa emerged in the late 1990s and after 2000 around female education, reproductive rights, violence against women, women's political empowerment, women in peace building, land rights, and many other concerns. Similar regional networks were found in other parts of the world.

In sum, at the beginning of the twenty-first century, most global networks were still based in the North. But global networks are increasingly initiated and led by women in the South, and even though much of their funding still comes from the North, the perspectives and priorities they offer are their own. For example, the Wise Women Process group, which started meeting at the Beijing+5 conference in New York in 2000 and was renamed Revitalising the International Feminist Movement at its 2002 Kampala meeting, is an informal network of activists that is one of the brain trusts of the international women's movement. This group involves activists, journalists, UN officials, and academics and is led by non-Western women; of its thirty-nine members, only five are from the global North. Its priorities, according to Mahnaz's Afkhami, were to revisit "the women's movement from the perspective of the women of the South" and to "rethink the movement's premises in ways that are more inclusive, more grassroots-oriented, more culturally relevant and nuanced, and more apt to appeal to a large segment of the world's population than West-focused and initiated efforts of the past that were shaped primarily by the experience of the women of the developed world" (Wise Women Process 2002).

Causes of the Shift in Momentum

Several factors have contributed to the shift in momentum in women's mobilization from the global North to the South. In the United States, for example, there is a growing complacency about the necessity of improving women's status and a greater need to defend gains already made. The demise of the labor movement, a deficit in the numbers of women activists holding political office, especially at the national level, a lack of femocrats in government positions, and the general strengthening of the position of conservative political forces have all contributed to a situation where the United States is falling behind in many key areas. The Bush administration's unilateralism in foreign policy has only reinforced these tendencies. The lack of media coverage of international initiatives that are adopted by feminist organizations contributes to the general lack of awareness of how far behind women in the United States have fallen.

In contrast, we have witnessed in the global South the vigorous use of transnational coalitions and networks, along with international treaties, platforms, and conferences to push new women's rights agendas. Intense regional networking in Latin America, Africa, and Asia around particular issues (trafficking, land reform, education, peace building, reproductive rights, violence against women, electoral quotas) has helped define these concerns and develop strategies to address them. Feminists in state and international policymaking positions have supported movement initiatives in these areas.

Some of the elements of this global shift have regional dimensions. Active or nascent women's movements have emerged in Africa, creating new energy around women's issues. The increased influence of femocrats within state institutions as in Latin America coupled with the NGOization or professionalization of women's activism have provided sustained interest in women's concerns that had been primarily the domain of women's movements in the 1970s and 1980s. New donor interest in supporting gender concerns as part of effective use of development aid has also contributed to the new momentum found in the global South.

The educational levels of women have changed dramatically around the world since the 1970s. The gender gap in literacy and school enrollment closed by half between 1970 and 1990. The gap between female enrollment at the tertiary level jumped from less than half the male rate in 1970 to 70 percent by 1990 (UNDP 1995, 33–34). This meant that the numbers of women with the necessary skills to lead national organizations and to hold decision-making positions increased dramatically, which had implications for women's participation in international forums. As Moghadam has observed, "Transnational feminist networks have emerged in the context of a growing population of educated, employed, mobile and politically aware women around the world" (2000, 79).

After the 1990s, the expanded use of the Internet, e-mail, faxes, and other forms of communication greatly facilitated networking globally. Governments were increasingly eager to demonstrate that they had modernized and were seeking to adhere to the emerging international norms regarding women. They had committed themselves to many international and regional treaties and conventions regarding women's status and needed to show progress in at least some of the goals ratified there. All these factors contributed to the shifting dynamics in transnational mobilization around women's rights that increasingly placed the momentum in the South.

Another factor contributing to the shift in the global momentum in advocacy for women's rights relates to the dynamics within the women's movements in the United States and Europe. In European and U.S. women's movement organizations there is surprisingly little discussion of how their countries' policies and economic practices affect women in other parts of the world. This is especially striking because the policies of the global North are a key subject of discussion in women's movements in the global South. The locus of global economic and political power resides in the industrially developed countries, and what happens in them has worldwide implications. There has yet to emerge a full appreciation of the way in which the policies of the North affect the South, and the interconnections between our mutual fates and futures. With a few important exceptions (e.g., political representation for women in Iraq and Afghanistan and development policy in Scandinavia), there is relatively little lobbying of the governments in the North by U.S. and European women's organizations to address concerns of women in the South, especially regarding global inequalities and the role of international financial institutions like the World Bank and International Monetary Fund.

The disconnect between the Northern and Southern feminist movements has implications for conditions for women in the North as well. There does not appear to be tremendous pressure on the U.S. government to ratify the CEDAW, which is used by women worldwide to advance their causes and concerns. The United States signed the convention in July 1980. The lack of urgency is especially strange when 90 percent (177) of the UN member countries have ratified it. As Charlotte Bunch (2002) noted: "There has been little interest here [i.e., in the United States] in using international human rights treaties like the Convention on the Elimination of All Forms of Discrimination Against Women (CEDAW), to advance domestic issues. There is a tendency not to see the international arena as adding anything to causes at home" (39). This is a striking difference with the earlier suffrage movements, which saw the adoption of the right to vote for women in other countries as an impetus for the United States to do the same.

American feminists seem little bothered by the fact that countries like Rwanda have 49 percent female representation in parliament (women hold 14.3 percent of the seats in the U.S. House and 13 percent of the seats in the Senate) and appear disinterested in the major ongoing worldwide debates about how to increase female legislative representation. U.S. feminists remain virtually untouched by these discussions. Moreover, the United States does not seem concerned about keeping up with other industrialized countries in terms of maternity and paternity leave, welfare benefits for single mothers, health care for uninsured women, and many other benefits that affect the well-being of women and of society. The 1993 Family and Medical Leave Act permits any employee who has worked for at least one year to take up to twelve weeks of unpaid leave a year to care for a newborn, adopted child, or another family member in need of care. There is little outrage at the limitations of this policy, perhaps because Americans are unaware of how far behind they have fallen when it comes to women's rights. Most women worldwide, even in the Middle East, enjoy paid maternity leave. For example, women have fourteen weeks maternity leave in Algeria, and twelve weeks in Morocco with 100 percent of their wages paid by social security.

Conclusions

This chapter has traced some of the changes in momentum at a transnational level and explored the consequences of these changes. It has evaluated the need to address these issues at a time when bilateral and multilateral aid is shrinking, and to consider the difficulties posed by continuing North-South gaps in approach and concerns. Even though feminists in North America and Europe have seemed to dominate transnational movements at particular moments, such as the early UN conferences on women in the 1970s, the closer one looks at particular movements, the more one finds that the influences on both agenda and organizations have always been multidirectional, even going back to the late 1800s. But one also finds that despite their transnational dimensions, women's movements define themselves and their vision of feminism with respect to local conditions. Non-Western countries continue to actively define their own agendas and have, in fact, claimed much of the momentum of feminist and women's rights advocacy globally, as movements in the global North have declined or become complacent or merely parochial. Global feminism is not a new phenomenon, but it is a more South-centered movement than ever before. This presents new challenges, of course, but there are also opportunities for women worldwide. The rights-centered approach to development offers a new and potentially powerful basis for cooperation. It is now up to feminist organizations in the global North to become more active participants in this worldwide movement.

Bibliography

Adams, Melinda. 2004. "Renegotiating the Boundaries of Political Action: Transnational Actors, Women's Organizations, and the State in Cameroon." Ph.D. diss., University of Wisconsin–Madison.

Boulding, Elise. 1977. *Women in the Twentieth Century World.* New York: Halsted Press.

Budlender, Debbie. 2000. "The Political Economy of Women's Budgets in the South." *World Development* 28:1365–1378.

Bunch, Charlotte. 2002. "International Networking for Women's Human Rights." In Michael Edwards and John Gaventa, eds., *Global Citizen Action,* 217–229. Boulder, Colo.: Lynne Rienner.

———. 2002. "Whose Security?" *Nation,* September 23.

Bunch, Charlotte, and Susana Fried. 1996. "Beijing '95: Moving Women's Human Rights from Margin to Center." *Signs,* August, 200–204.

Callaway, Helen. 1987. *Gender, Culture and Empire: European Women in Colonial Nigeria.* Urbana: University of Illinois Press.

Dahlerup, Drude, and Lenita Freidenvall. 2003. "Quotas as a 'Fast Track' to Equal Political Representation for Women: Why Scandinavia Is No Longer the Model." Paper presented at the annual meeting of the American Political Science Association, August 28 to 31.

Denzer, LaRay. 1992. "Domestic Science Training in Colonial Yorubaland." In Karen Hansen, ed., *African Encounters with Domesticity,* 116–139. New Brunswick, N.J.: Rutgers University Press.

DuBois, Ellen. 2000. "Woman Suffrage: The View from the Pacific" *Pacific Historical Review* 69:539–551.

European Commission. 2002. "Beijing+5: An Overview of the European Union Follow-up and Preparations." http://europa.eu.int/comm/employment_social/ equ_opp/beijdocen.pdf.

European Parliament Committee on Women's Rights and Gender Equality. 2004. the Secretariat, Brussels, June 29. http://www.europarl.eu.int/comparl/femm/ news_docs/presentation_en.doc.

Jayawardena, Kumari. 1986. *Feminism and Nationalism in the Third World.* London: Zed Books.

———. 1995. *The White Woman's Other Burden: Western Women and South Asia during British Rule.* New York: Routledge.

Keck, Margaret E., and Kathryn Sikkink. 1998. *Activists beyond Borders: Advocacy Networks in International Politics.* Ithaca, N.Y.: Cornell University Press.

Krook, Mona. 2004. "Reforming Representation: The Diffusion of Candidate Gender Quotas Worldwide." Paper presented at the meeting of the International Studies Association, Montreal, Canada.

Kymlicka, Will. 1995. *Multicultural Citizenship.* Oxford: Clarendon Press.

Labode, Modupe. 1993. "From Heathen Kraal to Christian Home: Anglican Mission Education and African Christian Girls, 1850–1900." In Fiona Bowie, Deborah Kirkwood, and Shirley Ardener, eds., *Women and Missions: Past and Present—Anthropological and Historical Perceptions,* 126–144. Oxford: Berg.

Lavrin, Asuncion. 1995. *Women, Feminism, and Social Change in Argentina, Chile, and Uruguay, 1890–1940.* Lincoln: University of Nebraska Press.

Moghadam, Valentine M. 2000. "Transnational Feminist Networks: Collective Action in an Era of Globalization." *International Sociology* 15, no. 1: 57–85.

Okin, Susan Moller. 1999. "Is Multiculturalism Bad for Women?" In Joshua Cohen, Matthew Howard, and Martha C. Nussbaum, eds., *Is Multiculturalism Bad for Women?* 9–24. Princeton, N.J.: Princeton University Press.

Pernet, Corinne A. 2000. "Chilean Feminists, the International Women's Movement, and Suffrage, 1915–1950." *Pacific Historical Review* 69:663–688.

Phillips, Ann. 2002. "Multiculturalism, Universalism, and the Claims of Democracy." In Maxine Molyneux and Shahra Razavi, eds., *Gender Justice, Democracy and Rights,* 115–138. Oxford: Oxford University Press.

Pietilä, Hilkka. 2002. *Engendering the Global Agenda: The Story of Women and the United Nations.* Development Dossier, UN/Non-Government Liaison Service, Geneva.

Ramirez, Francisco O., Yasemin Soysal, and Suzanne Shanahan. 1997. "The Changing Logic of Political Citizenship: Cross-National Acquisition of Women's Suffrage Rights, 1890 to 1990." *American Sociological Review* 67:735–745.

Ranchod-Nilsson, Sita. 1992. "'Educating Eve': The Women's Club Movement and Political Consciousness among Rural African Women in Southern Rhodesia,

1950–1980." In Karen Hansen, eds., *African Encounters with Domesticity*, 195–217. New Brunswick, N.J.: Rutgers University Press.

Snyder, Margaret C. 2003. "African Contributions to the Global Women's Movement." Paper presented to "National Feminisms, Transnational Arenas, Universal Human Rights," Havens Center Colloquium Series, Madison, Wisconsin, April 14.

Snyder, Margaret C., and Mary Tadesse. 1995. *African Women and Development: A History.* London: Zed Books.

Stienstra, Deborah. 1994. *Women's Movements and International Organizations.* New York: St. Martin's Press.

Strobel, Margaret. 1991. *European Women and the Second British Empire.* Bloomington: Indiana University Press.

Sullivan, Barbara. 2003. "Trafficking in Women: Feminism and New International Law." *International Feminist Journal of Politics* 5, no. 1: 67–91.

Tripp, Aili Mari. 2002. "Women's Mobilization in Uganda (1945–1962): Nonracial Ideologies within Colonial-African-Asian Encounters." *International Journal of African Historical Studies* 35:1–22.

UNDP. 1995. *Human Development Report 1995.* New York: Oxford University Press.

Weldon, S. Laurel, 2004. "Inclusion, Solidarity and Transnational Social Movements: The Global Movement against Gender Violence" Paper presented at the annual meeting of the American Political Science Association, Chicago, September 4.

Wise Women Process. 2004. *Revitalising the International Feminist Movement: A Report of the Consultations Held at Kampala, Uganda, July 22–25, 2002.*

Part II

Local Experiences
Encountering the Transnational

4

Turkey's Modern Paradoxes

Identity Politics, Women's Agency, and Universal Rights

Yakın Ertürk

The Turkish Republic, established in 1923, has experienced in the course of its history increased political pluralism, resulting in a diversification of images available for women, expanding space for autonomous individual initiative and for feminist organizational development. Parallel to this, divisions in formal politics along secularist, Islamist, and ethnic nationalist lines have encapsulated a women's agenda within their domain, thus potentially undermining the capacity for an autonomous feminist agenda. However, the growing aspirations in the country for individual rights and liberties, increased engagement of women's organizations with universal rights regimes, and the national consensus over European Union (EU) membership offer new opportunities for reinterpreting the parameters of national unity. Such reinterpretation may serve to transcend the domestic rivalries that arise in the alternative masculine political discourses. Paradoxically, women's status, which is at the center of current controversies, is perhaps the main point at which the "patriarchal knot" and thus the ensuing political tensions may be unraveled.

In this chapter, I address this paradox by looking at the competing forces of identity politics, gender mobilizations, and transnational political development. I suggest that the case of Turkey is particularly important because it incorporates Islamic and secular, modern and traditional, and democratic but authoritarian tendencies that shape the status of women around the world. Furthermore, it illustrates how women's agency can transcend domestic rivalries as a result of increased engagement in universal rights regimes.

Global Trends in Identity Politics

The trends observed in Turkey in identity politics and the representation of women in the public sphere correspond to global shifts in values towards the recognition of sociocultural pluralism. Since the early 1970s it has become evident that a diversified and plural competition for power gradually replaced the ideologically polarized world order between the East and the West that marked much of the twentieth century. This trend became particularly pronounced with the breakup of the Soviet bloc, which brought to the fore micronational and ethnic interests in redrawing of boundaries and conflict among groups within and between countries. Consequently, identity politics became central to the competition over power at national as well as international levels.

These developments revealed the fact that the modernization project, which most assumed would establish new contractual relationships free from the binding ties of the past, the family, tribe, or religion (Migdal 1997: 254), could not be realized. Instead, modernization became globalized, carrying the contradictions of national capitalisms to a transnational level.[1] While this resulted in deterritorialization of national borders for the flow of capital, new borders and new marginalities emerged for labor. The new tension between labor and capital has invigorated particularistic modes of identity and solidarity. The relations between the state, the community, and the individual are reconstituted around the communal group rather than the state as the focal point of loyalty, the provider of welfare, and the administrator of justice. While cultural fragmentation increasingly reinforces loyalties below and beyond the level of the national state, at the same time supranational institutions and transnational networks evoke other loyalties as they emerge as agents of change in the transformation from the national to the global market and link the local with the global.[2] Within this context, as the loyalty of individuals shifts to centers of power below and above the national state, the monopoly of the state over the representation of its citizens begins to erode, creating alternative norms and, at times, parallel normative systems that traditionally did not exist.

While transnational movements of the past two decades, such as environmentalism and feminism, offer the possibility for a global identity, the opportunity for inclusive membership in the transnational community for the masses of the world is jeopardized by several factors: (1) growing economic inequalities across the globe between nations, classes, ethnic groups, women, and men; (2) creation of new social marginalities and divisions among the working classes of the world, who are separated from one another in terms of language, culture, and religion; and (3) reconstitution of antagonisms tied to historical struggles in the form of a global conflict across imagined civilizations. Hence, globalization has proved to encompass equally strong tendencies toward standardization as well as fragmentation—and toward universalism as well as particularism—in restructuring the economic and political order.

Implications for Gender Equality

These trends have implications and give rise to tendencies that are contradictory for the identity formation of women and men. On the one hand, diversification implies greater options and autonomous space for women, and the weakened role of the state in determining identity allows for the expression of alternative lifestyles. On the other hand, politicization along ethnic/religious specificities poses a threat as women's public representation may be monopolized by traditional centers of power that claim legitimacy on the grounds of culture, ethnicity, and religion, thus overriding individual rights. Such spheres of power, whether in the North or in the South, are almost invariably biased against women. Women's identity carries the symbols of collective identity, such that the assertion of group boundaries necessarily suppresses women's individuality. Especially after September 11, the assertions of cultural particularism have deepened global antagonisms, "legitimizing" the power of conservative or even reactionary political actors, whether within or outside of the state apparatus. The global gender equality agenda and the capacity for women's collective action are adversely affected as a result (Ertürk 2004a).[3]

Paradoxically, parallel to these trends, there has also been a convergence over the value of universal human rights. This has been particularly marked in the area of the advancement of women. The UN-sponsored conferences of the 1990s—in particular, Vienna 1993, Cairo 1994, Beijing 1995, and Copenhagen 1980—placed gender equality and women's human rights on the public agenda across the globe. Moreover, emerging transnational feminist networks have been instrumental in simultaneously localizing global gender politics and globalizing local struggles. This creates a new *universalism* from below.

Conflicting demands emanating from group interests and interests of women as individuals continue to compete in the formation of women's identity. This issue has been central to debates on women's human rights. While some theorists have pointed to the incompatibility between women's rights and cultural diversity (Okin 1999), others have argued for the possibility of reconciliation (Kymlicka 1999). Still others, employing a dialectical approach, look at the contradictions that arise within the intersectionality of culture, material conditions, and relations of power that often underlie cultural justifications for women's subordination. As an advocate of the third approach, I aim to identify the sites where the struggle for change can be possible. From this perspective, women's liberation is better understood as a political problem than a cultural one (Ertürk 1991a, 2004a; Tripp 2002).

The critical question, then, is this: Given the global trend toward fragmentation along cultural lines, can universal human rights regimes help transcend paradoxical identity formations that subordinate women to a patriarchal gender order of competing masculinities operating locally, nationally, and internationally? Tripp (2002), in her study on Uganda, argues that universal norms reflect problems and solutions ingrained in the commonality of humanity. This conviction provides the underpinning for the global gender equality agenda, calling for human rights of women, equality between women and men, and commitment to change among women, linking them across discourses, cultural groups, classes, and nationalities. In what is to follow, this chapter provides an analysis of these trends in the case of Turkey, further exploring how local and global linkages are established in women's quest for transformative change.

Women's Identity Formation in Turkey

In analyzing women's identity formations in Turkey, my primary focus is on the politics of public representation of women within diverse discourses, resulting in the diversification of "legitimate" images available to them as the society moves from modernization to globalization. I argue that competing masculinities have dominated the political competition over identity politics in Turkey, representing alternative patriarchal conceptions of women's place in society, whether the ideological frame of reference is based on secular, nationalist, Islamist, or other principles.

While I identify similarities in the gender contract inherent in these alternative discourses, I also argue that the diversification of political discourse is accompanied by new contradictions that produce neutral zones—that is, ones undefined by the dominant competing paradigms—and rupture the traditional patriarchal order, resulting in greater space for women's autonomous movement. However, this is not an unproblematic process. Women's public representation is a convenient site where contending political groups negotiate their terms for an alternative societal project vis-à-vis one another. Today, while middle-class, educated women of all orientations enjoy more autonomous space, the secularist/Islamist polarization in formal politics sustains the contours of patriarchal dominance.

To establish the basis of these contradictory political forces shaping Turkish gender identities, I start with a discussion of the continuities and discontinuities in the transition from the Ottoman multinational Islamic world empire to the secular national state of the Turkish Republic. My attempt is neither to critique the Turkish modernization project nor to analyze the various forms of resistance and opposition to this project. Rather, at the risk of being categorical, I try to capture the specific discourse(s) defining women in successive time periods where men's competition over political power has been the defining characteristic.

My argument is that the political contest has been over the definition of the "modern" space. Therefore, in essence, all competing gender discourses are a by-product of the modernization project. Each political discourse, while reconfiguring and expanding modern space to include new symbols of representation, at the same time has generated its peripheral space of marginalities and excluded certain social groups. However, the latent consequence of this competition has been the broadening of space for autonomous individual action beyond what is intended by the various political discourses. The feminist movement and the liberalization of the economy in the 1980s have been both a consequence of and an instrument in the creation of an autonomous individual with a quest for an identity beyond what is prescribed by the competing discourses.

The impact of the global political processes on these developments cannot be overlooked. Most recently, Turkey's accession bid to the EU has complemented and reinforced the opening of new venues for individual liberties, particularly for women. Diverse women's groups, despite their mutual suspicion and seemingly irreconcilable differences, are joining to use both the regional mechanisms of the EU and the global ones of the UN in pushing their agenda forward.

Continuities and Discontinuities in State Formation

Turkey is located at the crossroads of two continents and many civilizations. It emerged as a modern secular national state by radically breaking from the multination Islamic Ottoman Empire and adopting a Western model of development. Ironically, a war for independence fought against Western powers after World War I made it possible for Turkey to diverge from its historical heritage and converge with the West. This process of transition carried with it elements of continuity and discontinuity, unity and diversity, tradition and modernity, which today still form the basis of political competition and identity politics.[4]

The elements of continuity from the Ottoman to the Republican era are ingrained in what has been referred to as "corporate identity" (Lewis 1961), which incorporated both religion and political power within state authority and historically facilitated the sustenance of a centralized political order. Keyder argues that "the historical genesis of the state tradition in Turkey determined the choices made by modernizers in their attempt to delimit the scope of modernity, thus undermining their avowed goal of Westernization" (1997: 39). Within this context, the collectivist community rather than the individual constituted the building block of society, thus suppressing any tendency toward heterogeneity in public discourse. This political culture, sustained through religion, state tradition, and economic order, is rooted in public consciousness, social convention, and the individual identities of men and women alike (Ertürk 1991a). These constitute the dimensions of continuity in the Turkish Republic, which assumed a centralized, authoritarian, statist character at its inception.

The process of modernization had already started in the late eighteenth-century Ottoman Empire. The *Tanzimat* (reorganization) reforms mark the beginnings of a shift from a theocratic sultanate toward a modern state. However, modernization became more far-reaching with the creation of the republic. The new national state entailed a restructuring of the relationship between state, community, and individual, by subordinating religion to state authority and adopting legal and institutional measures that would transform the individual into a citizen, loyal and responsible to the state rather than to the communal groups. At this juncture, the modernization project of the republic diverged from its past Ottoman counterpart, and a paradoxical tension between the state and civil society had emerged. Yavuz (2000) argues that, while Islam was used in the process of nation-building to unify diverse ethnolinguistic groups, at the same time, it was excluded from the representation of identity under a state-monitored public sphere. A major dilemma is created as an absolutist state is built on the corporate character of the populace rather than on individual citizens, an essential element for nation-building.

"The Woman Question"

The "woman question" formed one of the major sites where this transformation was both initiated and challenged. Analysts of women's emancipation in Turkey generally agree that the "woman question" as a political agenda dates back to the Ottoman modernization (*Tanzimat*), starting in 1839 (Kandiyoti 1991a). The modernizing elites perceived women's advancement to be part and parcel of Turkey's overall modernization. The founder of the Republic, Mustafa Kemal Atatürk, emphasized that the road to progress must include both sexes working together. In this regard, he took an uncompromising stand on the place accorded to women in official and popular conceptions of Islam. Thus, equality between women and men was given constitutional and statutory recognition. A number of reforms were undertaken, most significantly, the abolition of the caliphate and passage of the Unification of Education Law in 1924; the adoption of the Swiss-inspired Civil Code in 1926; and the extension of the right of women to vote and be elected in local elections in 1930 and in national elections in 1934.

Integrative Institutions

Lacking a significant bourgeois class around which to develop integrative market institutions, the modernizers relied basically on three institutions in their effort to create national integration: secular education, the nuclear family, and the military.[5] Education would transform subjects into citizens; the nuclear family would liberate the individual from traditional extended kinship ties; and the military, with its well-organized infrastructure, would disseminate and guard the goals and principles of the Republic throughout the country.

Secular Education

Education is often attributed a transformative capacity. According to Caldwell, "Schools destroy the corporate identity of the family, especially for those members previously most submissive and most wholly contained by the family: children and women" (quoted in Moghadam 1993: 125). Education was perceived to be the cornerstone of the republican reforms, through which modernization and the creation of a citizenry were to be achieved.[6] The Unification of Education Law of 1924, based on the principle of equal opportunity and free education for all, made the five-year primary school education free and compulsory for both sexes. Starting in 1924 with primary schools, coeducation was introduced to higher levels of education. In the process, although new schools for girls were opened, girls' education lagged behind. Despite the considerable progress achieved to date in universal compulsory education, which was increased to eight years in 1997, regional and gender inequalities in literacy, access to schooling, enrollment rates, and educational attainment continue to characterize the educational system (Abadan-Unat 1991; Ertürk and Dayıoğlu 2004).

Thus, the role of education in nation-building was constrained by gender inequality and unequal access to schooling. Due to the former, many girls and women were excluded from the process of becoming citizens in their own right. However, it was through the principle of education for all that the cadres of an urban middle-class society were formed and the participation of many women in public life as professionals was possible.

The Nuclear Family

Ziya Gökalp (1876–1924), the theoretician of Turkish nationalism, urged the proliferation of the nuclear monogamous family. This, he believed, represented the original Turkish family prior to Islam and is the means for women to reclaim their value and reestablish a balance of power (Fleming 1998: 137). The Civil Code, adopted in 1926, aimed at creating modern nuclear households and thus represents a paradoxical encroachment of modern state authority on communal and traditional forms of patriarchal power. The law outlawed polygamy and gave women equal rights to inheritance, divorce, and child custody, but the patriarchal nature of the family was preserved as households were deemed male-headed and defined patrilocally.

As Moghadam argues, "The relationship between the family and the state illustrates the fine line between the public and private spheres" (1993: 103). Modernized patriarchy represented state feminism in the private sphere (Tekeli 1986). Within the reconfiguration of paternity, masculinity was reconstructed in line with the new contours of citizenship. "The modern father had a special link to his daughters, who were valued, educated, and nurtured—men gave social birth to the new woman of the republic. . . . Atatürk's choice of daughters as his adopted children[,] in a society where male child preference was the uncontested norm, was also heavy with symbolic significance" (Kandiyoti 1997: 123).

The nuclear family, where modern fathers were to raise modern daughters, could not be universally realized, especially because of the resistance of traditional power blocs that reproduced themselves by exercising control over women through increased sex segregation, veiling, and paternal cousin marriages. A degree of autonomy for the traditional elites was tolerated by the state, especially with regard to the private sphere. In fact, the degree to which the Civil Code could influence the areas of social practice outside direct state control is an indicator of the balance of power between the state and local communities. In this regard, the modern republican institutions remained remote for some segments of the population. Moreover, the inability of the system to provide people access to formal means of social security and sources of livelihood left the masses with little or no alternative to kinship and traditional networks for their survival.[7]

The Military

Among the three institutions, the military was by far the primary modernizing agent, since its hierarchical, authoritarian, and highly developed organizational structure allowed it to penetrate the periphery. Universal conscription for men allowed the military, although in an authoritarian manner, to connect directly with every household. Through military service, men became acquainted with the state apparatus and their citizenship responsibilities. Until the early 1980s, when alternative practices were introduced, military service was regarded as a rite of passage into "real" manhood, after which, it was said, a boy became eligible for marriage. The military, with its universal conscription and role as the guardian of the Republic, revealed itself as the face of the "father state" across the country, generating both loyalty and dissent from the people. Ironically, it can be argued that the authoritarian "father" built a sense of "egalitarianism" or guardianship into the social consciousness, particularly of men.[8]

Given that the military was the primary vehicle through which citizenship expanded to the periphery, women, particularly in rural areas, remained marginal citizens, at best experiencing state membership indirectly via men.[9] Therefore, the female consciousness with regard to the military is considerably different and less problematic. Whereas women of the secularist urban classes may share men's positive inclination to the military as the safeguard of the modern secular system, women of the periphery are likely to be distant, even hostile, toward the military.

In short, all three modernizing institutions shared a gender bias as the modern secular reforms of the state were mediated mainly through men. Women's realities and engagement with modernity were established differently and depended on their patriarchal setting. This bifurcation put women at the center of competition over identity politics, since women's autonomous engagement in the modernization project could not be assumed to the same degree.

Competing Paradigms in Women's Identity Politics

State hegemony over identity politics continued until the 1960s. After this point, uneven development, exodus from rural to urban areas, and emergent urban marginalities carrying the seeds of opposition rapidly unfolded into an irreversible pluralism. Despite three military interventions (1960, 1971, and 1980) to protect the integrity of the regime, public opposition to the very foundation of the system heightened significantly by the 1980s. This posed a challenge to Turkey's identity politics, constructed on the basis of secular and unitarian principles excluding religious and ethnic distinctions. While the "woman question" was central to the national identity, women's role was defined in terms of their service to the state-building process rather than recognizing their autonomous personhood. Women's identity thus remained a site for political competition throughout recent history.

I distinguish four distinct periods embodying new and competing paradigms for public representation of women: (1) the 1920s to 1960s—hegemony of the nationalist/modernist paradigm; (2) the 1960s and 1970s—the emergence of a leftist or socialist paradigm; (3) 1980s to mid-1990s—diversification of discourses along religious and ethnic lines, on the one side, and the feminist movement, on the other; this was also a period of economic liberalism that favored market-oriented individual liberties; (4) mid-1995 to the present—engagement of the competing actors, including women, in universal human rights regimes and transnational networks.

The Nationalist/Modernist Paradigm

Although this period contains contradictory elements in terms of political discourse—mainly resistance movements with ethnic and religious underpinnings,[10] and the transition to a multiparty system in 1946—no significant shifts in the modernist paradigm can be said to exist from the point of view of the politics of women's status and identity.

The image of women as the markers of the modern nation was defined with reference to an idealized, original culture of the Turks before they accepted Islam. As Durakbaşa (1998) observed, "Gender equality was presented as part of national identity; in fact the equality of the sexes in the original nomadic culture of the Turks was the basic theme in the first generation of Kemalist women" (141). Afet Inan, a historian and Atatürk's adopted daughter, argues that Turkish women lost status with the transition to Islam in her book *Emancipation of Turkish Women*. Reference to the ancient Turkish values legitimized not only the active role envisaged for women by the state in national development but also a break with Islamic law and practice. The modernizing elites also relied on the legitimization won by victory in the war for national independence.

The new modern Turkish women were perceived as an integral part of the public landscape. As educated professionals they would assume their citizenship duties in serving the state, while within the context of the nuclear family as homemakers they would sustain sexual modesty and their reproductive responsibilities. These contradictory expectations set the standards by which women's self-worth and value in society were to be measured. The challenge for the newly created urban elite women was to distinguish themselves both from the traditional backward Turkish women through their professionalism and from Western women through their assumed sexual modesty. Indeed, "The traditional values of virginity before marriage, fidelity of the wife, and a particular public comportment and dress—was carried over with an even heavier emotional load to the new generations of Kemalist women and became the basic theme of the 'new morality' for the Kemalist elite" (Durakbaşa 1998: 148). Consequently, under the emerging new masculinity, the modern father—with the backing of the modern state—could give his daughter the right to participate in public life confident in her self-monitored sexual purity and moral conduct—a duty first-generation Republican women unquestionably assumed. *Erkek gibi kadın* (manlike woman) came to denote the virtue and enlightenment with which women paid back the privilege bestowed upon them. Thus, the integration of women into the public domain was accomplished without endangering the crucial aspects of patriarchal gender relations.[11]

Many success stories of women in the professions, in politics, and even in international beauty pageants mark the early decades of the Republic. These achievements testified that the "women question" in Turkey was resolved, leaving only the task of spreading modernization across the country to the masses, eliminating the rural/urban and traditional/modern differences (Ertürk 1991b). Kandiyoti notes, "The discourse on tradition and modernity acquired a new dimension, and the civilizing gaze turned inward. 'Tradition' was no longer used to designate Ottoman mores versus the West, but those of the urban elite versus villagers and tribesmen" (1991b: 312).

Expansion of modernity to the periphery, however, was constrained by the uneven penetration of capital to the periphery. By the 1950s the market integration of the agricultural sector had accelerated, thus uprooting labor from land. Rural to urban and international labor migration offered new opportunities for rural people, but the generation of urban jobs lagged behind the increasing number of people migrating to the cities, which resulted in the creation of urban ghettos. Here the seeds of opposition were sown, but for much of this period the authoritarian civil and military bureaucracy maintained a monopoly over political power.

The Marxist/Socialist Paradigm

The emergence of the Marxist/socialist paradigm corresponds to a period that started and ended with military interventions (1960 and 1980, respectively), with another in between (1971). This is an era in which "the state's ability to maintain a monolithic ideology and monopoly over political mobilization was seriously shaken and eclipsed by the emergence of new and ideologically distinct opposition groups" (Z. Arat 1998: 17). The Marxist/socialist paradigm, in its varying forms, expressed the mounting discontent experienced by these groups. As a result, during the 1960s and

1970s, the focus of political discourse shifted from building national institutions onto critiquing economic inequalities and redistributive processes. The Turkish left represented an alternative norm of masculinity vis-à-vis the modernizing elites. Similar to the nationalist paradigm, its intellectual frame of reference emanated from the Western tradition, albeit an alternative one. The ideology of third worldism, class cleavages, and student activism also provided a powerful international frame of reference to the aspirations promoted by the leftist groups. However, the main impetus was the 1961 constitution, which was quite progressive in terms of individual rights, welfare, and social obligations of the state. Vibrant debates around the socioeconomic structure of the country culminated in a rich literature. Political mobilization around economic and social justice also attracted much enthusiasm, particularly from the marginalized new urban dwellers and university students. The ethnic and religious cleavages, increasingly more conspicuous, were articulated in the rhetoric of both the left and the right.[12]

Within the left paradigm, women's emancipation was perceived as a dimension of the struggle against backwardness and feudal formations. Female university students were extensively mobilized and recruited into left organizations and were encouraged by male "comrades" to take part in revolutionary activism, which took violent forms in the 1970s. However, like the modern/nationalist women, the revolutionary women also had to submit to a new form of patriarchal domination. In her analysis of the gender politics of the Turkish left, Fatmagül Berktay (1991) argues that, since left ideologues perceived women as potentially corruptible by bourgeois values, they claimed jurisdiction over women's dress and behavior. A desexualized image of women was constructed by the left, symbolized through reference to female comrades as *bacı*, a provincial term that means "sister." The reliance on the "folksy" term was not only a way to link the left to the masses, but also a means of guarding against women's potential for dissent while countering the popular perceptions that communists are sexually promiscuous.

During this period women's issues were also ignored, and the leftist women functioned under the strict scrutiny of their male counterparts. However, these women lacked the support the nationalist women had been provided by the modern father and the modern state. The opposition against the establishment, which the women shared with their male counterparts within the left movement, distanced and placed them at odds with the institutions of the state, particularly the three integrative institutions. Yet participation in the left movement exposed these women to a new political reality involving conflict, opposition, and activism, clearly distinguishing them from the compliantly modern bourgeois women. Thus, despite the disillusionments and the cost of social upheaval, experience, and the contradictions of the left, political discourse in Turkey laid the ground for individual and feminist consciousness and women's issues to emerge in their own right under feminist leadership.

The 1980s: Fragmentation and Diversification of Identities

The decade of the 1980s is perhaps best described by Tekeli (1991: 7) as one in which a "civil society" was emerging out of divergent groups of conflicting interests all of which nonetheless formed a common bloc in demanding democratic guarantees from the state. This awakening from below occurred at a time when the heavy hand of the military was trying to systematically depoliticize the country. After the third military intervention in 1980, which had disproportionately suppressed political ideas and activism on the left, among labor unions and universities, a cautious but resolute defiance epitomized the mood. There was discontent with the repressive and antidemocratic nature of the 1982 constitution and the other measures imposed by the military.

In 1983, Turkey returned to civilian rule. Although the transition to "democracy" was carefully orchestrated by the military, the party of their choice lost the elections. Instead, Turgut Özal led the newly established Motherland Party (ANAP) to power. ANAP and its charismatic but controversial leader took office with an ambitious privatization and liberalization program, in line with what is often referred to as Reaganism and Thatcherism. The Özal period represents contradictory but striking elements, demystifying taboos but perhaps also leaving a vacuum in public and private life. Combining religious and conservative values with liberal and unconventional modes of behavior in his personal and political life, Özal injected a feeling, however false, of freedom in the people. A new entrepreneurial culture emerged; business administration, marketing, and economics became popular fields of study among university students. Özal's policies aimed not only to transform the urban middle-class way of life and support big business in the metropolises but also to strengthen the religiously oriented provincial small capital holders. He wanted to "revive the market by bringing Muslim capitalists, businessmen and small traders to compete with secular bourgeoisie, with their more enduring ties with Western-centered capitalism" (Navaro-Yashin 2002: 224).

By encouraging individual and entrepreneurial initiatives and launching deregulation programs, Özal's policies in many ways significantly eroded "statism" and unleashed competition within capital itself. Furthermore, unlike in the previous years, ANAP policy offered a degree of individualization of public space, allowing for divergent demands to be voiced.[13] According to Zehra Arat, the restrictions imposed by the military "allowed the previously circumvented issues and subsumed groups to find an opportunity to surface and organize around new causes or old ones rephrased in different political language" (2003: 10). The ANAP economic programs within a matter of four years proved to be unsustainable, and on the political front, ANAP fell short of fulfilling the expectations it gave rise to with regard to democratization. However, Özal's politics ruptured the secular and unitarian principles of the Republic, fostering not only economic competition but also public articulation of religious and ethnic aspirations.

Three main groups particularly stand out with their alternative claims for political space in the 1980s: Islamists, Kurdish nationalists, and feminists. The first two, while projecting alternative images for women, also significantly contested the secular and unitarian foundation of the Republic. Islamist political groups symbolize the claims for justice that they believed were compromised by secularism, and the Kurdish nationalists' clamored for recognition of an ethnic identity that they believed was repressed by the unitarian structure of the state. Both discourses represent alternative masculine ideologies competing for power and directly challenging the existing state formation. Though defined differently in each movement, women are similarly mobilized within the ranks of both to serve the wider cause. This creates two new dichotomies in women's public representation: Islamist versus secular and Kurdish versus Turkish women. The boundary of women's identity is still carefully guarded by masculine norms in both Islamist and the Kurdish discourses, as was the case with the modernist and socialist discourses.

The illegal Kurdistan Worker's Party (PKK) monopolized Kurdish nationalist aspirations,[14] and its encounter with the state mainly took the form of armed conflict from 1984 to 1999. Increasingly militarized, women took part in several suicide missions staged by the PKK in the 1990s. Although lack of reliable information on the internal dynamics of the PKK makes it hard to assess the full extent of women's involvement in its ranks, we know that Kurdish women in general had to deal with violence both from the rebels and from the state security forces. This situation politicized and moved them in the late 1990s to join political parties and to establish women's rights organizations throughout southeastern Turkey.

The Islamist groups used more diversified entry points into the public discourse.[15] According to Yavuz, the Islamic movement is a source of power for marginalized segments of the society that includes distinct identities framed in terms of the Islamic vernacular (2000: 28). Analysts differentiate the characteristics of Islamist discourses that became dominant in the 1980s from earlier right-wing movements (Gülalp 1997; Ilyasoğlu 1998). The growth of an Islamic bourgeoisie in the previous period not only constituted an alternative to the secular Western-oriented big business but also provided Islamist political parties with a material base (Z. Arat 2003: 14). Thereby, religion was brought from the margins to the mainstream and into modern terrain, challenging the modernist discourse on its own ground. This also had the effect of transforming Islamic discourse through altered lifestyles of the new social strata.

"The new veiling of Islamist women in Turkey is a part, and an essential part, of this new Islamism; it is the main instrument of identity politics" (Ilyasoğlu 1998: 243). As a matter of fact, it is argued that women's status, symbolized by the Islamic dress code—mainly the head scarf referred to as the *türban*—is the main marker of the Islamist movement. Without it, there would be little to distinguish it from other contestations for power (Toprak 1994). This issue also brought Islamist politics into a head-on collision with the secular establishment, since the *türban* is banned in public institutions.[16] In this regard, Islamist women, like the revolutionary women of the 1970s, differed from the secular modern women in terms of their antagonism toward the integrative institutions of the Republic. Yet they differed from the revolutionary women, insofar as being part of an opposition that was heavily entrenched within communal and family values, which made their struggle in the public realm harmonious with their private life. Their primary goal was to access mainstream institutions, from which they were excluded by their veiling.

Since the 1980s, the *türban* has come to symbolize contradictory claims in the public sphere. Although the meanings attached to it have at times shifted, *türban*, by and large, symbolizes cultural authenticity and defiance of the Republican modernization project for the Islamists and a fundamentalist reaction *(irtica)* to Republican principles for the secularists. Irrespective of the intentions of the Islamist women themselves, their bodies became the site where the Islamist versus secularist struggle manifested itself. Interestingly, neither discourse rejects modesty as an esteemed goal for women: secularists call for an "internalized veiling" of women's sexuality, whereas Islamists demand external veiling.

Feminism, as the third major discourse influencing women's identities from the 1980s onward, differs from the Kurdish and Islamist discourses in a number of ways. First, feminism seeks to define women's identities from within women's own experiences rather than identify a role for women within a wider political agenda. Unlike the other discourses that created dichotomies of women's images, feminists have argued that all women are oppressed by the patriarchal system and that it is continually reproduced in traditional as well as modern institutions. Though the movement was theoretically open to all women who considered themselves disadvantaged, in practice it remained restricted to a small group of educated middle-class women mainly in Istanbul and Ankara.

Second, although feminism offers a deep critique of the patriarchal gender order, it initially appeared less than challenging for the system. As a matter of fact, the movement was perceived by many observers as being promoted by the establishment to distract attention from "more fundamental issues" in the society (Tekeli 1991: 13). According to Kardam, "Women's groups themselves did not challenge the state authority, and, in fact preferred to have minimal interaction with the state. During this period, Turkish women began to explore the meaning of feminisms, as they had been discussed in the West since the 1960s" (forthcoming: 14). Disillusioned by their involvement in the left movement in the 1970s, they were eager to distance themselves from formal politics, confining their activities initially to consciousness-raising meetings and moving only slowly toward open public gatherings (Y. Arat 1994; Sirman 1989; Tekeli 1995). Also during this period, Western feminist classics were translated into Turkish, and women began to engage with international events more systematically. The UN Conference on Women in Nairobi (1985), unlike the Mexico City (1975) and Copenhagen (1980) conferences, was attended by women of diverse backgrounds. Their experience helped to link local issues with the global agenda, as reflected in the Nairobi Forward Looking Strategies for the Advancement of Women that were adopted to review and appraise the implementation of goals set by the conference.[17]

The lack of threat of the feminist movement did not last long. Feminism's transformative potential was revealed as the movement matured and the international momentum for gender equality began to have its impact. In 1987, the feminist platform organized the first street demonstration under military rule in protest of domestic violence, a strategically chosen theme. Fighting violence against women was moving to the top of the international gender agenda, as was manifest in the Convention on the Elimination of All Forms of Discrimination against Women (CEDAW),[18] which the UN General Assembly adopted in 1979. Turkey, as a result of commitments made in Nairobi, ratified the convention in 1985 with reservations on a number of its articles. Although the "no violence" demonstration was regarded with some cynicism, it opened the private sphere of life to public debate and helped legitimize the feminist movement in the eyes of many.

Perhaps more significant was the public uproar of women's groups in 1989, in connection with a rape case taken up by the Supreme Court, that challenged Article 438 of the Criminal Code, which granted the rapist of a prostitute a reduced sentence. The court ruled that the article was not in violation of the equality clause of the constitution, since it aimed to protect "respectable women." The mounting public reaction resulted in the abolishment of the article in the National Assembly. Women's groups have since become more diversified but acted in unison in demanding state accountability for equality between women and men, particularly after the Beijing conference (Kardam and Ertürk 1999).

Islamist women's activism became conspicuous toward the end of the 1980s through mass demonstrations against the *türban* ban at universities, developing an alternative women's movement in the following years. Although Islamist women defined their identity within a religious context, they began to make nontraditional demands. According to Ilyasoğlu, "Their public stance constitutes a subjective rupture from the roles defined within the boundaries of traditionalism, and Islamist women situate themselves within the modern condition" (1998: 245). Hence, Islamist women's identity is constructed not only in opposition to modern secular women, but also in opposition to traditional women. Aktaş (1988), an Islamist woman writer, distinguishes between enlightened and traditional Muslim women, where the latter, she argues, lack an Islamic view of themselves and of the world.

During this period, the encounter between Islamist and secularist, Kemalist and feminist women alike, entailed much mutual suspicion and led to countermobilizations. Islamist women challenged the secularist women for being elitist and antidemocratic, and the secularists—particularly the more mainstream Kemalist women—organized to counter the rising religious activism (Y. Arat 1994: 246). Despite this obvious mistrust and reactive orientation, the Turkish experience differed from that of other Muslim countries, such as Egypt, Algeria, and Iran, where the encounter among different groups has been more conflict ridden. Ye_im Arat argues that in Turkey the competition between Islam and secular ideology had long been won by the latter in the public realm.[19] Although the feminists disagreed with Islamist women and maintained that their position could not be considered feminism, some feminists acknowledged and respected the struggle of their Islamist sisters (1997: 107). However, for the majority of secular women as well as the society at large, Islamist women in the 1980s stood in stark contrast to the image of modern educated women in the Turkish society (Acar 1991: 60). Hence, the politicization of the *türban*, as discussed earlier, has served to keep women divided, a situation that continues to be a source of tension and an obstacle in forging a common women's agenda today.

In conclusion, greater integration into global markets, erosion of modernist/nationalist state ideology, and an increase of pluralism in identity politics (and the emergence of the individual as an autonomous economic and political actor) have characterized a new phase in Turkey's development since the 1980s.[20] Political pluralism offered women alternatives within conflicting discourses and at the same time allowed public space for autonomous initiatives to take hold.

As the new decade unfolded, the activism and fervor of the women's movement gave way to what many have called "project feminism" (Bora and Günal 2002), as women started organizing around specific issues and raising funds for their projects. Islamist women began to gain more visibility within the Islamist discourse with their distinctly female but religiously flavored orientation. At the turn of 1990s, the Kurdish women were yet to be heard.

As was already evident by the mid-1990s, institutionalization has gained further momentum in the new millennium. The most significant developments of the early 1990s were twofold: the establishment of the national machinery for women and women's centers and academic programs within universities, and recognition of the potential of women's issues in politics by political parties. This was reflected in the 1991 general elections when women's issues became visible in the campaigns and programs of major political parties. However, "contrary to the rhetoric of the political parties, women candidates were shunned in the electoral race" (Y. Arat 1994: 247).

Although women's low level of representation is a common feature of all political parties in Turkey,[21] it has become particularly contentious within the religiously oriented parties, which relied heavily on women in soliciting support, without allowing space for their equal participation. This was often justified by the *türban* ban. It is commonly acknowledged that women voters were the force behind the victory of the Welfare Party (WP) in 1994 local elections. However, in the 1999 elections the Virtue Party, which succeeded the WP after its closure, brought into parliament only three women. One of them, a *türban*-clad, U.S.-educated young professional, aroused much public controversy (Saktanber 2002: 77–79). She was prevented from taking her oath as a parliamentarian clad with her *türban* and subsequently stripped of her Turkish citizenship when it was discovered that she concealed her U.S. citizenship when registering as a candidate to stand election. Islamist women were angry both with their party and with the secularist women, as the latter condoned the discriminatory treatment of the first veiled woman to be elected into the parliament.

Toward a Consolidation of Diversities: 1995 and Beyond

As the momentum of the Beijing conference snowballed worldwide, the women's movement in Turkey was stimulated as well, benefiting from the increased availability of resources due to Beijing.[22] This particularly took the form of NGOization and was spurred by the steady buildup of governmental and nongovernmental institutional mechanisms since the turn of the decade. The national machinery for women (Directorate General of Women's Status and Problems), established in 1990 to coordinate public and civil activities for the advancement of women to fulfill Turkey's international obligations, played an important role in consolidating the emerging capacity in the country toward putting gender on the domestic political and public agenda. The directorate also led Turkey's active engagement with international gender equality regimes. Arguably, this was a significant enough turning point to delineate the period after the mid-1990s as a distinct phase in the identity politics and women's agency in Turkey.

The national machinery was first established as a unit within the Ministry of Labor and later restructured under the office of the prime minister

(Acuner 2002; Kardam forthcoming). Until 2004 the directorate functioned without any legal base and as a result suffered from poor financing and understaffing. Its weak structure, however, contributed to the growth and strengthening of the academic and activist capacity on gender issues in the country, since the bureaucracy had to rely on the voluntary contributions of expertise that existed outside itself. This collaboration between the state and civil society served several ends, for both the state apparatus and civil society.[23] It gave women's groups an institutional framework within which to penetrate and influence the state apparatus; to become familiar with the international gender agenda and women's rights instruments and mechanisms; to give inputs into Turkey's official reports prepared in accordance with international and regional mandates, including the European Commission mechanisms and intergovernmental bodies of the UN; and to provide a diverse set of women's groups a common platform for dialogue. Perhaps most important, it also gave women the ownership of the state's agenda on women's issues. For the state apparatus, it provided expertise and human resources in meeting its mandate and enabled the directorate to engender its political agenda and activities in relative independence from bureaucratic priorities.

The NGOization and the "project feminism" that emerged earlier in the decade dominated the agenda of women's groups after the Beijing conference.[24] While this has been criticized for fragmenting the feminist movement and thus being an obstacle in its development, it has also enabled the women's agenda to "trickle down" to the grass roots, bringing feminists into close encounter with "other" women (Bora and Günal 2002). In southeastern Turkey, as the impact of the armed conflict eased, Kurdish women came forth as autonomous agents, beginning to engage in the mainstream society through legitimate institutions and processes. In 1999, a women's center (KAMER) was established in Diyarbakır to address women's daily problems. Other such organizations followed throughout the region. In an article that chronicles the inception of KAMER, Akkoç wrote, "At every phase of our lives we implemented the decisions taken by others. Although we strove more than men, unless we behaved like them, we could not participate in decision-making processes" (2002: 206). Thus, the Kurdish women, in a struggle that had a dual character, targeted both the dominant Turkish society as members of an excluded ethnic entity and their indigenous patriarchal order as oppressed women. Precariously situated, they found themselves at odds with Turkish women's groups, as well as with their own ethnic community.

Association with the directorate not only provided a shared space for different women's groups but also paved the way for channeling feminist energies into the formation of pressure groups that sought to influence legislative change. Landmark legal reforms in this regard include the adoption in 1998 of the law on domestic violence; the removal in 1999 of the reservations placed on CEDAW; the entering into force of the new Civil Code in 2002 and the ratification of the CEDAW Optional Protocol; and the Criminal Code reform scheduled for adoption in October 2004.

The recent changes in both the Civil Code and the Criminal Code reflect significant shifts in the understanding of gender relations, modifying traditional patriarchy and bringing domestic law in line with CEDAW principles. The former establishes the principle of equality between spouses by replacing the concept of the male head of the conjugal union with equal partnership in decision-making authority and representational powers in the management of the household. The most significant amendment under the new Civil Code is the legal property regime, which stipulates that all property acquired during marriage shall be shared equally in the case of divorce, thereby recognizing the unpaid contributions of women to household sustenance. The criminal law reform is replacing the community with the individual as its focal point. In this regard, the definition of the word "women" on the basis of chastity has been abandoned in the draft law. Similarly, sexual crimes are now recognized as crimes against women's bodily integrity rather than against public morality as previously was the case.

It would, no doubt, be wrong to attribute these recent achievements in Turkey to the efforts of women alone. However, this is not the point here. Rather, the issue is that engagement in lobbying and advocacy, using universal norms and Turkey's international commitments as negotiating tools for leverage, has increased the opportunity for dialogue among women of different orientations. This is not to argue that women's groups have a common stand on all issues; rather, it is the process of dialogue around common problems negotiated within a common human rights framework that creates the possibility of transcending the diverse identities imposed within formal politics. Recently, the strong reactions provoked by so-called honor crimes have allowed women's groups and organizations to act together on a common platform against such acts. Honor crimes, in particular, and violence against women, in general, are the primary issues that unite women. In March 2004, women's organizations sent a joint complaint to the special procedures mechanism of the Human Rights Commission charging that the state failed to provide protection to a woman killed by her brothers, while in hiding.

These types of activities around common issues and seeking solutions on the basis of a common framework broaden the women's agenda and cut across divergent and irreconcilable differences among women. Turkey's EU candidacy serves as a catalyst in supporting this process, both in terms of the democratization measures undertaken by the government and in creating a momentum for greater rights and liberties. The ruling Justice and Development Party (AKP), elected to power with a majority in 2002, has incorporated EU membership and universal human rights norms in its government program as priority goals despite its Islamist orientation. It thereby engaged itself in a political agenda that was traditionally associated with the secularist political discourse. However, due to skepticism regarding AKP's intentions, particularly with regard to secularism, the Islamist/secularist tension continues to define formal politics. Interestingly, however, with an Islamist government in office, the tension is now brought into the state apparatus itself. Ironically, while the *türban* is excluded from state protocol, the wife of the country's prime minister is clad in one. Consequently, Islamist women, at least those in the mainstream, find themselves a part of the establishment—although in a rather awkward fashion. This situation brings to light the patriarchal contradictions in their lives, thus bringing them closer to their secularist sisters in their stance vis-à-vis patriarchy.

There are also contradictions associated with market mechanisms that offer risks as well as opportunities for rupturing traditional patriarchal structures and for diversifying women's identities. Liberalization of Turkey's economy gained momentum in the 1980s and has accelerated over the last two decades. Women's bodies have become commodities in advertisements and television programs, thus demystifying the emphasis on modesty over women's sexuality. Ironically, this is happening at a time when one of the major political battles is still about the *türban*. In the meantime, market commoditization has also reconstructed the *türban* itself as a fashion object. Interestingly, the market is providing a context shared by Islamists and secularists alike (Navaro-Yashin 2002: 222). Consumerism has further diluted the ideological premises that demarcated the boundaries of alternative female identities. Within the context of Turkey's integration into the global market, female modesty and arrogance, concealing and revealing of the female body, are in evidence simultaneously. The cosmetic and fashion industry is booming to cater to the modern bourgeois women, whether *türban*-clad or not.

Conclusion

I have argued here that the political contest over women's identity politics in Turkey has revolved around the definition of the "modern" space. Consequently, each competing political discourse resulted in reconfiguring and expanding modern space to include new symbols of representation, while at the same time generating its peripheral space for marginal and excluded women's groups. This competition, which reflects the diversification of the society in terms of sociopolitical cleavages, not only created alternative patriarchal images of women but also broadened the space for autonomous individual action beyond what was proscribed by the respective political discourses. The feminist movement and the liberalization of the economy in the 1980s have been both a consequence of and an instrument in the creation of an autonomous individual in the quest for expanded rights. In the process, women increasingly engaged with the human rights regimes in articulating their demands. This has naturally served as the node where all roads crossed, thus increasing the possibility that diverse women's groups engaged each other.

Increased interaction around common problems among women from different orientations—Islamist, nationalist, secularist, and so forth—has eroded the dichotomized boundaries that fragment women, while also disclosing the patriarchal nature of all existing societal discourses discussed in this chapter. Of course, the hard reality of economic disparities (locally and globally), pressures emanating from radical religious and nationalist movements (inside and outside Turkey), uncertainties with regard to Turkey's place in global political order, and the persistence of the polarized public discourse among competing masculinities continue to pose obstacles for sustaining a women's common agenda. Against these odds, women need to expand their networks domestically and internationally, enhance their skills in using international instruments to hold governments accountable, and develop strategies to resist identity politics that project women's images, making them a bone of contention and a form of ideological expression. The current political environment in Turkey, with a commitment to EU membership and universal human rights norms, offers an opportunity for women's human rights advocates to strategize for an inclusive understanding of rights, transcending their particularistic concerns as imposed by the identity politics of competing masculinities.

Returning to the question posed at the outset: Can universal human rights regimes be instrumental in transcending paradoxical identity formation? I argue that universal human rights regimes certainly provide a normative framework within which diversities can coexist and be reconciled. These regimes represent the highest level of international consensus, reflecting commitments governments have made in response to the demands filtering up from the local to the global and emanating from the intergovernmental forums. Translating these norms back into the local context to expand the rights of excluded social groups requires, first and foremost, due diligence on the part of the state and civil engagement on the part of the public, to hold the state accountable for compliance. As argued throughout this chapter, women stand at a strategic location in this regard. However, the global conjuncture cannot be overlooked. The effectiveness of these regimes and the sustenance of the gains achieved so far in the implementation of human rights and gender equality standards are dependent on the future direction of the world political and economic order. At the moment, there is a strong tendency at the global level toward a deviation from the rule of law toward the rule of power, while at the same time there has been a fortification of the relations between capital and labor in favor of the former. If this indeed is a predicament in the emerging new world order, then one can only expect that the existing economic disparities and cultural divisions will further deepen, thus intensifying conflicts at the local, national, and global levels. This will endanger the realization of the global agenda for gender equality worldwide. It would then be probable that the "clash of civilizations" will be a self-fulfilling prophecy!

Notes

1. Both concepts—modernization and globalization—are associated with the rise of modern capitalism. This point in human history involves the institutionalization of patriarchal class relations beyond the boundaries of the local and the traditional, creating uniform patterns and linking localities into a hierarchical "world system." As opposed to the overall standardizing tendencies of modernization (which aimed at creating national markets), globalization (the creation of a

global market) inherently contains the contradictory forces of both uniformity and diversity.

2. This is not to imply that the state is disappearing but that its role and sphere of sovereignty are changing. By adopting deregulation and privatization policies and measures, the state facilitates globalization.

3. Tripp (2002: 416) argues that cultural rationales are used to protect the status quo when it comes to women's rights. Ironically, this rationale cuts across cultures and religions. Such was the case during Beijing+5, when conservatives from diverse cultural backgrounds formed an alliance against the Beijing agenda (Ilkkaracan 2002: 753), declaring that the Beijing Platform for Action is a dangerous document.

4. For alternative interpretations of Turkey's modernization process, see Lewis (1961) and Bozdoğan and Kasaba (1997), among others.

5. After the war of independence (1919–1922), most non-Muslims, mainly merchants and industrialists, either left or were expelled, leaving the new republic in need of creating its bourgeoisie (Keyder 1997).

6. Moghadam (1993: 120) has argued that education for women in the "patriarchal belt" has had a revolutionary impact and demonstrated this with the experience of countries in the Middle East.

7. Patriarchal structures, while constraining the penetration of state authority, in some regards may relieve the state of the responsibility to provide welfare to its citizens.

8. This is a relatively unexplored aspect of the role of the military in Turkish modernization, which is important in understanding its current involvement in governance and the tolerance with which this has been accepted by diverse social segments, particularly by the secular nationalist elite.

9. It has been argued elsewhere that rural women of eastern Anatolia, the majority of whom did not speak Turkish at the time, have perhaps been the most marginalized by the republican reforms. Their participation in the institutions of the modern national state was literally mediated through men, whose own access—given the ethnic and tribal character of the region—was dependent on their place within the local power structure (Ertürk 1991b).

10. For a discussion of the challenges encountered by the Republic, see Keyder (1987).

11. Women's autonomous initiatives were discouraged. For example, the creation of a Republican Women's Party was prevented, and the Turkish Women's Federation was closed (Y. Arat 1997; Tekeli 1991). It was argued that feminist activism is not necessary, since women's rights are already granted.

12. The left/right fragmentation characterized political parties as well as other civil society organizations. In this regard, Sunni Islamist and ultranationalist groups represented right-wing politics as opposed to the left-wing political orientation of the Alevi Muslims and Kurdish groups.

13. Durakbaşa (1998: 150) argues that, although unintentionally, Kemalist socialization cultivated in women the first seeds of individuation, since women were confronted with the task of reconciling between modernity and tradition.

14. Although ethnic Kurds always participated actively in the political system and rose to high positions as ministers or even prime ministers, their representation in their own right continues to be a fragile issue. The first Kurdish political party was established in 1990 and represented in the parliament until banned in 1993. The succeeding parties could not make the threshold in the subsequent elections.

15. Although the Islamist groups have also been perceived as a threat to the system, their engagement with the state and its agents has varied. It is often claimed that it was the military itself that supported militant Islamist groups as a counterforce both to the leftists and later to the PKK (Z. Arat 2003: 11).

16. The first *türban* incident took place in 1968 when a female student in the Department of Theology at Ankara University was expelled because she wore a head scarf. In the 1980s, the issue gained greater attention. In 1982, the newly created Higher Education Council banned the head scarf in institutions of higher education. This provoked protests from Islamist female students and their supporters. The issue has occupied the agenda of the parliament and the judicial system and more recently has been taken to the European Human Rights Court, which in July 2004 ruled against the complainant. With the coming to power of the religiously based Justice and Development Party (AKP) in 2002, the head scarf has become a crisis in state protocol, since the wives of most AKP ministers and parliamentarians wear *türban*.

17. In the absence of a national machinery to disseminate the outcomes of the Nairobi conference, its impact was limited to the writings of journalists and academicians.

18. In 1992 the CEDAW committee adopted General Recommendation 19 defining violence as a discrimination against women and placed responsibility on the states to eliminate it. However, the most significant breakthrough with regard to violence against women came as a result of the persistent efforts of the women's movement, at the International Human Rights Conference in Vienna in 1993. The same year, the Declaration on the Elimination of Violence against Women was adopted as the formal normative framework on violence against women. The following year the post of a rapporteur on violence against women, its causes, and consequences was created with the mandate to document and monitor violence against women worldwide.

19. Given the ongoing friction over secularism at the level of the state—the office of the president representing secularism versus the current government representing Islamism—the tension no doubt is one that requires a cautious assessment of Arat's assertion.

20. Women's relatively low level of labor force participation constrains their autonomy.

21. A right-wing party (True Path) elected a woman as its chair in 1993; she later became Turkey's first woman prime minister. Today women's representation in the parliament is at a low of 4 percent.

22. In 1996, with UNDP funding, I organized rural women's workshops in two localities. The objective of the workshops was to provide a platform for rural women, the most invisible segment of the society, to voice their problems.

23. The directorate initiated a participatory approach to the preparation of inputs to national reports. The most significant of these was the preparatory workshop for the Turkish National Report in 1994 for the Beijing conference, bringing together seventy women from different backgrounds. As such, the report reflected views of women "themselves" rather than that of a government institution. Similarly, Turkey's second and third combined periodic CEDAW reports (1997), as well as the third and fourth combined periodic CEDAW reports (2005), were prepared in a collaborative manner. Official delegations of Turkey to the various international meetings were also composed of participants from academia and the NGO community.

24. For instance, of the 339 women's organizations listed in the *2004 Women's Organizations Guide in Turkey*, 196 were established in 1995 and after, which amounts to 58 percent of the organizations listed in the guide. Of the remaining, 92 (27 percent) were created between 1980 and 1995; 25 (7 percent) between 1960 and 1980; and 18 (5 percent) prior to 1960. No date was specified for 8 of the organizations. Forty-two percent of the NGOs are located in the three main urban centers: Istanbul (21 percent), Izmir (11 percent), and Ankara (10 percent).

BIBLIOGRAPHY

Abadan-Unat, Nermin. 1991. "The Impact of Legal and Educational Reforms on Turkish Women." In N. R. Keddie and B. Barrons, eds., *Women in Middle East History*, 177–194. New Haven, Conn.: Yale University Press.

Acar, Feride. 1991. "Women and Islam in Turkey." In Tekeli (1995), 46–65.

Acuner, Selma. 2002. "90'lı Yıllar ve Resmi Düzeyde Kurumsallaşmanın Doğuş Aşamaları" (The Phases of the Emergence of Formal Institutionalization in the 90s). In Bora and Günal, 125–158.

Akkoç, Nebahat. 2002. "Diyarbakır Ka-Mer'in Kuruluş Hikayesi ve Yürüttüğü Çalışmalar" (The Story of Ka-Mer's Establishment and Its Activities). In Bora and Günal, 205–216.

Aktaş, Cihan. 1988. *Sistem İçindeki Kadın* (*Women within the System*). Istanbul: Beyan Yayınları.

Arat, Yeşim. 1994. "Towards a Democratic Society: The Women's Movement in the 1980s." *Women's Studies Forum*. 17:241–248.

———. 1997. "The Project of Modernity and Women in Turkey." In Bozdoğan and Kasaba, 95–112.

Arat, Zehra, ed. 1998. *Deconstructing Images of "The Turkish Women."* London: Macmillan.

———. 2003. "Promoting Identities: Human Rights and Democracy within Cycles of Politics: The Case of Turkey." Paper presented at the annual conference of the American Political Science Association, Philadelphia, August 28–31.

Berktay, Fatmagül. 1991. "Has Anything Changed in the Outlook of the Turkish Left on Women?" In Tekeli (1995), 250–262.

Bora, Aksu, and A. Günal. 2002. *90'larda Türkiye'de Feminizm* (Feminism in Turkey in the 90s). Istanbul: Iletişim.

Bozdoğan, Sibel, and R. Kasaba, eds. 1997. *Rethinking Modernity and National Identity in Turkey.* Seattle: University of Washington Press.

Durakbaşa, Ayşe. 1998. "Kemalism as Identity Politics in Turkey." In Z. Arat, 141–155.

Ertürk, Yakın. 1991a. "Convergence and Divergence in the Status of Moslem Women: Cases of Turkey and Saudi Arabia." *International Sociology* 6:307–320.

———. 1991b. "Rural Women and Modernization in Southeastern Anatolia." In Tekeli (1995), 141–152.

———. 2004a. "Considering the Role of Men in Gender Agenda Setting: Conceptual and Policy Issues." *Feminist Review,* no. 78.

———. 2004b. *Towards an Effective Implementation of International Norms to End Violence against Women.* Geneva: Commission on Human Rights, Sixtieth Session (E/CN.4/2004/66).

Ertürk, Yakın, and M. Dayıoğlu. 2004. *Gender, Education and Child Labour in Turkey.* Geneva: ILO/IPEC.

Fleming, K. E. 1998. "Women as Preservers of the Past: Ziya Gokalp and Women's Reform." In Z. Arat, 127–138.

Gülalp, Haldun. 1997. "Modernization Policies and Islamist Politics in Turkey." In Bozdoğan and Kasaba, 52–63.

Ilkkaracan, Pınar. 2002. "Women, Sexuality, and Social Change in the Middle East and Maghreb." *Social Research* 69:754–779.

Ilyasoğlu, Aynur. 1998. "Islamist Women in Turkey: Their Identity and Self-Image." In Z. Arat, 241–261.

Kandiyoti, Deniz. 1991a. "End of Empire: Islam, Nationalism and Women in Turkey." In Deniz Kandiyoti, ed., *Women, Islam and the State,* 22–47. Philadelphia: Temple University Press.

———. 1991b. "Patterns of Patriarchy: Notes for an Analysis of Male Domination in Turkish Society." In Tekeli (1995), 306–318.

———. 1997. "Gendering the Modern: On Missing Dimensions in the Study of Turkish Modernity." In Bozdoğan and Kasaba, 113–132.

Kardam, Nuket. Forthcoming. *Turkey's Engagement with Global Women's Human Rights.* London: Ashgate.

Kardam, Nuket, and Y. Ertürk. 1999. "Expanding Gender Accountability? Women's Organizations and the State in Turkey." *International Journal of Organization Theory and Behaviour* 2:167–197.

Keskin, Burçak. 2002. "Confronting Double Patriarchy: Islamist Women in Turkey." In Paola Bacchetta and Margaret Power, eds., *Right Wing Women: From Conservatives to Extremists around the World,* 245–257. New York: Routledge.

Keyder, Çağlar. 1997. "Whither the Project of Modernity? Turkey in the 1990's." In Bozdoğan and Kasaba, 39–51.

———. 1987. *State and Class in Turkey: A Study in Capitalist Development.* London: Verso.

Kymlicka, Will. 1999. "Response to Okin." In J. Cohen, S. M. Okin, M. Howard, and M. C. Nussbaum, eds., *Is Multiculturalism Bad for Women?* 31–34. Princeton, N.J.: Princeton University Press.

Lewis, Bernard. 1961. *The Emergence of Modern Turkey.* New York: Oxford University Press.

Migdal, Joel S. 1997. "Finding the Meeting Ground of Fact and Fiction: Some Reflections on Turkish Modernization." In Bozdoğan and Kasaba, 252–260.

Moghadam, Valentine M. 1993. *Modernizing Women: Gender and Social Change in the Middle East.* Boulder, Colo.: Lynne Rienner.

Navaro-Yashin, Yael. 2002. "The Market for Identities: Secularism, Islamism, Commodities." In Deniz Kandiyoti and Ayşe Saktanber, eds., *Fragments of Culture,* 221–253. London: Tauris.

Okin, Susan Moller. 1999. "Is Multiculturalism Bad for Women?" In Joshua Cohen, Matthew Howard, and Martha C. Nussbaum, eds., *Is Multiculturalism Bad for Women?* 9–24. Princeton, N.J.: Princeton University Press.

Saktanber, Ayşe. 2002. "Whose Virtue Is This? The Virtue Party and Women in Islamist Politics in Turkey." In Paola Bacchetta and Margaret Power, eds., *Right Wing Women: From Conservatives to Extremists around the World,* 71–83. New York: Routledge.

Sirman, Nükhet. 1989. "Feminism in Turkey: A Short History." *New Perspectives* 3, no. 1 (Fall): 134.

Süpürge, Uçan. 2004. *Türkiye'de Kadın Örgütleri Rehberi.* 2004. (Guide for women's organizations in Turkey). Ankara, Turkey: British Embassy.

Tekeli, Şirin. 1986. "Emergence of the Feminist Movement in Turkey." In D. Dahlerap, ed., *The New Women's Movement,* 179–199. London: Sage.

———. 1991. *Women in Modern Turkish Society.* London: Zed Books.

———, ed. 1995. *Women in Modern Turkish Society.* London: Zed Books.

Toprak, Binnaz. 1994. "Women and Fundamentalism: The Case of Turkey." In Valentine Moghadam, ed., *Identity Politics and Women: Cultural Reassertions and Feminisms in International Perspective,* 293–306. Boulder, Colo.: Westview Press.

Tripp, Aili Mari. 2002. "The Politics of Women's Rights and Cultural Diversity in Uganda." In Maxine Molyneux and Shahra Razavi, eds., *Gender, Justice, Democracy and Rights,* 413–440. New York: Oxford University Press.

Yavuz, Hakan. 2000. "Cleansing Islam from the Public Sphere." *Journal of International Affairs* 54:21–42.

5

Working Women of the World Unite?

Labor Organizing and Transnational Gender Solidarity among Domestic Workers in Hong Kong

Sarah Swider

In 1998, in the midst of the Asian financial crisis, segments of the Hong Kong government and public singled out foreign workers as scapegoats for their economic pain. The Hong Kong employers association (which represents both employers and agencies that place migrant domestic workers) demanded that the minimum wage for domestic workers be cut by 35 percent, and the government proposed a 20 percent wage cut. In response, the Coalition of Domestic Workers Unions (CDWU) organized a demonstration during which an estimated 22,000 migrant women took to the streets, handed out flyers, and collected more than 50,000 signatures on petitions against the proposal (Asian Migrant Centre 1999). As a result of their strong mobilization, the proposals for wage cuts were tabled.

This demonstration was just one of many campaigns that the CDWU has orchestrated, and not the first policy change it has won. The strategies of the CDWU include petitions, lawsuits, marches, formal complaints with international organizations, and lobbying both their home countries and the Hong Kong government. The CDWU also does much more than political campaigning. It provides English, leadership, and computer skills training to its members and education classes covering topics such as feminism, migration, and the global economy. The union coalition also runs investment projects (called reintegration projects) by which domestic workers form investment groups, save money, and then send group members back home to start a joint business. This coalition is, I argue, a new organizational form that successfully mixes characteristics of both a labor union and a transnational women's movement. Such a strong, well-organized group of women migrant domestic workers is quite an anomaly. Generally speaking, as a result of globalization, most labor unions are today facing declining membership and decreasing effectiveness. Furthermore, domestic workers are some of the most difficult workers in the world to organize. Their working conditions are in themselves stigmatizing and isolating; class, race, nationality, and gender are constructed in ways that divide them (Gill 1994). Moreover, in most countries, the state uses regulations such as labor and immigration laws to create additional barriers to organizing (Giles and Arat-Koc 1994; Glenn 1992; Colen 1989). So the success of domestic workers in Hong Kong is remarkable. Their unusual level of organization takes them well beyond the individual acts of resistance that are usually seen as their only recourse (Salzinger 1991; Constable 1997; Romero 1992).

The Hong Kong case shows that domestic workers, under certain conditions, can effectively change their working conditions. In this chapter I explore the conditions leading to the formation of this alternative women's economic organization and attempt to explain why it has been uniquely successful. First, I review the research on domestic workers, focusing on the barriers to organizing they face and how they nonetheless attempt to resist their exploitation. Second, I look at how the CDWU in Hong Kong challenges some of our ideas about domestic workers, social movements, and the constraints on organizing women. I argue that it is a new type of women's economic organization, unlike labor or feminist movements of the past. In the third section, I examine two campaigns, one focused on maternity benefits and one on "underpayment," that provide insight into how these organizations work and what contributes to their unlikely success. I argue that the CDWU has organizationally managed to overcome essentializing notions of women, without devolving into particularism or ignoring the significance of gender.

Why Are Migrant Domestic Workers So "Unorganizable"?

Studies on domestic workers identify three sets of variables that make them seem virtually unorganizable: the characteristics of domestic work itself; the ways in which gender, class, race, and ethnicity shape the labor market, the industry, and the employment environment; and the active state regulation of immigration and domestic work. I consider each of these barriers in turn.

Characteristics of the Work

Domestic work is highly stigmatized, representing one of the lowest positions in societies across the globe (Palmer 1989; Cohen 1987). This stigma makes it difficult to organize domestic workers because they attempt to distance themselves from (rather then identify with) their occupation (Van Raaphorst 1988; Parreñas 2001). The stigma and lack of career mobility in the occupation make it more appealing to look for other types of work rather then improve the conditions within the occupation (Hondagneu-Sotelo 2001).

The hours worked and tasks performed by domestic workers vary according to their employment arrangements.[1] In most cases, they work very long hours doing difficult labor with few days off (Gill 1994; Ruiz 1987). Despite this, they are poorly compensated for their work (Childress 1986; Giles and Arat-Koc 1994). The combination of long hours and low pay leaves these women with few resources of time or money to dedicate to collective organizing. Moreover, domestic workers do not share a common physical workplace and have no common employer to target, nor does collective action minimize risks to individuals who confront their employers (Chang 2000; Hondagneu-Sotelo 2001), all factors that make collective action around labor conditions harder (Burawoy 1982; Moody 1988).

Furthermore, migrant domestic workers (MDWs) are doubly isolated. In many cases, their families remain in their home countries, and the workers have limited opportunities to develop new interpersonal networks (Hondagneu-Sotelo 1994a; Menjívar 1999). As a result of their spatially dispersed workplaces, domestic workers must travel (sometimes long distances) in order to congregate and participate in collective action. Employers of domestic workers may foster isolation more or less deliberately, by limiting workers' access to various forms of communication, such as the phone or Internet (Chin 1998; Salzinger 1991), tools that have become important in organizing collective action.[2] The live-in situation intensifies the control that the employer has over the domestic worker (Constable 1997), which is sometimes semishrouded in the form of a "maternalistic" relationship (Rollins 1985; Dill 1994; Fairchilds 1984).[3] Isolation plus a complex one-on-one relationship make it difficult for domestic workers to advocate for better working conditions.

Conflict and Division

Another set of barriers arises from the ways in which race, class, and gender are made salient to the worker through the organization of work, and the local, national, and global labor markets in which this occupation is situated. Class, race, ethnicity, nationality, and gender have created divisions among domestic workers, between domestic workers and women's movements, and between domestic workers and the labor movement (Hondagneu-Sotelo 1994b; Cohen 1987; Chin 1998).

In many countries domestic work is done by racial/ethnic minority women both because of the disadvantages they face in finding other work and the cultural appropriateness seen in having low-status work done by low-status women. As native-born minority women's opportunities in employment increase, paid domestic work typically becomes the province of immigrant women, segmenting the stratification of the labor market along the lines of race, ethnicity, and/or nationality (Glenn 1992; Gill 1994; Cheng 1996). This intensifies divisions among domestic workers by creating different problems and concerns for each national/racial group. Organizing domestic workers requires that they recognize these differences, deal with language and cultural differences, and overcome these divisions to act with solidarity.

Class, race/ethnicity, nationality, and gender also interact to create divisions between domestic workers and women's movements (Pereira de Melo 1989; Macklin 1994). Although domestic workers are primarily women, and their associations and organizations share some goals with their respective national feminist movements, there is typically an estranged relationship between domestic workers and these movements (Schecter 1998). In part, this distance is created because domestic workers struggling to improve their situation place many women employers in a contradictory location. Women play a large role in determining the pay and working conditions of domestic workers. Women employers are also dependent on domestic workers as a solution to the burdens of the "double day," their gendered responsibility for housework and paid employment, that allows them to enter into the formal paid workforce.

This contradiction has led some to argue that feminists' complaints about the "double day" seem more rhetorical than real (Chaney and Castro 1989). At the very least, the structure of paid domestic work has made the gendered nature of such work and the unequal burden it places on women less of a "universal" issue. When feminist movements mobilize middle- or upper-class women of the dominant race or nationality, many of whom are reliant on domestic workers, their contradictory interests make it difficult for domestic workers to either participate in these movements or gain their active support.

Finally, class, gender, race, and nationality have always played an important role in defining workers' relationships with the labor movement. In many contexts, unions have been male-dominated and have ignored, or even been hostile toward, women workers (Kessler-Harris 1982; Deslippe 2000). Most unions aim to protect their current members, and while some unions have become more attentive toward organizing women and immigrant workers, MDWs remain outside of their purview in most countries (Milkman 2000; Louie 2001).

State Regulation

The state also plays a significant role in creating barriers to organizing (Cheng 2003; Pratt 1999; Momsen 1999). The state interventions are important on both the international and the national level. Sending and host states along with international governmental and nongovernmental organizations (NGOs) all play a role.[4]

Immigration and labor laws are two of the most important ways in which the host states impact domestic workers' ability to organize (Silvey 2004; Hondagneu-Sotelo 2001).[5] In the "host" countries, immigration laws regulating MDWs fall into three types: unregulated systems, highly regulated systems, and highly regulated systems with stipulations.[6] Labor law protection falls along a continuum from considerable labor law applicability and enforcement, to applicability but little enforcement, to a lack of labor law protections. There is much variation in the combination of these regulatory regimes. Each has different repercussions for organizing among domestic workers.

In countries where immigration is unregulated, such as the United States (Chang 2000; Hondagneu-Sotelo 2001), MDWs usually are undocumented and located in the informal economy (Mattingly 1999). In these regimes, the barriers to organizing include the fear of repatriation, lack of access to formal institutions, and lack of recognition by the state. This shadow existence makes it difficult to demand rights or make claims on the state.

Singapore and Malaysia have a regime characterized by rigid guest worker programs, with tight immigration laws reinforced by the absence of labor rights for MDWs (Huang and Yeoh 1996). Their laws provide employers with incentives to maintain strict control over MDWs, such as requiring employers to pay security bonds and making it illegal for MDWs to change employers. Furthermore, these countries provide no avenues for MDWs to obtain permanent status. Such systems make MDWs very reliant on employers, increasing the power inequality between them and making it very difficult to challenge this relationship.

The regimes of some countries, such as Canada, are not so lawless or so tightly controlled. MDWs are highly regulated by immigration laws but these laws offer avenues for becoming permanent residents and moving into other occupations (Pratt 1999; Bakan and Stasiulis 1994). For example, under Canada's Live-In Caregiver Program, MDWs can apply for permanent status. However, domestic workers are not protected by Canadian labor laws, and because their change in status is dependent on two years of prior domestic service, they are particularly vulnerable to mistreatment during this two-year period. Hong Kong's regime is also intermediate in stringency but in a different way. It has a guest worker program that highly restricts women from changing their temporary status. As a result, many women work in Hong Kong for decades but remain without rights and privileges, and their family must remain in their home country. However, domestic workers are covered by labor laws and a mandatory standard contract.

The countries from which the domestic workers come also play an important role in regulating MDWs. These sending countries rely heavily on exporting workers as a way to earn desperately needed foreign currency. To make their "exports" more attractive, they often have policies that facilitate host countries' control over workers, such as visa systems and requirements that all domestic workers use state-sanctioned labor intermediaries to obtain overseas work (Heyzer, Lycklama à Nijeholt, and Weerakon 1994; Anderson 2001).

There are nonetheless potential spaces in the transnational opportunity structure in which unions and movements can be formed. Since many countries are signatories to international conventions and care about their reputation in the international arena, transnational NGOs can offer MDWs opportunities to make claims about their rights as women, migrants, workers, and humans. The different state systems of regulation interact with local conditions, sometimes to create or reinforce class-based, gendered, ethnic, and racial practices on the local level, but in other situations they create opportunities to organize against these practices.

Individual Resistance and Collective Organizing

Although domestic workers face daunting obstacles, they are not passive victims. They actively participate in shaping domestic work and resisting exploitation (Romero 1992; Salzinger 1991). Individual resistance can be indirect, such as chicanery, tricks, silence, and manipulation (Constable 1997). More direct strategies include structuring work time and tasks to increase control over their work, negotiating pay and benefits, and minimizing demeaning contact with employers (Romero 1992; Dill 1988). Yet, while domestic workers have creatively utilized a wide range of individual forms of resistance, and sometimes thereby improved their individual situations, their individual resistance does not affect the overall system. As Constable's (1997) study of such individual acts of resistance among Filipina domestic workers in Hong Kong concludes: "The overall 'success' of Filipina domestic workers in improving the structure of domestic work or the reputation of domestic workers has been extremely limited. The rules and policies that control domestic workers, especially the two-week rule and the policies regarding full-time, live-in work, remain serious impediments and a constant source of frustration" (179). Constable (1997) makes two important points: that there are large structural factors arrayed against migrant domestic workers, and that individual acts of resistance are not effective in changing these sources of oppression.[7]

Scholars have begun to examine the relationship between different regulatory regimes and the opportunities and/or barriers they create for collective action among MDWs. Some argue that strict guest worker programs hinder MDWs' efforts to organize. For example, Hondagneu-Sotelo (2001) claims that the loose regulatory environment of the United States has created more opportunities for collective organizing than the more strict regulatory environments in places such as Hong Kong. In the United States, she argues,

> Domestic work remains an arrangement that is thought of as private: it remains informal, 'in the shadow' and outside of the purview of the state and other regulating agencies. On the other hand, the absence of state monitoring of domestic jobs contracts and of the domestic workers' personal movement, privacy, and bodily adornment suggests an opening to upgrade domestic jobs in the United States. . . . The absence of a neocolonialist, state-operated, contractual system for domestic work thus represents an opportunity to seek better job conditions. (22)

The successful collective organizing of MDWs that I found in Hong Kong, achieved in the context of such a contractual system, challenges her conclusions. While it would seem that strict regulations on MDWs should prevent organizing, my case study suggests that this type of regulatory regime presents a different set of opportunities and barriers for organizing. In this context, the transnational NGOs support new and potentially effective collective forms of resistance.

Defining the Movement and Its Organizations:
Transnational Feminism

The particular organizational form created by MDWs in Hong Kong is central to their success.[8] The Coalition of Domestic Workers Unions in Hong Kong does not fit any of the common labor union models, although it calls itself a union, nor does it fit the traditional definitions of women's or feminist organizations. The CDWU is instead a creative hybrid of both these classical forms, one I suggest is best seen as a new type entirely: a *women's alternative economic organization.* Such groups not only undermine notions of women workers in informal and contingent employment as being "unorganizable" but also challenge our categorization of women's organizations as merely middle-class. They combine new ways of organizing as women workers of specific national/ethnic groups with demands that speak to improving the conditions of MDWs as both women and workers.

Earlier work on feminist organizations argued that collective identity affects the types of organizational structures that are created, which in turn shapes discussions, goals, and activities of the group. Feminist organizations are often classified into a typology with the "bureaucratic strand" at one end and the "collectivist strand" at the other (Riger 1994; Ferree and Hess 1994; Barnett 1995).[9] Case studies relating feminist identity to organizational forms have elaborated on this association of form and group identity, but the relationship is unidirectional: collective identity impacts organizational form, but not vice versa (Ferguson 1984; Rodriguez 1988; Thomas 1999).

Recent feminist literature recognizes that there is neither a single feminist collective identity nor a singular women's movement. There is a wide diversity, especially along lines of class, race, and ethnic identity (Tripp 2000; Beckwith 2000; Ferree and Roth 1998). As a starting point, I define an organization as feminist if its goals *include* challenging structures of gender oppression or altering gender power relations. This definition allows me to include organizations that have multiple goals, such as the migrant women's unions. In this case study I focus on how the organizational form adopted helped to *create* a common identity and allowed women to work together effectively despite their diversity.

The Hong Kong CDWU also does not fit a standard definition of labor unions. Hondagneu-Sotelo (2001) offers three different "union models" that have been used to organize domestic workers in the United States: professional associations, job cooperatives, and traditional unions. None of these fit this case, which is multilevel and coalitional.

Women's alternative economic organizations are therefore distinctive structurally, ideologically, and strategically from both labor and feminist organizations. Although they are formally structured, they avoid the hierarchical and bureaucratic characteristics of unions and formalized feminist advocacy groups by putting their emphasis on process and democratic practices. Women's alternative economic organizations expand issues beyond the classical "bread and butter" concerns of economic unionism or the gender-based claims of classic feminist movements (Bullock 1994; Jhabvala 1994; Rowbotham and Mitter 1994). Thus they frame the issues facing migrant domestic workers in such a way that they are not distinctly "feminist" or "worker" issues.

Women's alternative economic organizations use a host of strategies, including relying on networks and relationships with other organizations, many of which are transnational (Martens and Mitter 1994; Kidder and McGinn 1995); providing services and assistance that are usually the purview of NGOs (Date-Bah 1997; Rose 1992); pressuring governments through protests, campaigns, and invoking international treaties and standards (Chhachhi and Pitten 1996); broadening their targets to include the state, the public, employers, and unorganized workers (Roth 2003; Rowbotham and Mitter 1994; Bullock 1994); and creating alternative economic and financial institutions such as alternative lending institutions, hiring halls, and employment services (Rose 1992; Jhabvala 1994). Women's alternative economic organizations, I argue, gain political leverage by using gender and race/ethnicity as well as occupational identities to mobilize collective resistance. They neither demand the subordination of "other" identities to an occupational or class solidarity, such as unions have done, nor force women to chose between gender claims and other interests, as feminist movements have done. These women's alternative economic organizations use multiple intersectional identities as a source of strength.

Methodology

This case study relies on data collected during the summer of 1999 in Hong Kong and the Philippines. The snowball sample was developed through initial contacts with a labor research NGO that had worked closely with the migrant unions. In-depth and semistructured interviews were conducted with sixty-one individuals. Most interviews were taped and transcribed, and most were conducted in English.[10] The interviewees belonged to a wide range of organizations: 23 union members, 12 members of migrant associations, 3 government employees, 12 NGO workers, 2 local union employees, 1 service provider, 2 employees of migrant-owned businesses (former migrant domestic workers) all in Hong Kong, and 6 NGO workers in Philippines.

Primary documents gathered from the organizations and unions included membership records, meeting notes and records, and recruiting literature. Participant observation was also important. I was at the union offices daily and kept a journal. Some days, I just observed activities, and other times I joined in meetings, social activities, court proceedings, campaigning, and demonstrations. I also spent time with nonunion organizations and with domestic workers who were non-union members.

Before examining the CDWU, it is necessary to review some of the legal, social, and political background that defines the regulatory regime and labor market in Hong Kong. I then present the case of MDWs' organizing efforts and the difficulties they encountered, and offer a detailed account of the resulting changes in their approach that created their new organizational form. Finally, I describe two campaigns undertaken in the summer of 1999 that reveal the distinctive features of these women's alternative economic organizations and their success.

Hong Kong's Legal Framework

In Hong Kong, domestic work is regulated through four tools that define it as formal work: the standard employment contract, the Employment Ordinance (EO, Hong Kong's general labor law), the labor tribunes, and immigration law. The standard domestic worker contract and the EO apply equally to all MDWs. The mandatory labor contract reflects legislated working standards and covers hours, pay, overtime, holidays and sick pay, insurance, and conditions of legal termination. Issues not covered by the contract fall under the more general EO. Maternity benefits are part of the EO and are granted to the MDWs because they are part of the formal labor market. Labor tribunes provide a possible venue for enforcing both types of regulations. These three parts of the regulatory regime apply to all domestic workers, regardless of national origin.

In contrast, immigration laws vary for domestic workers depending on their respective home country. Immigration is regulated not only by Hong Kong law but also by the sending countries and international politics (Cheng 2003; Huang and Yeoh 1996). These differences are partly responsible for the stratification in the labor market. For example, the Indonesian government requires that Indonesian MDWs use a government-approved agency to obtain overseas employment. These agencies are known to confiscate passports, overcharge on fees, and intentionally violate numerous other laws. In contrast, Filipinas can use informal networks or agencies to find employers, making them less vulnerable to exploitation by intermediaries. While the Hong Kong government allows MDWs two weeks to change jobs and locate new employment, the Indian and Indonesian consulates immediately deport any domestic worker who leaves her contract, requiring her to return home to change employers. The Philippine and Thai governments allow domestic workers to remain in Hong Kong while looking for a new employer. Such variation affects the working conditions and organizing efforts of each group of domestic workers. The diversity of origins among the immigrant domestic workers also matters socially.

Social Conditions: Increasing Diversity and Division

In 1973, Hong Kong received the first group of Filipino migrants entering the country under the Standard Domestic Helper Contract. There are no limitations on the number of MDWs who can be contracted to work in Hong Kong, which has allowed for exponential growth. In 1986, there were 37,800 MDWs in Hong Kong. By 1992, this number had reached 101,000, and by 2000, the number was 202,900 (Asian Migrant Centre 2001). While in the 1980s, Filipina women accounted for more than 93 percent of all domestic workers, larger numbers of Thai and Indonesian women entered in the 1990s. By 2002, women from the Philippines constituted only 60 percent of the MDWs, while Indonesian women accounted for more than a third.

This change was the result of a number of factors. Most important, the increasing strength and organization of Filipina immigrant domestic workers led to improvements in their working and living conditions, increased wages, and better protection from abuse. As a result, the Hong Kong government, the employers association, and segments of the population encouraged bilateral agreements that allowed the importation of women for domestic work from other countries. The growing ethnic and racial diversity was supported by racially discriminatory attitudes in Hong Kong, as one NGO worker explained, "People are getting more accepting toward domestic workers from different countries, Indonesians, mainland Chinese, and Indians, because they are cheap and they don't cause much trouble. Before they wanted a domestic worker [who] could speak English, so comparatively Filipinos are better, but Indonesians are more obedient and quiet and accept lower wages" (Shum, personal interview, 1999). Employers of domestic workers, the general public, and governments treated the domestic workers differently based on their nationality. For example, even though Hong Kong has a government-mandated minimum wage for domestic workers, as the diversity of the labor market has increased, an informal wage scale emerged. At the top of the wage scale were Filipinas, who were usually paid the minimum wage of HK$3,860 per month (1998), whereas the standard wage for Indonesians was HK$2,000 per month, and Thais were paid somewhere in between. At the bottom of the wage scale were Indian and Sri Lankan domestic workers, who were paid as little as HK$500 per month (roughly US$65).

The Political Environment: International and National

The social and political currents in Hong Kong became favorable for organizing in the 1980s and early 1990s as tensions about the impending "handover" of Hong Kong increased. On the one hand, there was an overall revitalization of the labor movement because of concern among both migrant and local workers about the potential competition from an influx of mainland Chinese immigrants. On the other hand, the pro-democracy movement drew strength from concern about the limited democracy that existed and possible changes in the political system once under mainland rule. During this period, the labor movement developed political independence and created the Hong Kong Confederation for Trade Unions (HKTUC). New NGOs and labor unions flourished. All the eighteen migrant organizations listed in an NGO migrant directory were founded after 1980, only two of these before 1985. Both domestic workers unions and migrant rights NGOs drew strength from this politically unsettled situation.

The MDWs union movement began in 1989, marked by the founding of the Asian Domestic Workers Union (ADWU).[11] The ADWU grew in strength into the early 1990s, then quickly declined, and was practically defunct by 1996. As ADWU waned, the Filipino Migrant Workers Union (FMWU) started organizing. In 1998 it officially registered as a union and created the CDWU, formed from separate organizations representing Indonesians, Thais, Indians, and Chinese. The shift from the earlier union, the ADWU, to the new union, the CDWU, shows how the women strategically overcame barriers to their organizing and became unusually successful in representing women MDWs.

Turning Diversity from an Obstacle into a Strength

Organizational characteristics explain the decline of the ADWU and the rise and success of the CDWU. The characteristic "union" structure of the ADWU, its goals and issues, and its internal struggles were influenced by the organizations that assisted in its creation. After the ADWU failed, the CDWU was created with the benefit of the lessons drawn from its decline and therefore chose a deliberately different, innovative form.

Negative Lessons

The founders of the ADWU had constructed it as a hierarchical organization, typical of unions. There were three advantages to organizationally taking the characteristic form of a "union." First, it is fairly easy to gain recognition as a union in Hong Kong.[12] Second, the legal designation of being a union allowed it to conduct a wide range of activities. Finally, the labor laws and labor contract, which applied to the domestic workers, were possible targets for organizing. In this standard union form, individuals join the union and then elect members to their country committee (each nationality has a country committee), which in turn elects a certain number of representatives to the union's nine-member executive committee. Because the organizational structure and processes follow the concept of proportional representation, the nationality that represents the most members dominates the executive committee. Minority groups' representation occurs both through their country committees and through the fact that every country must have at least one member on the executive committee.

At its peak, the ADWU held rallies and demonstrations, joined in broader labor struggles occurring in Hong Kong, handled more than a hundred labor cases a year, and operated two shelters for foreign domestic workers who had lost their live-in jobs and thus their places to stay (Asian Domestic Workers Union 1993). Yet, in 1993, only four years later, the ADWU faced serious problems. During its 1993 annual general meeting, which was attended by more than 500 members, open conflict between the Thai and Filipino members erupted. As a result, more than half of the executive committee walked out, later followed by almost the entire Thai membership (ADWU 1993).

This dispute between the Thai and Filipino members, at least in part, occurred because the union structure created unequal representation for the minority ethnicities (Thai and other nationalities). Their concerns and issues were subordinated to those of the Filipino migrant workers. In terms of organizational issues, such as selecting leaders, the Filipino vote was more numerous, and the Filipino voice was louder. As one NGO observer noted, "I feel, in the Asian Domestic Worker's Union, the language barrier became a major barrier . . . it becomes difficult in organizing the different groups. But somewhere along the way, because the Filipinos form the majority, hence the focus is always on that group and that drives the others, the minorities, . . . to form a different association" (Committee for Asian Women, personal interview, 1999). The union structure also affected the organization's choice of priorities. Due to immigration policies, the most important issues for domestic workers from Thailand differed from those for workers from the Philippines or from Indonesia. However, the union structure was such that the Filipina majority decided which issues were important. In practice, Filipino MDWs' issues were represented as universal. Ineffectual representation and the lack of influence on priorities eventually led most non-Filipino members to leave the union. This produced concerns about how representative and democratic the union was, which made it more difficult to maintain and organize membership. This meant that by 1995, ADWU had lost all its international funding.

As the ADWU declined, the domestic workers themselves were already reorganizing, creating a new coalition led by the FMWU. This new coalition quickly surpassed the ADWU's former strength, with each major rally bringing out tens of thousands of workers. The CDWU also raised a broader spectrum of issues. As of 2006, it has managed to maintain itself for more than ten years. How did it succeed when the ADWU failed?

Positive Growth

The new organizational model mixed NGO-like and unionlike characteristics. The coalition organized domestic workers into associations composed of five to forty women from the same hometown in a particular country. These associations joined together to create a union from the bottom up. Initially this union called itself the Filipino Migrant Workers Union. In a similar process, women from Indonesia created local associations that banded together to create the Indonesian Women's Migrant Union (IWMU). These two unions, along with the Thai Women's Group, the local Chinese Domestic Workers Union, and the Indian Association, then created the Coalition of Domestic Workers Unions. These organizations remained formally separate despite their intense interaction. Many use the same office space and have meetings in the same building, share resources, and network with the same national and transnational NGOs.

The organizational structure of the CDWU deliberately meets needs that the earlier ADWU neglected. In the ADWU, the members were individuals, and this single union claimed to represent all domestic workers regardless of their nationality. In the new coalition, hometown associations join the union. And, while each nationality forms its own union, the unions then join together into a coalition. The hometown associations provide support, education, and advocacy at the grassroots level for individual women. At the coalition level, this structure creates spaces where issues of race and nationality and legal issues specific to the union can be addressed. Since participation is based on equal representation of all the member unions, rather than proportional representation, it is difficult for any single union or nationality to dominate the coalition, and issues of concern to minorities reach the top organizational level, where they can be acted upon.

Two campaigns from the summer of 1990 illustrate the effectiveness of this intersectional strategy: maternity benefits and underpayment.

Two Campaigns and Conditions for Their Success

The maternity benefits issue is about protecting rights that already existed for all MDWs under labor law and the standard domestic worker contract. The "underpayment" issue is about how the immigration regulatory regime creates unequal pay for domestic workers of different nationalities. I have chosen these two issues for a number of reasons. The "underpayment" issue is a sign of solidarity because the majority of domestic workers are Filipinas who generally face no such problem. Therefore, when the Filipinas dominated the domestic workers union movement, underpayment relative to the statutory minimum was not addressed. However, in the new organizational structure this became a priority issue. Contrary to classic union approaches, the CDWU frames maternity benefits as a universal right and underpayment as particular to a segment of the labor market, but it campaigns strongly for both.

Both these issues are typically classified as economic, but in the CDWU campaigns neither maternity benefits nor minimum wages were framed as economic issues. The maternity benefits campaign used gender as the primary organizing principle. This allowed the domestic migrant women workers to gain support across movements rather then rely only on the solidarity of male unionists. The minimum wage (underpayment) issue organized around issues of racial and ethnic discrimination, highlighting the differences rather than the commonalities among domestic workers. Strategically, these two issues highlight the importance of the international arena and so the roles of transnational and transmovement cooperation, networks, and coalitions. Comparison of these two campaigns shows how the regulatory regime of the state has shaped the CDWU activities.

Maternity Benefits on Paper and in Practice

In Hong Kong, maternity benefits have been provided under the Employment Ordinance since 1968. When, in June 1997, the EO was amended to provide improved protection, the government decided to revisit how the law should apply to live-in domestic workers.[13] The EO entitles all women who have worked for one employer for forty continuous weeks to ten weeks of paid maternity leave, protection from dangerous work and time off for medical appointments, and protection from dismissal once they have notified the employer of their pregnancy. The broader environment in which they are instituted limits the impact of these protections. Lack of provisions in immigration law for family reunification, marriage restrictions, and temporary status all create a situation in which it is difficult for MDWs to have children.[14] Despite the limited use made of maternity benefits, the Labor Department concluded that "there is a need to introduce some flexible arrangements because when a live-in domestic helper becomes pregnant, her pregnancy would cause some practical inconveniences to the employer and his family and may adversely affect the latter's daily life" (Labour Department Report, June 1999). The more "flexible" arrangement proposed by the Labour Department would allow the employer and domestic worker to "mutually" agree to end the contract, holding the employer liable for only a few months' salary but not for unlawful dismissal.

When the government circulated this memo, the response on behalf of domestic workers was swift. Various social movements mobilized, including long- and short-term coalitions of organizations ranging across migrant and local NGOs and unions at the local, national, and international levels. The Coalition for Migrants' Rights in Hong Kong, of which the CDWU is a member organization, took the lead role and organized a meeting of NGOs and labor unions to discuss the government's proposal.[15] During the meeting they decided to put together a temporary coalition to deal with this one issue. This new coalition would include women's organizations, representatives from national unions, local NGOs with other target populations, and regional migrant organizations. The coalition devised a calendar of response actions, with groups at different levels taking on different responsibilities. The long-term coalition, the Coalition for Migrants' Rights, already had an infrastructure that allowed its member groups to give an immediate response, while the broader temporary coalition widened the potential actions that could be used by others. Finally, the multiplicity of grassroots organizations provided a mobilizing structure to quickly educate and activate the woman workers.

Each group also had a specific target. The Coalition for Migrants' Rights exerted pressure on "sending country" governments to discuss the issue with the Hong Kong government. Local organizations and unions focused on lobbying legislators and elected officials. Regional migrant, labor, and women's organizations directed their efforts toward exploring opportunities presented by international conventions. Finally, the domestic workers' unions and local unions (the CDWU), along with service NGOs, worked on mobilizing both migrants and the local population.

The successful formation of such a broad coalition that traversed such different groups depended on how the issue was framed. Framing this issue as an attack on "all" women, and on national and international standards and universalistic norms, was very important in soliciting participation from this wide range of organizations.[16] The formal response sent to the government focused on how this issue affected *all* women:

> Our first objection is that any practice that is short of complete and unconditional applicability to all women and strong enforcement would be discriminatory against women and, depending on the conditions, against foreigners. All women have the basic right to conceive a child without fear of direct or indirect reprisal or punishment. All women, not just Hong Kong women, not just women with a certain status, not just women from a particular country or of a particular background should be afforded complete protection of their basic rights recognized by both the Hong Kong government and the international community. (Coalition for Migrants' Rights 1999)

The group organized demonstrations, as well as filing a complaint with the International Labor Organization that the proposed amendment was in violation of the International Labour Convention No. 97, a convention to which Hong Kong was a signatory. The campaign ended with the Legislative Council not acting upon the recommendations of the Labour Department.

Unequal Pay

In Hong Kong, the minimum wage for MDWs is dictated by the standard domestic workers contract. Every year the government, the employers associations, and the domestic workers negotiate this wage level. In reality, the minimum wage has been circumvented by the development of an informal wage scale, with Filipinas earning the top wage (the legal minimum wage), and other nationalities earning progressively less. Indonesian domestic workers are the fastest-growing segment of foreign domestic workers (a 20 percent increase in 1998–1999) and among the most vulnerable. These women usually arrive in Hong Kong in debt. The language barrier and lack of institutionalization of the immigration process place them at the mercy of employment agencies that are notorious for using illegal methods of control such as confiscating passports and having the women sign for money they did not receive. But when problems arise with an employer, the Indonesian consulate, rather than facilitating access to NGOs, labor courts, or unions, immediately deports the domestic worker.[17]

The creation of the Indonesian Group in 1998, a migrant organization that later became the Indonesian Women Migrants Union, addressed these underlying conditions. The IWMU spent time in the parks where Indonesian workers gathered on Sunday, their only day off, talking to women and identifying the details of their situation. In this process the issue of "underpayment" came to light. The group followed up by conducting a survey of Indonesian domestic workers, revealing that 80 percent of the workers were paid less than the statutory minimum wage.[18] It also found that placement agencies in Hong Kong were charging Indonesian domestic workers fees in excess of the maximum charge (10 percent of one month's salary).

In April 1998, the IWMU published its findings in pamphlets and held press conferences that were covered by major newspapers. The press sensationalized the situation by printing stories that exemplified the worst-case scenarios. In May, accompanied by local NGOs and the Filipino migrants union, the IWMU representatives met with the Hong Kong Immigration Department and convinced the department to conduct an investigation and set up a hotline. The IMWU reached out to workers through Kartini Day, a cultural celebration named after a heroine in Indonesia who fought against exploitation. The event uses theater, dance, and art and is more accessible to women who usually are either afraid of or unfamiliar with overt political activity (Nelsey, personal interview, June 6, 1999). The first Kartini Day drew a few hundred women; three years later, more than 5,000 women attended the event. By 2003, more than 2,000 Indonesian domestic workers participated in a march protesting their consulate's practice of immediate deportation of domestic workers who have problems with employers and protesting against the consulate's requirement that they return home to change employers, which increases the costs of leaving an employer (Asian Migrant Centre 2003). Three years earlier this kind of action on behalf of Indonesian domestic workers would have been unimaginable.

Such events not only reached out to and politicized Indonesian domestic workers but also made other domestic workers more aware of the issues facing Indonesians. At Kartini Day, representatives from Filipino, Thai, Indian, Sri Lankan, and Nepalese migrant organizations and unions gave messages of support. As a Filipino domestic worker describes it, "The Indonesian Group started the 'Year-Long Campaign,' which was supported by the FMWU, and it raised awareness among the Filipino domestic workers" (personal interview, June 19, 1999).

Under this new form of union organizing embraced by the CDWU, where each nationality had its own union, a political space emerged where the differences in their situations could be recognized. New issues thus emerged as priorities. The organizational structure also allowed Indonesian women to use a strategy that relied more on cultural symbols and art, which spoke to women who had less political experience than the Filipinas. The CDWU's form as a women's alternative economic organization allowed the MDWs to recognize and organize around difference and diversity.

Conclusions

This case study provides a clear example of the "unorganizable" organizing. Migrant domestic workers in Hong Kong organized and changed their working conditions with the help of broader coalitions. The Coalition of Domestic Workers Unions provides an example of how women's organizations that are both transmovement and transnational create opportunities to work in such broader coalitions, draw upon larger constituencies, and operate in different arenas. In these cases, the "unorganizable" provide a new model for organizing that offers both the labor and the women's movements a practical strategy for overcoming difficulties they face in the globalizing world.

This case study also shows how transnational organizing around gender issues has challenged universal and essentializing notions of women. Women have multiple identities and historically contingent positions that organizers need to take into account if they are to be successful (Tripp 2000; Ferree and Roth 1998; Beckwith 2000; Basu 1995). Although challenging a simple universalism, the organizing strategy seen here also did not end in disintegration or particularism, as some have feared. As illustrated by the maternity benefits issue, appealing to gender as a universal, affecting "all women," remains an important organizing tool. But addressing this commonality through difference appears to be more effective than trying to make it an organizational prerequisite.

The successful organizing of MDWs in Hong Kong also shows how the state shapes organizing opportunities, particularly through regulatory regimes. However, it challenges the idea that strict state-operated contractual systems for importing immigrant labor make it impossible for immigrant workers to organize. Different types of regulatory regimes create different types of opportunities and barriers, and organizational strategies must differ accordingly. The diverse membership and complex situations of domestic workers situated in the gendered transnational economy complicate the ways in which these regulatory regimes actually play out in specific places. The transnational nature of the work relation, no less than of organizations and movements, allows a new approach to organization that crosses national boundaries, as the maternity leave case showed. In this now transnationally governed space, women's alternative economic organizations have the flexibility and coalitional potential to support effective strategies that are attentive to both commonality and difference.

NOTES

1. Although live-in domestic workers are the focus of this chapter, it is important to note that there are also "day workers," women who perform paid domestic work for a specified number of hours over a specified period. Also, both live-in and day workers can have a specialty or specific task, for example, child care, or they can be hired under conditions in which their job combines a wide range of tasks, such as child care, cleaning, and cooking. In some cases employers also add in things like pet care, yard work, cleaning cars, and even assisting with work at their small businesses.

2. As a result, alternative forms of communication have developed, such as a heavier reliance on written publications, radio broadcasts, and posters.

3. Hondagneu-Sotelo's (2001) study of domestic workers in the United States notes that today this relationship between the domestic workers and her employer is more often characterized as being quite distant and cold. However, this less maternal relationship also creates issues for the domestic worker, such reinforcing her low status and denying her recognition.

4. Host states are the states that receive immigrant workers, and sending states are those that export large numbers of workers.

5. In certain states access (or lack of access) to state welfare programs also plays an important role in shaping opportunities for migrant domestic workers (Ching 2001). However, in states where migration of domestic workers is highly regulated and predicated on their having a job, the question of social welfare services become moot.

6. The United States and Hong Kong (Hondagneu-Sotelo 2001; Constable 1997) represent countries that provide some labor law protections (although levels of protection and enforcement vary); Canada and Singapore (Arat-Koc 1997; Cheng 1996, Chin 1998) represent countries in which labor laws do not apply to domestic workers.

7. However, since her focus was on individual acts of resistance, the union organizing occurring in Hong Kong at this time fell outside the purview of her study and is mentioned only briefly.

8. The migrant domestic workers in Hong Kong are often referred to as foreign domestic workers (FDWs), a term designated by the state. I use the more general term migrant domestic workers (MDW) because I am discussing both legal and illegal immigrant women working as domestic workers across many countries.

9. Some scholars have used other terms to describe the bureaucratic model, or forms of it, such as formalization (Riger 1994), the legal rational model (Gottfried and Weiss 1994), hierarchical form (Leidner 1991), and the professionalized organization (Lebon 1996). The collective strand has also been assigned a number of terms, such as the consensual-egalitarian (Gottfried and Weiss 1994), participatory (Leidner 1991), and nonprofessionalized models (Lebon 1996).

10. In a few cases translators or recorders were not used due to either the sensitivity of the topic, request of the interviewee, or not having access to the equipment. A few interviews utilized translators for interviewees who only spoke Thai.

11. The migrant domestic workers union movement has a history that spans more than a decade and includes seven domestic workers unions that were organized between 1982 and 1999. However, the mobilization of domestic workers has been led by these two main unions, the ADWU and the FMWU.

12. Creating a union and organizing/mobilizing a union are two different processes in Hong Kong. Creating a union simply requires pulling together seven or more people who have some relationship (for example, in the same industry). They agree to form a union and are willing to hold a position in the union. They have a physical space where they can post their union certificate.

13. In Hong Kong almost all live-in domestic workers are migrant domestic workers; therefore, the review of how maternity protections should apply to live-in domestic workers was really a review of how the maternity protections should apply to migrant domestic workers.

14. According to a 1998 survey, there were more than 175,000 MDWs, of whom roughly 44 percent were married. However, of the total MDWs, only .09 percent (159) of them gave birth in that year (Hong Kong Labour Relations Service 1998).

15. The Coalition for Migrants' Rights consists of roughly fourteen organizations, including migrant NGOs, domestic workers unions, migrant associations, and local NGOs that provide services to migrants.

16. The response argued that such an amendment would violate international norms and treaties that the Hong Kong government has signed, including the International Labour Convention No. 97 (ILC 97), the Convention on the Elimination of All Forms of Discrimination against Women (CEDAW), and the UN Convention on the Protection of the Rights of All Migrant Workers and Members of Their Families.

17. The political situation in their home country, the lack of protections and regulations of recruitment agencies and other aspects of the labor export industry, and the lack of support from their government representatives in Hong Kong have all contributed to a precarious situation for these women.

18. This was later supported by an estimate of 90 percent given by the Indonesian Manpower Department.

BIBLIOGRAPHY

Abella, Manolo, and Hiromi Mori. 1996. *Structural Change and Labour Migration in East Asia: Development Strategy, Employment and Migration Country Experiences.* Cambridge, Mass.: Harvard University Press.

Anderson, Bridget. 2000. *Doing the Dirty Work? The Global Politics of Domestic Labour.* London: Zed Books.

———. 2001. "Different Roots in Common Ground: Transnationalism and Migrant Domestic Workers in London." *Journal of Ethnic and Migration Studies* 27:673–683.

Arat-Koc, Sedef. 1997. "From 'Mothers of the Nation' to Migrant Workers." In A. B. Bakan and D. Stasiulis, eds., *Not One of the Family: Foreign Domestic Workers in Canada.* Toronto: University of Toronto Press.

Arnold, Gretchen. 1995. "Dilemmas of Feminist Coalitions: Collective Identity and Strategic Effectiveness in the Battered Women's Movement." In M. M. Ferree and Patrica Yancey Martin, eds., *Feminist Organizations: Harvest of the New Women's Movement,* 276–291. Philadelphia: Temple University Press.

Asian and Pacific Development Centre. 1989. *Trade in Domestic Helpers: Causes, Mechanisms, and Consequences.* Kuala Lumpur: Asian and Pacific Development Centre.

Asian Domestic Workers Union. 1993. *ADWU Update.* Hong Kong: Asian Domestic Workers Union. Summer.

———. 1995. ADWU Update. Hong Kong: Asian Domestic Workers Union. Summer.

———. 1996a. *Evaluation Meeting and Camp.* Hong Kong: ADWU, internal document.

———. 1996b. *Hong Kong Report and History.* Hong Kong, ADWU, internal document.

Asian Migrant Coordinating Body (AMCB). 1997. *Joint Submission on the Proposed Wage Cuts for Foreign Domestic Helpers.* Hong Kong, internal document.

———. 1999. *Minutes of the Advocates' Meeting.* Internal documents.

Asian Migrant Centre. 1996. Asian Migrant Forum. Hong Kong, AMC.

———. 1998. *Asian Migrant Yearbook.* Hong Kong: Asian Migrant Centre.

———. 1999. *Asian Migrant Yearbook.* Hong Kong: Asian Migrant Centre.

———. 2001. *Asian Migrant Yearbook.* Hong Kong: Asian Migrant Centre.

———. 2003. *Asian Migrant Yearbook.* Hong Kong: Asian Migrant Centre.

Asian Pacific Mission for Migrant Filipinos. 1997. *News Digest.* Hong Kong: APMMF. January–February.

———. 1998. *News Digest.* Hong Kong: APMMF. March–June.

———. 1999. *News Digest.* Hong Kong: APMMF. January–March.

Bakan, Abigail B., and Daiva Stasiulis. 1994. "Making the Match: Domestic Placement Agencies and the Racialization of Women's Household Work." *Signs* 20:303–332.

———. 1997. "Foreign Domestic Worker Policy in Canada and the Social Boundaries of Modern Citizenship." In A. B. Bakan and D. Stasiulis, eds., *Not One in the Family: Foreign Domestic Workers in Canada,* 29–52. Toronto: University of Toronto Press.

Barnett, Bernice McNair. 1995. "Black Women's Collectivist Movement Organizations. Their Struggle during the Doldrums." In M. M. Ferree and P. Y. Martin, eds., *Feminist Organizations: Harvest of the New Women's Movement,* 199–219. Philadelphia: Temple University Press.

Basu, Amrita. 1995. "Introduction: The Challenge of Local Feminisms." In A. Basu, ed., *Feminisms: Women's Movements in Global Perspective,* 1–21. Boulder, Colo.: Westview Press.

Battistella, Graziano, and Anthony Paganoni, eds. 1996. *Asian Women in Migration.* Quezon City, Philippines: Scalabrini Migration Center.

Beckwith, Karen. 2000. "Beyond Compare? Women's Movements in Comparative Perspective." *European Journal of Political Research* 37:431–468.

Bullock, Susan. 1994. *Women and Work.* London: Zed Books.

Burawoy, Michael. 1982. *Manufacturing Consent: Changes in the Labor Process under Monopoly Capitalism.* Chicago: University of Chicago Press.

Chaney, Elsa, and Mary Garcia Castro. 1989. *Muchachas No More: Household Workers in Latin America and the Caribbean.* Philadelphia: Temple University Press.

Chang, Grace. 2000. *Disposable Domestics: Immigrant Women Workers in the Global Economy.* Cambridge, Mass.: South End Press.

Chant, Sylvia. 1992. *Gender and Migration in Developing Countries.* London: Belhaven Press.

Cheng, Shu-ju Ada. 1996. "Migrant Domestic Workers in Hong Kong, Singapore, and Taiwan: A Comparative Analysis." In G. Battistella, A. Paganoni, and Scalabrini Migration Center, eds., *Asian Women in Migration,* 109–122. Quezon City, Philippines: Scalabrini Migration Center.

———. 2003. "Rethinking the Globalization of Domestic Service: Foreign Domestics, State Control, and the Politics of Identity in Taiwan." *Gender and Society* 17:166–186.

Chhachhi, Amrita, and Renee Pittin. 1996. "Multiple Identities, Multiple Strategies." In Amria Chhachhi and Renee Pitten, eds., *Confronting State, Capital and Patriarchy: Women Organizing in the Process of Industrialization,* 93–130. New York and The Hague: St. Martin's Press, in association with the Institute of Social Studies.

Childress, Alice. 1986. *Like One of the Family: Conversations from a Domestic's Life.* Boston: Beacon Press.

Chin, Christine B. N. 1998. *Service and Servitude: Foreign Female Domestic Workers and Malaysian "Modernity Project."* New York" Columbia University Press.

Ching Yoon Louie, M. 2001. *Sweatshop Warriors: Immigrant Women Workers Take on the Global Factory.* Boston: South End Press.

Coalition for Migrants' Rights (CRM). 1999. "Unsolicited Submission to the Hong Kong Labor Department Regarding the Proposed Amendment to the Maternity Protection for Live-In Domestic Helpers." Document submitted to the Hong Kong Legislative Committee Panel on Manpower and Labour Department. July 21.

Cobble, Dorothy Sue. 1993. *Women and Unions: Forging a Partnership.* Ithaca, N.Y.: ILR Press.

———. 1996. "The Prospects for Unionism in a Service Society." In C. L. Macdonald and C. Sirianni, eds., *Working in the Service Society,* 338–358. Philadelphia: Temple University Press.

Cohen, Rina. 1987. "Women of Color in White Households: Coping Strategies of Live-In Domestic Workers." *Qualitative Sociology* 14:197–215.

Colen, Shelle. 1989. "'Just a Little Respect': West Indian Domestic Workers in New York City." In E. Chaney and M. G. Castro, eds., *Muchachas No More: Household Workers in Latin America and the Caribbean,* 171–194. Philadelphia: Temple University Press.

————. 1990. "'Housekeeping for the Green Card: West Indian Household Workers, the State, and Stratified Reproduction in New York." In R. Sanjeck and S. Colen, eds., *At Work in Homes: Household Workers in World Perspective* 89–118. Washington, D.C.: American Ethnological Society.

Collins, Jane Lou, and Martha Giminez. 1990. *Work without Wages: Comparative Studies of Domestic Labor and Self-Employment.* Albany: State University of New York Press.

Committee for Asian Women. 1988. *Beyond Labour Issues: Women Workers in Asia.* Hong Kong: Committee for Asian Women. Summary of conference held in Hong Kong October 4–11, 1987.

Constable, Nicole. 1997. *Maid to Order in Hong Kong: Stories of Filipina Workers.* Ithaca, N.Y.: Cornell University Press.

Cox, Rosie, and Paul Watt. 2002. "Globalization, Polarization, and the Informal Sector: The Case of Paid Domestic Workers in London." *Area* 34, no. 1: 39–47.

Date-Bah, Eugenie. 1997. *Promoting Gender Equality at Work: Turning Vision into Reality for the Twenty-first Century.* London: Zed Books.

Deslippe, Dennis A. 2000. *Rights, Not Roses: Unions and the Rise of Working-Class Feminism, 1945–80.* Urbana: University of Illinois Press.

Devault, Marjorie L. 1991. *Feeding the Family: The Social Organization of Caring as Gendered Work.* Chicago: University of Chicago Press.

Dill, Bonnie Thorton. 1988. "Making Your Job Good Yourself: Domestic Service and the Construction of Personal Dignity." In A. Bookman and S. Morgen, eds., *Women and the Politics of Empowerment,* 33–52. Philadelphia: Temple University Press.

————. 1994. *Across the Boundaries of Race and Class: An Exploration of Work and Family among Black Female Domestic Servants.* New York: Garland.

Ehrenreich, Barbara, and Arlie Russell Hochschild. 2002. *Global Women: Maids, Nannies, and Sex Workers.* New York: Metropolitan Press.

Fairchilds, Cissie C. 1984. *Domestic Enemies: Servants and Their Masters in Old Regime France.* Baltimore: Johns Hopkins University Press.

Ferguson, Kathy E. 1984. *The Feminist Case against Bureaucracy.* Philadelphia: Temple University Press.

Ferree, Myra Marx, and Beth Hess. 1994. *Controversy and Coalition: The New Feminist Movement.* Boston: G. K. Hall.

————. 2000. *Controversy and Coalition: The New Feminist Movement across Three Decades of Change.* New York: Routledge.

Ferree, Myra Marx, and Silke Roth. 1998. "Gender, Class, and the Interaction between Social Movements: A Strike of West Berlin Day Care Workers." *Gender and Society* 12: 626–648.

Foner, Philip Sheldon. 1979a. *Women and the American Labor Movement: From Colonial Times to the Eve of World War I.* New York: Free Press.

————. 1979b. *Women and the Labor Movement.* New York: Free Press.

Fonow, Mary Margaret. 2003. *Union Women: Forging Feminism in the United Steel-workers of America.* Minneapolis: University of Minnesota Press.

Freeman, Richard B., and James L. Medoff. 1984. *What Do Unions Do?* New York: Basic Books.

Gabin, Nancy F. 1990. *Feminism in the Labor Movement: Women and the United Auto Workers, 1935–1975.* Ithaca, N.Y.: Cornell University Press.

Giles, Winona, and Sedef Arat-Koç 1994. *Maid in the Market: Women's Paid Domestic Labour.* Halifax, Nova Scotia: Fernwood.

Gill, Lesley. 1994. *Precarious Dependencies: Gender, Class, and Domestic Service in Bolivia.* New York: Columbia University Press.

Glenn, Evelyn Nakano. 1986. *Issei, Nisei, War Bride: Three Generations of Japanese American Women in War Service.* Philadelphia: Temple University Press.

————. 1992. "From Servitude to Service Work: Historical Continuities and the Racial Division of Paid Reproductive Labor." *Signs* 18:1–43.

————. 2002. *Unequal Freedom: How Race and Gender Shaped American Citizenship and Labor.* Cambridge, Mass.: Harvard University Press.

Gottfried, Heidi, and Penny Weiss. 1994. "A Compound Feminist Organization: Purdue University's Council on the Status of Women." *Women and Politics* 4, no. 2: 23.

Heckscher, Charles C. 1988. *The New Unionism.* New York: Basic Books.

Heyzer, Noalleen, Geertje Lycklama à Nijeholt, Nedra Weerakon, and the Asian and Pacific Development Centre. 1994. *The Trade in Domestic Workers: Causes, Mechanisms, and Consequences of International Migration.* London: Zed Books.

Hochschild, Arlie Russell. 1997. *The Time Bind: When Work Becomes Home and Home Becomes Work.* New York: Metropolitan Press.

Holter, Darryl. 1994. *Reorganizing Labor: Can Unions Come Back?* Los Angeles: University of California, Institute of Industrial Relations.

Hondagneu-Sotelo, Pierette. 1994a. *Gendered Transitions: The Mexican Experiences of Immigration.* Berkeley: University of California Press.

————. 1994b. "Regulating the Unregulated? Domestic Workers' Social Network." *Social Problems* 41:50–64.

————. 2001. *Doméstica: Immigrant Workers Cleaning and Caring in the Shadows of Affluence.* Berkeley: University of California Press.

Hong Kong Government. 1998. *Hong Kong in Figures.* Hong Kong: General Statistics Section.

Hong Kong Labour Department. 1999. "Labor Department Report." Section on Proposed Amendments to the Conditions of Applicability of the Maternity Provisions under the Hong Kong Employment Ordinance. June.

Hong Kong Labour Relations Service. 1998. Survey of Domestic Helpers' Labor Disputes.

Huang, Shirlena, and Brenda S. A. Yeoh. 1996. "Ties That Bind: State Policy and Migrant Female Domestic Helpers in Singapore." *Geoforum* 27: 479–493.

―――. 1999. "Spaces at the Margins: Migrant Domestic Workers and the Development of Civil Society in Singapore." *Environment and Planning* 31:1149–1167.

International Confederation of Free Trade Unions. 2003. *Labour Flash,* no. 1090. Hong Kong: ICFTU, Asian Pacific Regional Office.

Jhabvala, Renana. 1994. "Self-Employed Women's Association: Organising Women by Struggle and Development." In Sheila Rowbotham and Swasti Mitter, eds., *Dignity and Daily Bread,* 114–138. New York: Routledge.

Johnston, Paul. 1994. *Success While Others Fail: Social Movement Unionism and the Public Workplace.* Ithaca, N.Y. Cornell University ILR Press.

Katzman, David M. 1978. *Seven Days a Week: Women and Domestic Service in Industrializing America.* New York: Oxford University Press.

Kessler-Harris, Alice. 1982. *Out to Work: A History of Wage-Earning Women in the United States.* New York: Oxford University Press.

Kessler-Harris, Alice, and Karen Brodkin Sacks. 1987. "The Demise of Domesticity in America." In L. Benería and C. R. Stimpson, eds., *Women, Households, and the Economy,* 65–85. New Brunswick, N.J.: Rutgers University Press.

Khagram, Sanjeef, James V. Riker, and Kathryn Sikkink, eds. 2002. *Restructuring World Politics: Transnational Social Movements, Networks, and Norms.* Minneapolis: University of Minnesota Press.

Kidder, Thalia, and M. McGinn. 1995. "In the Wake of NAFTA: Transnational Workers Networks" *Social Policy* 24, no. 4: 14–21.

Lang, Sabine. 1997. "The NGOization of Feminism." In J. W. Scott, C. Kaplan, and D. Keates, eds., *Transitions, Environments, Translations: Feminisms in International Politics,* 101–117. New York: Routledge .

Lebon, Nathalie. 1996. "Professionalization of Women's Health Groups in San Paulo: The Troublesome Road towards Organizational Diversity." *Organizations* 3:588–609.

Lee, Joseph S., and Su-Wan Wang 1996. "Recruiting and Managing of Foreign Workers in Taiwan." *Asian and Pacific Migration Journal* 5:281–302.

Leidner, Robin. 1991. "Stretching the Boundaries of Liberalism: Democratic Innovation in a Feminist Organization." *Signs* 16:263–289.

Lim, Lin Lean, and Nana Oishi. 1996. "International Labor Migration of Asian Women: Distinctive Characteristics and Policy Concerns." In G. Battistella, A. Paganoni and Scalabrini Migration Center, eds., *Asian Women in Migration,* 23–55. Quezon City, Philippines: Scalabrini Migration Center.

Loh, Cheng Koi, Choi Wan Cheung, Maria Rhie, and the Committee for Asian Women, eds. 1991. *Many Paths, One Goal: Organising Women Workers in Asia.* Kowloon, Hong Kong: Committee for Asian Women.

Louie, Miriam Ching Yoon. 2001. *Sweatshop Warriors: Immigrant Women Workers Take on the Global Factory.* Cambridge: South End Press.

Macklin, Audrey. 1994. "On the Inside Looking In: Foreign Domestic Workers in Canada." In W. M. Giles and S. Arat-Koç, eds., *Maid in the Market: Women's Paid Domestic Labour,* 13–39. Halifax, Nova Scotia: Fernwood.

Mansbridge, Jane. 1996. "What Is the Feminist Movement." In Myra Marx Ferree and Patricia Yancey Martin, eds., *Feminist Organizations: Harvest of the New Women's Movement,* 27–33. Philadelphia: Temple University Press.

Martens, Margaret H., and Swasti Mitter. 1994. *Women in Trade Unions: Organizing the Unorganized.* Geneva: International Labour Office.

Martin, Patricia Yancey. 1990. "Rethinking Feminist Organizations." *Gender and Society,* no. 4: 182–206.

Martin, Patricia Yancey, Andrew Mason, and Nagayama Toshikazu. 1996. "Introduction." *Asian Pacific Journal of Migration* 5:163–173.

Mattingly, Doreen J. 1999. "Job Search, Social Networks and Labor Market Dynamics: The Case of Paid Household Work in San Diego." *Urban Geography* 20:46–74.

McBride, Theresa. 1976. *The Domestic Revolution: The Modernization of Household Service in England and France, 1820–1920.* London: Croom Helm.

Menjívar, Cecilia. 1999. "The Intersection of Work and Gender: Central American Immigrant Women and Employment in California." *American Behavioral Scientist* 42:601–628.

Milkman, Ruth. 1985. *Women, Work, and Protest: A Century of US Women's Labor History.* Boston: Routledge and Kegan Paul.

———. 2000. *Organizing Immigrants: The Challenge for Unions in Contemporary California.* Ithaca, N.Y.: ILR Press.

Mission for Filipino Migrant Workers. 1995. *Migrant Focus.* Hong Kong: Mission for Filipino Migrant Workers.

———. 1998. *Filipino Migrant Workers in Hong Kong.* Hong Kong: Organization document.

Momsen, Janet Henshall. 1999. *Gender, Migration and Domestic Service.* New York: Routledge.

Moody, Kim. 1988. *An Injury to All: The Decline of Industrial Unionism.* London: Verso.

Moody, Kim, and Mary McGinn 1992. *Unions and Free Trade: Solidarity vs. Competition.* Detroit, Mich.: Labor Notes Book.

Mueller, Carol. 1995. "The Organizational Basis of Conflict in Contemporary Feminism." In Myra Marx Ferree and Patricia Yancey Martin, eds., *Feminist Organizations: Harvest of the New Women's Movement,* 249–263. Philadelphia: Temple University Press.

Munro, Anne. 1999. *Women, Work, and Trade Unions.* London: Mansell.

Ostrander, Susan A. 1999. "Gender and Race in a Pro-feminist, Progressive, Mixed-Gender, Mixed-Race Organization." *Gender and Society* 13:628–642.

Palmer, Phyllis. 1989. *Domesticity and Dirt: Housewives and Domestic Servants in the United States, 1920–1945.* Philadelphia: Temple University Press.

Parreñas, Rhacel Salazar. 2001. *Servants of Globalization: Women, Migration and Domestic Work.* Stanford, Calif.: Stanford University Press.

Pereira de Melo, Hildete. 1989. "Feminists and Domestic Workers in Rio de Janeiro." In E. Chaney and M. G. Castro, eds., *Muchachas No More: Household Workers in Latin America and the Caribbean,* 221–245. Philadelphia: Temple University Press.

Pesotta, Rose, and John Nicholas Beffel, eds. 1987. *Bread upon the Waters.* Ithaca, N.Y.: ILR Press.

Pratt, Geraldine. 1999. "From Registered Nurse to Registered Nanny: Discursive Geographies of Filipina Domestic Workers in Vancouver, B.C." *Economic Geography* 75:215.

Richardson, Laurel, and Verta A. Taylor. 1993. *Feminist Frontiers III.* New York: McGraw-Hill.

Richardson, Laurel, Verta A. Taylor, and Nancy Whittier. 2001. *Feminist Frontiers V.* Boston: McGraw Hill.

Riger, Stephanie. 1994. "Challenges of Success: Stages of Growth in Feminist Organizations." *Feminist Studies* 20:275.

Rodriguez, Noelie Maria. 1988. "Transcending Bureaucracy: Feminist Politics at a Shelter for Battered Women." *Gender and Society* 2:214–227.

Rollins, Judith. 1985. *Between Women: Domestics and Their Employers.* Philadelphia: Temple University Press.

Romero, Mary. 1992. *Maid in the U.S.A.* New York: Routledge.

Rose, Kalima. 1992. *Where Women Are Leaders: The SEWA Movement in India.* New Delhi: Vistar Publications.

Roth, Silke. 2003. *Building Movement Bridges: The Coalition of Labor Union Women.* Westport, Conn.: Praeger.

Rowbotham, Sheila, and Swasti Mitter. 1994. *Dignity and Daily Bread: New Forms of Economic Organising among Poor Women in the Third World and the First.* London: Routledge.

Ruiz, Maria Luz Vega. 1987. "By the Day or the Week": Mexicana Domestic Workers in El Paso." In Carol Groneman and Mary Beth Norton, eds., *To Toil the Livelong Day: American Women at Work, 1780–1980.* Ithaca, N.Y.: Cornell University Press.

Salzinger, Leslie. 1991. "A Maid by Any Other Name: The Transformation of 'Dirty Work.'" In M. Burawoy, ed., *Ethnography Unbound: Power and Resistance in the Modern Metropolis,* 139–160. Berkeley: University of California Press.

Schecter, Tanya. 1998. *Race, Class, Women and the State: The Case of Domestic Labour.* Montreal: Black Rose.

Silvey, Rachel. 2004. "Transnational Domestication: State Power and Indonesian Migrant Women in Saudi Arabia." *Political Geography* 23:245–264.

Smith, Barbara Ellen. 1995. "Crossing the Great Divides: Race, Class, and Gender in Southern Women's Organizing, 1979–1991." *Gender and Society* 9:680–696.

Snow, David A., and Robert D. Benford. 1988. "Ideology, Frame Resonance, and Participant Mobilization." *International Social Movement Research* 1:197–217.

Thomas, Jan E. 1999. "Everything About Us Is Feminist." *Gender and Society* 13:101–119.

Tripp, Aili Mari. 2000. "Rethinking Difference: Comparative Perspectives from Africa." *Signs* 25:649–675.

Van Raaphorst, Donna L. 1988. *Union Maids Not Wanted: Organizing Domestic Workers 1870–1940.* New York: Praeger.

Wail, Howard. 1993. "The Emerging Organizational Structure of Unionism in Low Wage Services." *Rutgers Law Review* 45:671.

Waldinger, Roger C., Christopher Erickson, Ruth Milkman, Daniel Mitchell, Abel Valenzuela, Kent Wong, and Maurice Zeitlin. 1997. "Justice for Janitors: Organizing in Difficult Times." *Dissent* 44:37–44.

6

Women's Organizing
in Post-Yugoslav Countries
Talking about "Donors"

Aida Bagić

This chapter stems from an attempt to interrogate my personal involvement in feminist organizing in the former Yugoslav space, and the need to understand the transformation of that activism—as social movements in the context of war and external assistance—into nongovernmental organizations (NGOs). The focus of the analysis is on the process of relationship-building between "donors" and "recipients" of aid, understood as a series of complex encounters. This chapter discusses the ways in which international assistance has influenced the development of women's movements in the post-Yugoslav region by looking at how external influence has been conceptualized by feminist activists and members of women's organizations in the region.

International assistance in various forms has had a profound impact on the organizational development, agenda, and emergence of women's organizations in the region in the last decade. This chapter utilizes an ethnographic approach, within which the primary methodological problem has not been so much one of "entering the field of inquiry" as "exiting the field" or, more precisely, of reconceptualizing the site as a field of inquiry instead of a field of action. Normally, the "field" is understood as "a place where we do our work but do not live." The field for a Western consultant or researcher may be visits to the offices of various organizations in a country that is not his or her own, while for those working in the same offices, it may be represented by rural communities they visit occasionally, Roma settlements, refugee camps where self-help groups are being held, and so on. Clearly, what is to count as the field depends on the position of the researcher, not on an objectively defined reality.

In my research I have combined several types of data collection and analysis: first, materials produced by women's organizations themselves and an analysis of their self-representation; second, interviews and personal conversations with feminist activists and members of women's organizations; and third, participant observation since 1989 of women's organizations in several post-Yugoslav countries, namely, Croatia, Serbia, Macedonia, Bosnia-Herzegovina, and Kosova.

My focus is on complex interrelationships between two sets of actors: international aid organizations as "donors," and various forms of local women's organizing as "recipients." I introduce these terms here within quotation marks because a division that seems simple at the first glance— "donors" as those offering financial or some other kind of support, and "recipients" as those that are using "donor" resources—turns out not to be so simple in reality. The donor-recipient juxtaposition appears as only one among many features displayed in the process of relationship-building. Thus, the relations between donors and recipients are framed within simultaneous encounters between the local, the regional, and the global; between the margin and the center, and at the intersections of nontranslatable and multiple languages or codes.

In their portfolios, donors emphasize a "regional" or "global" approach while at the same time claiming an impact on "local women." Myriad intermediary organizations reproduce this emphasis, and actors who are perceived as local by their own donors may, in another context, be seen as having a regional or global perspective. Though "marginal" in their own social context, encouraged and amplified by outside interveners and donors, recipients may begin to reconsider their potential to reach the mainstream. Hence, interventions from the outside reconfigure internal boundaries between the "margin" and the "center." Encounters between donors and recipients are made possible by those who are able to operate in multiple codes, who are skillful translators (not just in terms of language), and who can make incoherent life experiences appear as a coherent text, as purposeful, goal-oriented activity.

Women's Organizing in Former Yugoslavia and the Post-Yugoslav Countries

Much of women's organizing through the 1990s, and the international assistance associated with it in post-Yugoslav countries, has been affected by war and its aftermath. In all the post-Yugoslav countries, the 1990s have seen a proliferation of women's organizations, partly due to the new political environment that has encouraged the free association of citizens, and partly due to the often-observed phenomenon of women's organizing as a reaction to crisis situations. One model of the emergence and growth of women's movements suggests that there are three important conditions for social movements to emerge: group consciousness, resource availability, and sense of efficacy (Chafetz 1990: 167). Women's organizations in post-Yugoslav countries do indeed have a potential to create those conditions: by the very fact of organizing as women, they contribute to the creation of gender consciousness. The organizations themselves represent important mechanisms for mobilizing human and financial resources. Furthermore, achievements in improving the status of women under socialism permitted them to continue forging a sense of efficacy, and a potential for success in influencing and changing the broader sociopolitical context.

There is a general agreement that prewar Yugoslav society differed from that in other Eastern European countries in its openness to the free flow of ideas. This openness allowed for new social movements to emerge in the 1980s. Feminism grew independently from the official socialist women's organizations, and in opposition to it. Benderly (1997: 184) suggests three main periods of Yugoslav feminism based on specific goals and actions: (1) 1978–1985, the period of feminist discourse; (2) 1986–1991, the period of feminist activism; and (3) 1991 and onward, the period of feminist opposition to the war.

In many ways, 1978 marks the beginnings of the new feminist movement in Yugoslavia. In that year an international feminist conference Drug-ca Žena: Žensko pitanje—novi pristup (Comrade [female] Woman: The Woman Question—A New Approach) was held in the Yugoslav capital of Belgrade. It led to the formation of feminist discussion groups, most notably Žena i društvo (Woman and Society) within the Croatian Sociological Association in Zagreb, and another group with the same name within the Students' Cultural Center in Belgrade (Papić 1995; Feldman 1999; Benderly 1997). Many of the participants in the conference and in the groups inspired by it are still active in women's organizing, some as leaders and some as supporters.

In the middle to late 1980s, a new generation of women became more interested in direct social activism. The first SOS hotlines for women victims of domestic violence were opened in Zagreb, Ljubljana, and Belgrade. The Yugoslav Feminist Network was formed in 1987, in order to exchange experiences in establishing SOS hotlines and to raise public awareness about violence against women. In the same period the first lesbian groups were formed in all three cities. With the first multiparty elections in 1990, a number of feminists actively engaged in various political parties. The Yugoslav Feminist Network had its last gathering in March 1991 in Ljubljana. The outbreak of the war in 1991 was preceded by various women's peace actions. Subsequent events brought divisions, among feminists from the-states-to-be, as well as within the states. From then on, the history of feminism in Yugoslavia cannot be described without describing the particularities of the each of the new states. Still, despite the divisions, many continued to cooperate across borders, and the feminists formed the core of the antiwar initiatives in the entire region.

The feminist opposition to the war extended well beyond 1991, however. Despite attempts to maintain links across the borders, the goals and strategies of feminism in each of the observed countries became so different that each would need a periodization of its own, more congruent with the political context of the new states. In addition, as has become clear from this brief overview, Yugoslav feminism was based in three urban centers: Zagreb (Croatia), Ljubljana (Slovenia), and Belgrade (Serbia), although individual participants from Sarajevo (Bosnia-Herzegovina) and Skopje (Macedonia) and from other parts of former Yugoslavia were also active.

Preceding the new feminist initiatives that developed after the Belgrade conference in 1978, and continuing parallel to them, were various forms of official socialist women's organizations. The most notable of these was the Conference for Social Activity of Women (CSAW) that grew out of the Antifascist Women's Front (AWF). As a mass organization directly linked to the Communist Party, the CSAW functioned primarily as the mechanism of women's mobilization on the part of the communist elite. For many women, however, it did provide a space for emancipation from traditional roles. Especially in rural areas and small towns, active women's groups provided an opportunity for women to participate in local politics and in humanitarian work.

These two major lineages of women's organizing in former Yugo-slavia—through feminist initiatives and through socialist women's organi-zations—were important points of reference for the groups emerging in the 1990s. In Croatia and Serbia, or, more precisely, in Zagreb and Bel-grade, contemporary organizations refer to the feminist initiatives as their immediate "foremothers." In Macedonia, however, the most visible groups are those claiming continuity with the Conference for Social Activity of Women, though at the same time emphasizing that under the "new sys-tem" they are independent of any political party and associated ideology. In Bosnia and Herzegovina, where the war was most intense and long-last-ing, most of the currently operating organizations emerged directly as projects of international organizations. This phenomenon of international "spin-offs" is present to varying degrees in all the countries mentioned. Although in Croatia, to my knowledge, there is only one organization founded in this way, in Macedonia and Bosnia-Herzegovina there are many more. In Serbia, as yet, there are no such organizations. This is, in part, perhaps due to the relatively recent arrival there of large interna-tional NGOs.

Recounted Encounters: From Solidarity-Based "Gifts" to "Implementing Contracts"

Fund Heinrich Böll gives me solidarity aid of 100 German marks to survive through the NATO bombing
    That is how much there was in a white unsealed envelope that I received. In gratitude I recited to her a biblical sentence by Böll. . . . I didn't look into the envelope immediately. I have postponed my joy for the privacy of my own room. She didn't understand anything, she was just a treasurer of that fund and some other funds. (Markunova 2001: 19)

There are few descriptions of the aid relationship that are so telling as a piece of writing by Štefi Markunova, a poet of Croatian origin living in Belgrade. "The 100 German marks" are received from a representative of a donor whose funding portfolio comprises half "women's projects" (Rodenberg and Wichterich 1999) and which, in its earlier incarnation as FrauenAnStiftung, was one of the first agencies to support independent women's groups in post-Yugoslav countries. This hundred-mark donation epitomizes how assistance initially reached women's movement(s): small amounts of money under circumstances of extreme need, primarily as an expression of transnational women's solidarity. No service, or anything else, has been required in return. Gratitude for receipt has been met with gratitude for the ability to give, "thank you" was exchanged for "it was nothing." The simplicity of verbal interaction corresponded to its nature: money transferred from one person to another as a (small) "gift." The ensuing processes transformed the relationship between those on the giving end and those on the receiving end from a simple gift-giving relationship to a more complex contractual one.

In this section, I analyze narratives of the "aid encounter" following the major themes that have emerged in the course of interviewing nine members of women's organizations and/or participants in feminist organizing in post-Yugoslav countries. Semistructured interviews included open-ended questions covering four broadly defined topics: a general assessment of the influence of international assistance; more specific influences on the organization of the respondent (or on organizations in which the respondent has been involved with in the past); memories of women's organizing prior to encounters with international assistance; and reflections on the future sustainability of women's organizations (and movement[s]). Excerpts from the interviews have been organized under the following subthemes: (1) classifying the donors, (2) negative assessments, (3) positive assessments, (4) (reflections on) the learning process and memory, (5) strategies of influencing the donors, and (6) future sustainability. The interviewed women represent, except for two representatives of donor agencies, the post-Yugoslav "feminist elite" in that all of them play important roles in their respective communities, as well as in transnational feminist networks. All have had direct experience in negotiating with donors; some are members of the advisory boards of international donor agencies; and most have participated in feminist organizing prior to the transitional period, the dissolution of Socialist Yugoslavia, and the wars that followed.

Classifying Donors

In asking for a general assessment of the international assistance, I did not try to elicit responses about specific donor agencies or a specific donor category. Instead, I wanted to arrive at a classification that emerges out of the *perception* of those on the receiving end, one that is different from the classification that those on the giving end may have about themselves. The terms "donor," "funder," or "foundation" are often used interchangeably, covering a wide variety of organizational forms involved in transferring international assistance. From the position of women's organizations "in the field," the distinction between donors and implementing agencies seems to be irrelevant, since the major characteristic through which donors are identified as donors is simply their willingness to provide direct financial assistance. While there is awareness that technical assistance through seminars, workshops, training, or consultancy also represents a form of assistance, organizations that are primarily operating in that way are often not perceived so much as playing a donor role as just implementing their own programs.

The women I interviewed used two major criteria in their classifications of the donors: first, an assumption about a shared solidarity base (women as the primary target group versus women as an element in some larger issue), and, second, physical presence versus absence in the field. Feminist groups have most often been the first to arrive, their "gifts" being based on the idea of international women's solidarity. Those most commonly referred to during the interviews have been women's foundations whose primary target are women's groups. Their advantage, in the perception of those on the receiving end, is their "genuine interest in the cause":

> International assistance to women's organizations was more piecemeal, not really big. There are, however, different organizations involved. One should single out those really feminist organizations, those who are really doing it from their hearts. They are doing it because they really believe in it.
>
> Some feminist organizations . . . really helped us when we had the most difficult time, when we didn't expect assistance, when we were under sanctions. That means it was impossible, it was difficult even to come here, and nobody really showed interest in coming. They did come and brought some little aid, but it meant a lot to us. It may be that it meant a lot to us because they were not themselves in a very good material position, but still. . . . They really did help us, sisterly, in a feminist way. [They] really helped us from their hearts, helped us because they believed in the women's movement and because they knew that it has to spread everywhere and every place. (Respondent 3)

Presence in the field has usually been achieved through setting up so-called field offices, or through the presence of the donors' representatives without an office infrastructure, mostly through regular visits lasting from a few days to several weeks. The assessment of physical presence, which entails the potential for developing personal contact, is contradictory. On the one hand, this presence seemed to offer easier accessibility. On the other, the presence in the field and the personal contacts that it enabled often posed a challenge to the perception of objectivity in the grant-making process: "I had much better experiences with foundations that didn't have their offices [here], objectivity was greater, criteria seemed simpler to me. Sometimes they were very bureaucratic, but somehow they were much clearer in advance" (Respondent 9).

The funders appearing as "distant bureaucratic structures" may seem "thrifty," since they do not need to fund offices in the country, and are therefore less subject to criticism by those on the receiving end. On the other hand, all the expenses associated with long-distance operations, although they may be higher than those with field offices or representatives, remain hidden from the recipients.

When staffed by local women, field offices may cease to seem *foreign*, especially if the representatives are perceived as personally committed to the same cause as the recipients:

> You know why I treat it as local? Our women are in it. That's the reason I really consider [a particular foundation] as a local one. Now, if the situation with personnel would change, most likely everything would be different. For now, it is as it is. We received great help from [them] for women's projects, for things that have been important to us—that is, for small, newly founded, powerless women's groups that need to move on and get strengthened. (Respondent 3)

Negative Assessments

Solidarity-based donors initially offered money without a lot of bureaucratic requirements concerning project proposal writing and reporting. On the other hand, such funders demanded a different kind of additional energy in the form of time-consuming meetings, emotional investment in developing friendships, and occasionally even love relationships. There is no reason to doubt the sincerity of feelings; there is, however, reason to doubt whether this mixture of personal friendships and emotional attachments, coupled with an imbalance in financial power, always led to the most beneficial use of resources. The initial enthusiasm over shared beliefs and vision often faded under the pressures of limited resources, no matter what size, and the external bureaucratic requirements for financial transfers:

> We were not aware that they were part of some strange political game which they could not influence, so I do not see a conflict of interests as the major problem but rather, the conflict between two concepts of power. They came to us as persons who would prefer cooperation based on horizontal power, but they themselves were part of a hierarchical, I would call it trans-state, or maybe state, power structure, and that is where the major conflict emerges. We didn't get it at the beginning. I remember exactly when one of them came to us and said they got the money and that we will be able to change all of what has been written according to our needs. Then it became clear that we won't have a chance to change anything, that at least one-third of that money will go back to some American funds. (Respondent 9)

The memories about the first encounters are impregnated with feelings of not being listened to and not being understood:

> I always had the impression that this was similar to some, let's say, English charity mission coming to India, you know . . . and then there are some natives there who arouse amazement by being able to speak Latin, that is English. . . . So they come and they don't listen to you at all. You can talk, endlessly. . . . They have a system, they send very young women and men who went to schools which are probably good schools, but they do not have any idea about where they are coming . . . about what it is like here. . . . Then they tell you stories about the Iron Curtain, the Eastern Bloc, some nonsense . . . you know. We lived here under circumstances that were different from what they saw in movies, in their own American movies about Russia. They come with James Bond stories. So it takes time before you can explain it to them. . . . You can explain yourself to death. They can't really get it. The best is if you don't explain anything. You let them to tell their story and you see what they want. If we can find some common point that suits us and suits them, fine. If not, then ciao. We say bye to one another, exchange our business cards, and that's it. (Respondent 3)

> [International organizations] didn't have any knowledge or sense about the perception of money under socialism—what did money mean for women, for women's organizations, for civil initiatives which did exist under social-

ism. It is not accurate to say that there was nothing. [The donors] just threw that money on our heads and we had to find the ways to come to terms with it. (Respondent 9)

These are descriptions of personal contacts in which "the foreigner" and "the native" mutually produce each other as "foreign" and "native." While the native perceives the foreigner's understanding as mediated (and therefore biased) through cultural production (James Bond movies), her lived experience appears to her as nonmediated. The idea that someone distant may know more about us than we know about ourselves, at least in terms of the ability to articulate that knowledge, seems to be frightening and to cause resentment. Therefore, an attempt is made to dismiss the knowledge (good schools) on the grounds of immediate experience.

Members of local women's movements lodge the ubiquitous accusation against external actors of their inability to differentiate the post-Yugoslav context from the rest of Eastern Europe. This impression, which relies on the popular self-image of "Yugoslavs" as being different from the rest of the socialist world, is counterbalanced with an awareness (achieved in hindsight) about their own isolation from the experiences of women exposed to international assistance in other regions:

What I can see now is that we lived in complete isolation, not just from foundations. I think that in '91 and '92 we would have benefited tremendously from the experiences of women from the Third World, and yet we had absolutely no contact with them. We didn't know what had been happening to them, and all of those stories that already happened ten, fifteen, or twenty years earlier, like the story of microcredit and about cows and milk in Asia. All of that was well known, and there was an attempt to transfer all of those things mechanically, especially to Bosnia. I read all of that later, and I think that type of experiential knowledge would really have helped us at the time.

We didn't know how to negotiate at the time, we didn't have negotiation skills, and we actually didn't know whether we were allowed to negotiate. We didn't know whether the funders were our partners, our collaborators, or our superiors; none of these things have ever been clear. I think that it came to the collision of different images and different expectations and different perceptions, and that we didn't have the knowledge that could have helped us at the time, especially regarding negotiations. (Respondent 9)

Exchanging experiences with other parts of the world that were exposed to international assistance could have enhanced the learning process. This "experiential knowledge" should not be confused with using examples from development manuals designed for the less developed countries. Rather, it refers to power relationships: the question that could have been discussed at such an encounter would be not How did you organize work with women war victims? but How did you negotiate the roles between your organization and the donors? or How did you influence their agenda, if at all?

The presence of the local (as opposed to the foreign), as well as the implied women's solidarity, is not necessarily assessed positively:

> It is good to have local staff, but not local staff that is at the same time financing themselves. In my opinion, that is completely inadmissible, both legally and morally. You cannot apply for funding for your own projects and for the projects of your own company. It should also be required that the applicant isn't an NGO where some of your relatives are working, or your former group, or whatever. (Respondent 1)

The reasons for the absence of field offices or donors' representatives differed from one country to the other. Absence did not prevent them or the potential recipients from establishing personal contacts that, combined with both an unsafe and a financially restrictive environment, often created grounds for mutual suspicion and the perception of bias:

> The money couldn't simply have been transferred to the bank account, so it was given in cash. So, did the woman to whom the money was given—and she brought it in her pocket (or, as we used to say, in her "left sock")—give all of it to her group? We don't know that. There were often suspicions about whether somebody put some money "to the side," whether somebody used the money for this or that. The groups where women spoke English, had computer skills, and e-mail communication, usually did the best. (Respondent 1)

> What I never liked (when I happened to be on that side) was when somebody in some other country, on some other continent, imagined what we would need to do in [our country], and then they send us their guidelines and that's it: we finance this and this and this. So we start to adjust. In order to get the money, groups often did what they would have never been doing,

simply because the funders would provide financing. Instead of the other way around, that the group does something because there is a genuine need for it, and because they know that they have the human resources, and the experience. . . .

Very often there was jumping from one theme to another. That means that now for three months we will do a project, let's say, on conflict resolution, and after that we'll work on, I don't know what, combating violence against women, then afterward we'll do some publishing . . . something like that. . . . So, now all of us know everything, and in fact nobody knows anything. And so we remain amateurs in everything. (Respondent 1)

Women's foundations that have been coming here very often felt that they have to invent something new, so they did try to create something new. Very often they didn't have an interest in the motivations of those women or in whether these new organizations made any sense; their mission has often been to create something new, something that would give them some kind of legitimacy. So very often they didn't have sympathy for existing organizations. They didn't want to listen to their needs, they didn't want to finance something that was grounded, that was genuine, that made sense within a certain context. (Respondent 9)

The criticism of donors based on the role of personal relationships as a key factor in obtaining grants, on the lack of transparency, and on unclear roles and the lack of accountability to the communities they are working in mirrors, to a large extent, the negative features of women's organizations themselves. Personal relationships, friendship as the basis of establishing the group and/or organization, is still the dominant way that groups operate; the recruitment of new women is still predominantly through personal initiation, and examples of employing women through open competition are rare.

Positive Assessments

The overall assessment of international assistance is by no means a negative one. There is an acknowledgment that the needs that existed in times of humanitarian crisis were partially alleviated by international assistance. Assistance encouraged women's initiatives, and many of the ideas that have been floating around since the beginnings of (neo)feminism in this region were given a chance to develop into specific projects, programs, and, in many instances, new organizations:

> International foundations had a positive role in the sense that they brought in humanitarian aid under war circumstances (it is a different question how and where they brought in humanitarian aid). Second, they encouraged some women, that is, some women's groups, by supporting some of their initiatives, some of their beginnings. (Respondent 9)

> Although the money came in rather bad, irregular ways, it was still the money that stimulated many movements, many moves within the women's movement. Many projects have started, many groups have started, and that was good. (Respondent 1)

There have been positive outcomes on the personal level in terms of increased knowledge and skills that are transferable to other sectors (including specific managerial skills, such as conflict resolution, strategic planning, and evaluation skills, and more broadly applicable interpersonal skills). While this kind of personal (and personnel) development can be regarded as an indicator of the capacity of women's organizations to contribute to the wider society, its downside manifests itself in the trend of women leaving their organizations for better-paid or more prestigious jobs in governmental structures or international organizations. The nongovernmental sector also seems to entail a potential for the development of more inclusive structures and nondiscriminatory organizational cultures that are, in part, reflected in the use of gender-sensitive language:

> A large number of people got trained in various things. We went through an incredibly large range of education and training. I wouldn't be able to count them all, but it seems to me that for a certain period of time, let's say in '92, '93, '94, we sat in classrooms and learned something. When I compare ourselves with people working in various ministries, we are much ahead of them. . . . Another thing, people in the NGO sector are much more politically correct, they are much more gender sensitive, in using language, for instance. Also, a nationalist, racist way of behaving is avoided. The moment you get out of that circle of nongovernmental organizations, it hits you in the face.
> Then, we acquired a whole range of technical skills. Some learned to make photocopies, to send a fax, to drive, to use various computer pro-

grams. Some learned a variety of interpersonal skills. Many people learned how to run a meeting, how to talk in public, how to conduct an evaluation, how to do a needs assessment, how to do many things that are needed in this country. So it is no wonder that some people from the nongovernmental sector entered into governmental bodies—not yet enough, since the salaries are still not attractive; more people are going into international organizations, for as long as they last. (Respondent 1)

The transparency of the transfer mechanisms is crucial in attributing positive, as well as negative, outcomes to external assistance. Public announcements and clear conditions are singled out as preferred modes of identifying grantees. Securing wide participation has been achieved by relying on local women as advisers, or by using local and regional advisory boards that meet regularly or communicate with each other from a distance:

As a symbol of fair play I could single out [an international NGO]. They made a public call, specifying conditions very clearly. They were clear about the amount they have at their disposal, the time period in which the activities need to take place, what the documentation should look like: project proposal, interim report, final report. That was the kind of transparency I liked very much. I think other organizations should use it. Not that I should know the boss of the organization so and so, so that I can somehow make her give money to my group, but that the organization should make a public call once a year, or for any other time period, and clearly give conditions for grants. Afterward it should publish a list of those who got the grants, so everybody can see who got what, for what kind of activities. So that there are no ideas about hidden intentions. In that case, no criteria are difficult. (Respondent 1)

When I look at [a U.S.-based women's foundation] over the last few years, I think that the way they are functioning is quite transparent. I consider them to be one of the most interesting women's foundations . . . because they don't give a lot of money, because they rely on a large women's network worldwide, and they have a large number of advisers who are doing it voluntarily. That means they want to hear many diverse opinions before making a decision on whom to finance. They don't run around the world; they want to hear opinions of women who live in that part of the world. (Respondent 9)

Sincerity of interest and even love are often invoked as elements that make a difference between the donors that are making a real contribution and those that are "just pursuing their own interests." What is especially appreciated is the possibility of engaging in direct dialogue, of having a space for negotiation and influence, along with flexible requirements and permission to change and learn from mistakes:

> I have a positive example. They didn't just ask us to set up priorities, but within the project framework they gave us absolute flexibility to change things. You plan something, you put it on paper, then you start working and you see that you got it wrong. So we changed; they gave us absolute freedom. It really turned out to be a beautiful project. At the final evaluation of all the projects in Washington, D.C., we were given an opportunity to say what was good and what wasn't, everything was fantastic. Unfortunately, they don't come to this region anymore. (Respondent 5)

The Learning Process and Memory

Encounters within the aid relationship have definitely provoked a learning process, both among the recipients and among donors:

> The situation is completely different depending on whether it is the first foundation that appeared or whether it is the tenth. If it is the first one, then it has great expectations of the recipients, and the recipients have great expectations of the foundation. I would say there is some kind of idealistic confusion on both sides, and since the expectations are great, the frustrations are great as well. . . . I think disappointments decrease along with the expectations and that roles are becoming more transparent. (Respondent 9)

At the same time, the learning process has been hindered and enhanced by the memories of the participants involved in relationship-building. In the course of the last decade, through each of the encounters, memories of the women on the recipient side collided with the memories of those on donor side. While there is a widespread conception among international researchers that the socialist system primarily used civic associations, if it did allow them at all, as a means of social control instead of individual empowerment, the testimonies from feminist activists under socialism demonstrate that there was a space for debating and challenging socialist solutions to the "woman question." Although the first feminist voices were publicly accused of introducing bourgeois ideology, most of their activities were financed by the state, either directly (meeting space) or indirectly (the system of social security provided the first activists with enough free time for their volunteer activities):

> The system completely softened sometime in the 1980s. We had some discussions on TV with those women . . . the socialist conference of women. We went on TV, they were telling their ideological story, we were telling our story. And that was OK. (Respondent 3)

> Something that was perceived as socially valuable could receive [state] funding. It was not a problem to find free space; if you had an idea you could do something. . . . The whole story revolved around some of our ideas, fantasies, and a desire to change something, to have an influence. I think it was partly connected with the self-management story. In some strange way self-management opened up space—not so much for activities, but for the feeling that you can influence something. You could discuss endlessly; everybody had a right to their opinion, and the only question was whether you wanted to channel it somehow, whether you had an interest. In general, I don't think one could have done it within the structures of work or the structures of authority; the rules were very clear there. But the fact or illusion that you can do something, that you can have your own opinion and that that is all right, did influence some of the possible organizing at the very beginning. At that time we financed ourselves in various ways: we invented for ourselves our own membership fees. I remember that in the section Woman and Society we had been paying membership fees regularly, from some kind of pocket money. Even women who had not been working were able to contribute, and that was considered completely normal because what we were doing was extremely important. (Respondent 9)

Respondents' reflections on the learning process and their memories of the time "before the internationals arrived" point the way toward more beneficial ways of developing relationships. These learning processes are also closely interlinked with strategies for influencing donors.

Strategies of Influence

Participants in feminist movements and members of women's organizations in the post-Yugoslav countries often see themselves as objects of donor agendas, caught in a power relation where the only leverage on their part is an awareness that the "other side" needs them as much as, and sometimes even more than, they need the donors. Activists did, however, adopt various strategies to influence the donors, sometimes on their own initiative, sometimes due to the readiness of the donors to create a space for such an influence.

The most successful strategic tools appear to be clarity of goals and sufficient confidence in one's own capacity, accompanied with the ability to take on the donors' perspective:

> First of all, you have to know exactly what you want. Second, you have to be strong enough to position yourself as a political subject. In that case you have the right, if they need you, if they think you are going in a direction that is interesting to them, then you have all the creative capacity, you can do everything as you want to do it. But first you have to decide for yourself, who you are, what you are, what you want. . . . Then you can negotiate with the donor. You can move a little bit here and there, but you have to keep your line. (Respondent 2)

> My project proposals usually got accepted because I wrote them in a studious way. . . . I also tried to imagine, at the time I worked in the women's movement, that if I would have been the donor, what things would I have liked to hear, what would have interested me about a project. So I wrote it, even though nobody asked me to. I guess that made a good impact on the donors, and I was successful. (Respondent 1)

Clarity of goals allows for a move away from the opportunistic approach, even if the choice is simply refusal:

> You can refuse. I remember that the representatives [of a particular foundation] fell down when I said no. Although we knew there was big money in it, we had our agenda that we dealt with and we didn't want to give up. We would rather not exist in that case, we would prefer to put much more effort into dealing with a funder who is interested in giving us the money. You cannot always run after good opportunities; there is enough of that. (Respondent 5)

Direct involvement in creating a donor agenda is a rare and appreciated opportunity:

Up to now we have very good experiences with [a particular foundation], they listen and they are willing to talk. Recently I spent seven days with them, they were doing their strategic planning for the next two years, and they invited us, a few women whom they thought are working well, from good organizations, and they let us set priorities ourselves, so they might look for projects that fit those priorities. So there are those, a few of them, who are open to dialogue and conversation and will ask you for an opinion. (Respondent 5)

The initiative seems to remain with the donor agency ("they invited us, they gave us the absolute freedom, they invited those of us they think are working well"), although there is definitely an emerging awareness that women's organizations themselves can take a more active approach. As noted by Respondent 5, "It would be good if all of us could sit together, make an arrangement and initiate contact with funders instead of waiting all the time for the funders to come to us."

Future Sustainability

Future sustainability is a question that usually comes at the end of the grant proposal guidelines. The potential recipients are asked to offer insight into their own future. Predictions by the women I interviewed follow two main directions. First, they expect a loss of outside financial sources due to the reallocation of international funding toward the state (with a concomitant loss of human resources, as women seek employment in the state sector or in international organizations). This trend could lead to the disappearance of these organizations: As Repondent 5 described it, "The funders are withdrawing, and since these states are impoverished, I think the organizations will disappear unless they find some new ways to finance themselves and find some income of their own" Genuineness of interest, although seen as a positive trait when assessing the donors, does not seem to be perceived as a guarantee of organizational survival:

I think that the best groups, the strongest ones in the sense of being professional, will survive. There is no strength in an ideological sense—some of "the most fabulous feminists" will survive, some not . . . that is not one of the criteria. Criteria include professionalism, respectability/reputation, quality of work . . . the groups with the highest profiles will survive, those who are clearly recognized for their work on certain things. . . .

Second, the sources of financing will change. Instead of charities, those providing humanitarian aid, there will be other agencies, e.g., the European Union. What I want to say is that this will never stop. I can see that non-governmental organizations in the U.S. and Western Europe also need to compete for funding. Any decent state will want to finance civil society. (Respondent 1)

Second, a change in the purpose of aid, from emergency to development work, may lead to the need for more professional organizations (and subsequently to NGOization), along with an increased reliance on state funding. Skills and knowledge obtained within nongovernmental women's organizations can potentially be transferred into other areas:

I also think that the financial support that is coming for various educational and research projects, including some other activities, will get reallocated from the nongovernmental sector to the state sector. In the future, people who have numerous and rich experiences gained in the nongovernmental sector, who have a decade of experience, will enter some ministries, or state offices. We may think at the moment that we don't want to belong to state institutions, but in the future that may be the best way to apply our knowledge and to continue to receive international funding. (Respondent 1)

There is also awareness about the role of the international feminist movement in pressuring individual governments and intergovernmental organizations to demonstrate gender sensitivity in resource allocation. Respondent 3 explained, "I believe that all that money that goes for women's projects is made available due to the pressure of women's movements and associations on the global level. So, if that's some kind of good image, the ruling establishment will follow it, if not, they won't." There are also those who think about sustainability, beyond financial and organizational imperatives, in terms of raising gender consciousness in order to guarantee women's involvement in the future, regardless of the financing of particular organizations or the generally difficult economic situation:

That network is most important to us, since it is the basis of the movement . . . When soon there will be no money, and there won't be, when poverty increases generally, as it seems it will, these women will already have some kind of consciousness, and they will know what we want. They won't get depressed and go back home; they will continue doing something. (Respondent 3)

Encounters as Analyzed: NGOization and Policy Shifts

The process of establishing a donor-recipient relationship in the post-Yugoslav context resembles Wedel's depiction of Western assistance to Eastern Europe as divided into phases of triumphalism, disillusionment, and adjustment (Wedel 2001). It is difficult to ascribe any feeling of triumph to the time of war and large-scale humanitarian crisis. Hence, a more appropriate name for the first phase in this context, the period when most of the donors approached women and women's organizations in the post-Yugoslav countries, would be "great expectations." The first phase was marked by high and, more often than not, unspoken expectations among all actors involved.

The phase of disillusionment brings the first frustrations and resentments, when expectations are not fulfilled so easily. In the process of getting to know each other, recipients sometimes realize that the rationale for giving is not purely altruistic, while donors have to face the fact that the needs expressed by recipients are often merely desires, programs, and projects drafted in haste, with no capacity for implementation. During the adjustment phase, an awareness of the contractual nature of the relationship becomes predominant, opening up the possibility for partnership instead of dependency.

If we conceive of "local" and "international" as separate spheres that do not necessarily interact with one another, as an "outside" and an "inside," we may identify three main points of entrance for an outside intervention in the form of assistance: (1) supporting existing structures, such as organizations, groups, and sometimes individuals, without intending to change them (in this case, there is trust in the capacity of the structure to influence change in its broader environment); (2) supporting existing structures in order to change them (this is the case when assistance is dependent on the modification of the existing structure, since there is no trust in its current capacity to influence change in the broader environment); (3) initiating a completely new structure (this mode of intervention may include looking for "novelty" projects within existing organizations, or setting up completely new organizations).

Currently, there are several hundred women's organizations in the post-Yugoslav region. Whether they would have emerged, and how many of them would now exist, without international assistance is a complex question. According to feminist respondents, perhaps up to 80 to 90 percent of them would have never appeared without foreign financial support, or if they had appeared, their subsequent development would have been very different.

The general trend toward the NGOization of the women's movement has been observed in various parts of the world. The term "NGOization" can imply two different things. The first refers to the increasing tendency of the state to contract nongovernmental organizations to work on social problems that the state feels unable or is unwilling to address. The other meaning refers to the process of transformation of social movements into professionalized organizations. The two processes are of course interconnected. In Western Europe, the phenomenon of NGOization has been described by Sabine Lang (1997) for Germany. Sonia E. Alvarez (1999) explores "the NGO boom" in the Latin American context, which seems strikingly similar to the processes in all of the post-Yugoslav countries. The main similarity can be seen in the fact that, unlike Germany (and other Western countries), where the state appears as the major donor, in Latin America and the post-Yugoslav countries, international organizations are the most important instigators of NGOization.

In terms of strategies and programs, NGOization leads to issue-specific interventions and pragmatic strategies with a strong employment focus, rather than the establishment of a new democratic counterculture. In terms of ideology, the "traditionally" complex feminist agenda of emancipation and equality gets translated into specific, single issues with a state-oriented focus (the recent trend in post-Yugoslav countries is an increased pressure on the third sector to cooperate with government). In terms of structure, professionalized (and decentralized) small-scale organizations, with more hierarchical structures, become dominant, replacing overarching movements focused on the politicization and mobilization of feminist publics. By the same token, feminist organization-building and institutionalization replace movement activism (Lang 1997: 102–103).

The process of NGOization has been fostered through various practices. Along with a variety of measures designed to increase "organizational capacity-building," the most prominent and explicit mechanism is the transfer of NGO management skills. The concept of "capacity-building" often resembles "compliance-building" in the sense that knowledge and skills gained through training aim primarily at increasing the capacity of participants to comply with the requests of others. While training is provided under the assumption that strengthening NGOs will contribute toward strengthening civil society, the downside of this is that participants often see a well-run NGO as the equivalent of activism for social change. The idea of "a small group of citizens that can change the world" very often gets lost in the process of "strengthening organizational capacity." In addition, the concepts of "civil society," "NGO," and "women's or feminist movement" undergo transformations according to specific local contexts that are not taken into account by those who intervene from the outside.

Pressure from donors has changed the working style of many organizations. For instance, many organizations did not have hierarchical structures prior to the receipt of a significant grant. Grant application forms, however, often require a role such as president or vice president, and even if a group has decided to delegate that role to one of its members for that particular occasion, if the grant is awarded, the "hierarchy-for-the occasion" may become the real structure, creating new, not necessarily harmonious, relationships within the group.

A common development within social movements that attempt to raise public awareness about deficiencies perceived by movement initiators is transformation of parts of the movement into organizations. Outside interventions in the context of post-Yugoslav countries seem to have worked from the other end: organizations are being supported (sometimes even created) with the idea that they will incite and sustain the movement. Foreign donors should consider whether the concentration on women's NGOs should be the primary vehicle for achieving gender equality. The effects are ambiguous. The support offered is too short for the organizations to reach full sustainability, and therefore the constant pressure to keep the organizations running decreases the capacity of the organization (and the women involved) to mobilize broader public support for a feminist agenda of social change. Whether the movements can indeed be strengthened, even created, through strengthening of organizational development skills remains to be seen.

International funding policies regarding gender issues in general, and women's organizations in particular, are more appropriately conceived from a notion of policy as "authorized choice," as distinct from a conception of policy as "structured interaction" (Colebatch 1998: 102). Policy as authorized choice assumes a simple definition of policy as "governments making decisions," following a linear process defining the problem that needs to be solved, identifying possible options, and establishing rational criteria for making a choice. In contrast, policy as structured interaction makes no assumption about a single decision maker or the clarity of a policy problem. It allows for the emerging pattern of activity not to be seen as collective effort to achieve known and shared goals. There is no single decision maker in the field of international assistance, regardless of the level on which we focus our attention. There is a range of "players" having diverse understandings of the situation and the problem.

There is no united set of donors' agendas, and no united set of agendas on behalf of women's organizations. To say this does not imply that there should have been such a set. In the period of emerging movements, in time of war and humanitarian crises, the immensity of the problem may function as the unifying factor. As soon as tensions calm, or as soon as the choice becomes more complicated than that of satisfying immediate needs, agendas also become more diverse.

All actors involved in the process of relationship building between donors and recipients are simultaneously players in policymaking processes influenced by many other factors in their environment, most notably by the sociopolitical context in which the relationships are being built. What kind of guidelines can be given for policymaking processes aimed at achieving gender equality through women's empowerment?

All the issues supported are valuable causes: eliminating violence against women, economic empowerment, political participation, and so on. They are usually interlinked in the sense that one heading can easily subsume others. The simple question, What is the most important issue for women in country X today?—whatever the answer may be—cannot provide guidelines on *how* the most important issue should be dealt with. If the answer is "violence against women," this does not imply whether it is necessary to provide shelters (how many, who should run them, what kind of support should be available in the shelter, how the quality of support will be assessed); to run public campaigns' or to educate policemen, social workers, and health care providers on dealing with victims of violence. In the search for "best practices" and "innovations," actors engaged in social change for gender equality often neglect local memories that play a crucial role in the implementation of models based on success in another location.

In order not to foster "practice without language" (Husanović, 2001), it is necessary to allow sufficient time for needs to be articulated, for an "incubation period" during which actors have an opportunity to develop their ideas and adjust their perceptions without immediate pressure to produce results. On a practical level, this implies direct financial support for activities such as needs assessment, planning, and developing cooperation. In addition, it means giving more attention to the question of how— that is, to the mechanisms for transferring financial and technical assistance. Through this chapter, I have tried to show how an ethnographic analysis of donor-recipient encounters can provide a fuller basis for understanding how this how can be imagined.

Note

My presentation at the Ninth Interdisciplinary Congress on Women was based on a research project on international assistance to women's organizing conducted during an Open Society Institute International Policy Fellowship in 2001 and 2002. More information on the OSI IPF program is available at http:// www.osi.hu/ipf. This article has been published in Jeremy Gould and Henrik Secher Marcussen, eds., *Ethnographies of Aid,* Occasional Paper Series no. 24, International Development Studies, Roskilde University, 2004.

Bibliography

Alvarez, Sonia E. 1999. "Advocating Feminism: The Latin American Feminist NGO 'Boom.'" *International Feminist Journal of Politics* 1:181–209.

Benderly, Jill. 1997. "Feminist Movements in Yugoslavia, 1978–1992." In Melissa K. Bokovoy, Jill A. Irvine, and Carol S. Lilly, eds., *State-Society Relations in Yugoslavia 1945–1992,* 183–209. London: Macmillan.

Chafetz, Janet Saltzman. 1990. *Gender Equity: An Integrated Theory of Stability and Change.* London: Sage.

Colebatch, Hal K. 1998. *Policy.* Minneapolis: University of Minnesota Press.

Feldman, Andrea. 1999. "Uz dvadeset godina neofeminizma u Hrvatskoj." /Twenty Years of Neo-feminism in Croatia / Kruh i ruže 10. Zagreb: Ženska infoteka, 3–8. Available at www.zinfo.hr/hrvatski/stranice/izdavastvo/kruhiruze/kir10/ 10neofeminizam.htm.

Husanović, Jasmina. 2001. "Practice with No Language." *International Feminist Journal of Politics* 3:124–130.

Lang, Sabine. 1997. "The NGOization of Feminism." In C. Kaplan, W. Keates, and J. W. Wallach, eds., *Transitions, Environments, Translations: Feminisms in International Politics,* 101–120. London: Routledge.

Markunova, Štefi. 2001. "Fund Heinrich Böll Gives Me Solidarity Aid of 100 German Marks to Survive through the NATO Bombing . . ." *Labris,* special issue no. 12, 19–21.

Papić, Žarana. 1995. "Women's Movement in Former Yugoslavia: 1970s and 1980s." In *What Can We Do for Ourselves?* 19–22. East European Feminist Conference, Belgrade, June 1994. Beograd: Centre for Women's Studies, Research and Communication.

Rodenberg, Birte, and Christa Wichterich. 1999. *Empowerment: A Study of the Women's Projects Abroad.* Hamburg: Heinrich Böll Foundation.

Wedel, Janine R. 2001. *Collision and Collusion: The Strange Case of Western Aid to Eastern Europe.* New York: Palgrave.

7

Women as Agents for Development
Learning from the Experiences of Women in Finland?

Hilkka Pietilä

This chapter presents the road the Finnish women's movement took toward achieving feminist goals. Today, Finland—together with the other Nordic countries, Denmark, Iceland, Norway, and Sweden—appears as one of the most advanced countries vis-à-vis gender equality and the status of women. Not so long ago, however, it was an agricultural and "underdeveloped" country, and Finnish women faced the same subordination that many women around the globe know. Although Finland is not perfect, it has come a great distance in a short time, and thus offers some possibly useful models and considerations for development struggles elsewhere.

Early Finnish feminists interpreted late nineteenth-century national interests and goals as adaptable to their purposes. Therefore, they joined in campaigning for national independence and a new constitution. This strategy brought Finnish women full political rights in 1906, as the first country in the world to do so. A similar strategy also worked later in the twentieth century as the state was building the welfare society in Nordic fashion.

In fact, over these past hundred years the Finnish women's movement has more or less consciously pursued a dual strategy. The women's movement has, on one hand, consciously worked for feminist aims and, on the other hand, treated women as a constituency to mobilize actively to support political, economic, and social progress in the country. By empowering women around the country as national political actors, the women's movement made a remarkable contribution to eradicating poverty in Finland.

The question is whether this kind of a dual strategy would be more widely useful today. In many countries of the global South, women are struggling for both feminist aims and the general socioeconomic development of their countries. Can the methods that the Finnish "Marthas" used for eradicating poverty not so long ago provide models for women's emancipatory struggles today?

The literature on development shows that the advancement of women and the progress of the country go hand in hand. This is not surprising. On the one hand, the status of women cannot be significantly improved without comprehensive political, social, and economic development in the country as a whole. On the other hand, making general progress in any country requires all possible contributions of women, too, and thus the empowerment of women benefits the whole nation.

Considering Finland as a fairly recently developed country provides a different angle of vision on such transnational organizations like the United Nations and the European Union. Usually the development role of the multinational institutions is studied only from the point of view of the South—as if development in the northern countries did not have to proceed further. From the point of view of women, how have such organizations helped or hindered the gendered process of development as it has taken place in Finland?

In my view the United Nations (UN) and the European Union (EU) are two very different—even contradictory—realizations of transnationalism. The UN conventions and programs for women have lent impetus to Finnish women's efforts against discrimination and toward further advancement. However, in the past decade, the effects of membership in the European Union have brought the situation to a standstill or even to a backlash. Neoliberal pressures from economic globalization as codified in the EU have put at risk the well-developed welfare society that is the foundation both of the good standard of living and of gender equality in Finland and the other Nordic countries.

The UN is a global institution for increasing the cooperation of states toward achieving justice and decreasing disparity between countries and peoples. It is a forum for sovereign states to cooperate and negotiate to bring about peace and a more equitable world. It did not aim to become a world government. The EU is a regional union of states for making rich Europe even richer and stronger in economic competition with other economic blocs around the United States and Japan. This kind of economic "warfare" only increases disparity, injustice, and the exploitation of people and natural resources. Politically the EU is on its way toward becoming a federation, a United States of Europe, much bigger than the United States of America.

From the transnational feminist point of view, the distinction between transnationalism as cooperation and as competition is crucial, making it easy to take a stand on which model is to be preferred. There is a great need for cooperation. The status of women differs greatly in various countries of the EU today, and so do the member states' policies for advancing equality. The differences are accentuated by the accession of ten new member states from Eastern and Central Europe in spring 2004.

In this context, it is easy to foresee what women in Finland, Sweden, and Denmark can expect from a union of twenty-two countries, less advanced than their own in gender equality politics. As someone who has lived through many of the transformations that Finnish women have undergone in the past hundred years, I hope that displaying the processes and strategies of Finnish women in their advancement in this one fairly newly developed country may find resonance among women in other countries in assessing and promoting their own progress.

Two Finnish Pathbreakers

The beginning of the women's movement in Finland occurred in the late nineteenth century, as nationalism was emerging in Europe, the Russian Revolution was approaching, and the labor movement and modern political parties were becoming institutionalized. At that time Finland was an autonomous grand duchy under the Russian czar, after having been a province of Sweden for centuries. Finland became autonomous in 1809 and an independent state in 1917.

The most important women's organizations in the last decade of the nineteenth century were the feminist Unioni Women's Movement (Unioni Naisasialiitto) and the Martha organization (Martta-liitto), both of which are still doing well today. Both were established by well-educated, young women activists, drawn mainly from the Swedish speaking intellectual families.

The Feminist Union was established in 1892 by a group of intellectual women, formalizing what had been for some time their informal discussion club. Here they developed their critical thinking and shared impressions and inspirations from other countries. Many of these women had traveled abroad, met activist women, and obtained feminist books.

A good example was Elise von Alftan, an active member of the club, who called for free discussion about sexuality in general. She wanted to eliminate the teaching of Christianity from the schools and substitute comparative studies on religions, history of cultures, and ethics. She also found it degrading for women to use the husband's surname and titles after getting married. The issue of condemning the man who bought sexual services rather than woman who sold sex was already being discussed. As early as 1895 the Union made proposals to the Senate about social and political reforms.

The two issues that drove political discussion all over Finland at that time were (1) resistance against curtailment of autonomy and suppression of citizen's rights by the Russian authorities and (2) a campaign for constitutional reform that would provide universal political rights for all, including women. Across all political and class distinctions, women, as well as men, campaigned for these aims.

As the oppressive measures of the Russian regime accelerated and tensions in the political climate increased, a second major women's organization was initiated, with the aim of working with women throughout the country. The first name this group proposed for itself was "Civilization into the Homes." When this was rejected by the authorities as too subversive, a new name was picked directly from the Bible, the "Marthas." This name dispelled the fears of the authorities, and the bylaws of the organization were approved in 1900.

The initiator of both these organizations was Lucina Hagman, rector of the first Finnish-language coeducational secondary school and later a professor and a member of parliament. Her idealism and enthusiasm are evident in her description of the purpose of these organizations: "The treasures of knowledge and skills should be carried directly to the Finnish homes, to the actual one who cares for and tends to the family, the Finnish woman, to bring her forward to become a strong protector of Finnish culture and a conscious defender of the rights of her country" (Haltia, 1949: 10). The strategy of the Marthas was very practical and simple, taking particular account of the situations of the women they wanted to address. The plan was to send educated women—often teachers and home economists—as "missionaries" to travel around the country, visit homes and women, organize meetings, seminars, and courses with them, and teach and train them. The aim was twofold, first to train women in practical household skills to raise the quality of life of their families and, second, to mobilize women against oppression and to use their forthcoming political rights. In the beginning the "missionaries" were volunteers, who used their vacations and whatever time they could find for performing this work.

This "Martha method" was effective in reaching women around the countryside and in improving the health and well-being of people through their households. It did not require big public investments in a poor country, but it required much commitment, solidarity, and hard work from the women. Along with the increasing skills and knowledge, rural women gained status in their families and communities, and their self-confidence and respect increased. It also helped them to acquire personal earnings, to which they often had had very little access at that time. Very similar situations and experiences have been faced in recent years in the Southern countries (Pietilä, 2001).

At that time of rising national consciousness and dawning political independence, a particular aim of the Marthas as well as of the Feminist Union was to prepare women for political participation. These women's organizations brought up the particular importance of political rights to women. In spite of the times of oppression, in 1906 the new constitution was adopted in Finland, granting general and equal franchise to all.

Because Finland gave women both the right to vote (1906) and the right to run for political office at the same time (1907), it was the first country in the world to give women full citizen rights. When the first modern parliamentary elections took place, the advance training given to women by Marthas and the Feminist Union meant that nineteen women were elected into the parliament of two hundred members in 1907, making women's share almost 10 percent. Seven of these women were founders and activists in the Marthas and the Feminist Union. It is also noteworthy that these women parliamentarians were dispersed throughout all parties represented in the legislature (Haltia, 1949; Koskelainen, 1999).

In the past century, the Marthas have had ups and downs in membership, ranging from one hundred thousand in the 1960s to about fifty thousand today, but their organizational network has covered the whole country. The Marthas' ideal was from the beginning to build bridges across class and political lines. In the early years they especially worked to raise the quality of life in the poorest and most remote parts of the country, and so to decrease inequalities among counties and families.

The Marthas played a pioneering role in eradicating poverty in Finland, and they were the initiators of building a welfare society thirty to forty years before the state systematically took on the responsibility (Pietilä, 2001). Since poverty and social welfare are still the biggest problems at the global level, a sense of sisterhood and solidarity has led the Marthas to share their experiences and methods of eliminating poverty with women in developing countries such as Kenya, Zambia, Zimbabwe, and Burkina Faso.

The Feminist Union had a somewhat more elite membership and remained a small organization, having today only about 1,300 members. Its activities have mainly been centered in Helsinki, although at times it has had a good deal of influence in public debates about women's issues and has stimulated and encouraged the openly feminist fractions of parties and movements in Finland. In its spacious premises in the middle of the city, it has hosted active groups like Women for Peace, groups on development cooperation and feminist radical therapy, and meetings of feminist mothers and young feminists. It has also provided services such as a legal rights advisory service, a help line for women victims of violence, and a rape crisis center.

In a very interesting piece, Ellen Marakowitz (1996) compared the impact of these two organizations on the formation of Finnish identity, how they helped in writing the national narrative in those formative years before national independence 1917. Both groups belonged to the broad front for national independence and universal suffrage, and both emphasized the particular importance of political rights for women. The Marthas' work addressed the larger family of the nation, whereas the Feminist Union's efforts were for women only. The gender approach in the Union's framework was one of sisterhood, and the Marthas' approach was that of interdependence between women and men. "As the history of the two groups unfolds, it becomes apparent that it is Martha's female imagery which takes hold in the Finnish nationalist narrative," says Marakowitz.

Marakowitz also speaks about "the domestication of the state" by Marthas. The role of the state as caretaker was female in the imagery of the Marthas, who ultimately became closely aligned with the Finnish state. Marakowitz suggests that the image of the state as a caring and sharing female institution was written into Finnish national narrative as the Marthas moved the framing of women's activities from household to voluntary organizations to government. The concept of a "caring society" has since then become a comprehensive, overarching reality in the form of a Nordic-style welfare society.

To expand on the biblical metaphor, one can say that these two organizations have worked like the two biblical sisters Martha and Mary. They even had the same mother, Lucina Hagman. Whereas Martha is a practical activist in the everyday life of families and people all over Finland, Mary is an intellectual, providing inspiration, radical ideas, and stimulus for generations of women seeking space for feminist debate and sharing experiences and thoughts. In today's terminology, the Marthas have *empowered* women by strengthening their capabilities and self-confidence in the former years of poverty and today by helping cope with problems of waste and environmental destruction in affluent Finland. The Marys of the Union develop feminist thinking for today's needs, strengthening and encouraging further efforts toward profound changes in patriarchal culture. It is also noteworthy that, even today, neither one of these organizations has ever been allied with a political party. Such cross-class autonomous women's organizing remains a powerful way of making change in the society.

By looking at some of the more recent Finnish debates about gender, equality, freedom, political power, and social welfare, I hope to show how this groundwork laid early in the last century remains fertile for feminism. I outline some of the most significant questions facing feminist organizers around the world today.

Formal Equality or Gender Perspective?

Although the English term "gender" is impossible to translate into a single word in Finnish, research on gender roles started early in Finland. The pioneers of Nordic women's research—Harriet Holter in Norway, Rita Liljeström in Sweden, and Elina Haavio-Mannila in Finland—published studies of gender roles that became classics in the 1960s, with the global resurgence of feminism.

In Finland, too, after decades of low-profile equality discussions, a new kind of organization, the Society of 9, was established in 1966. It was an organization of both women and men members, primarily academics and intellectuals. Its membership remained small, and its active life was short, but it had tremendous impact on discussions of gender equality in Finland.

The Society of 9 argued that only paid work and individual income could give women the prerequisites for equality. Its aim was to abolish the gender division of labor and eliminate the need to choose between family and career. The issue of equality became a part of the political agenda, since a claim for equal access to paid work for married women required the state to establish new social arrangements like day care services, family planning, and rationalization of the household chores. While the expanding economy and labor market needed workers, bringing more women into the labor force drew widespread political support.

The policy of the Society of 9 was that the distribution of labor both in households and in the labor market should be changed toward more similar tasks for men and women. Men should share household work equally with women, and the division of paid labor into women's and men's jobs should be eliminated. This implied that women's roles should be changed toward similarity with male roles, although it was also understood that even male roles should become less competitive (Jallinoja, 1983: 161–162). But since the organization did not define any "neutral" role model, the unspoken ideal was the prevailing male role.

The politicization of the equality issue defined the solutions also as political ones. With appropriate legislation, gender equality would be achieved. Therefore, the main task of the Society of 9 was to introduce the equality target into the programs of political parties, which would then lead to new legislation. The whole issue of gender was framed as an issue of public policies, and relations between men and women were not relevant anymore. Jallinoja argues that the incorporation of equality issues and equality policies fully into the public sphere implied that "private life and issues were pushed more and more aside," and the perception that "private life and public life were strictly separate spheres of life" became a general understanding (Jallinoja, 1983: 190).

In this climate, the first official instrument for advancement of equality, the National Equality Council, was established in Finland in 1972. It was to be a political advisory body for the cabinet, offering initiatives and giving comments on gender issues. The Society of 9 considered its task completed, since the advancement of equality between women and men had become part of the regular policies of the state.

The most important international instrument for codification and legal protection of rights of women, the Convention on Elimination of All Forms of Discrimination against Women, usually known as CEDAW, was adopted by the United Nations in 1979 and came into force in 1981. It became a significant step forward in official equality policies also in Finland, where all legislation on the status of women and discrimination against women was carefully checked before the convention was ratified. After this process, CEDAW came into force in Finland in 1986.

As consequences of the ratification of CEDAW, Finland adopted the Equality of Opportunity Act in 1987, some changes and revisions were made in the family laws, and the position of equality ombudsman, with a staff, was established. Thus ratifying CEDAW significantly strengthened the official instruments for gender equality and their juridical legitimacy. These new instruments made equality even more a political and legal issue, and addressed only formal inequalities between women and men.

Feminist Liberation Instead of Equality

In 1983, a group of Nordic women researchers, politicians, and activists prepared the first study on the quantity and quality of political participation of women in the Nordic countries, *Unfinished Democracy* (Haavio-Mannila and Skard, 1985). As they saw it, women's organizations founded in late nineteenth century had an equality policy based on the belief that the equality between women and men will be achieved through elimination of all forms of discrimination that prevent women from achieving the same education, political power, and leading positions in society as men have.

In the 1970s a new kind women's movement emerged that spoke about women's liberation instead of equality. The aim of this movement was not to get women into the power positions within male hierarchical structures but to dismantle that kind of power. The suppression of women was seen as just one mode of operation of capitalist industrial society. In this view, it did not make sense to struggle for equality in this kind of structure; women had to strive for changing the structures and roles of men and women.

This was the beginning of modern Finnish feminism, directed now at change from below through conscientization of women instead of using existing political institutions. In claiming that the "private is political," feminists now linked the suppression and violence against women in private life with the prevailing patriarchal socioeconomic system. The 1983 study also argued that equality policies were inadequate, since the equal treatment of the unequals does not promote equality. Even equal access to work or education does not help if there are no jobs or schools.

Because the new women's movement was not very interested in equality, the issue of having more women in politics was framed instead as being "not just as an end in itself, but in order to bring about change" (Haavio-Mannila and Skard, 1985: 167). In their conclusion to *Unfinished Democracy*, Elina Haavio-Mannila and Drude Dahlerup ask the following crucial questions: "Will increasing numbers of women in politics lead to change? Do wider women's representation and increased participation automatically involve anything new? Do women enter politics only when they already have adopted the elitist terms of the political life? Imagine the frightful scenario in which women's representation finally rose to the magical figure of 50%—and nothing changed!" (160).

Today, with the proportion of women legislators at 38 percent in Finland, the pertinent question is: "Under what conditions can women in politics create social change by means of political action?" One answer is that a certain "critical number" of women politicians is required before a substantial difference will become possible. A second "critical condition" is that "women's policies must be backed up by strong women's organizations and by a critical, radical and visionary women's movement which stands outside the system" (166).

Bitter proof of the crucial importance of the latter condition was provided when Finland at last had a woman as prime minister (March 2003), but that condition was lacking. Anneli Jäätteenmäki took office as prime minister after the victory of her party in elections and said she would like to change the political culture in Finland. She set up a cabinet with equal numbers of women and men. However, due to some careless statements she made, male politicians found an excuse to combine forces and start working against her to an extent never seen before against any male politician. Since there was no dynamic, conscious political women's movement to rally behind her, women stood by helpless and silent, watching men push her out after only three months in office.

A Hidden Catch in the Welfare Society?

Finland approaches the state as a caring and sharing institution from the point of view of gender equality and the status of women. The feminist notion of "domestication of the state" is very close to the terms often used about the welfare society in Nordic countries in general. *Folkshemmet,* "a people's home," was politically popular in Sweden for decades, and idea of "the public family" as parallel to the private family was introduced by Swedish researcher Ulla Olin in the 1970s (1979). Anneli Anttonen (2001) speaks about "a maternalist citizenship" in Finland. Since the welfare state here shares with families both the burden and the expenses of raising children, it is sometimes called "the third parent in every family."

All these characterizations frame the state as a caring institution. The notion of the state as a caring institution appropriately applies to the Nordic model of a welfare society, an overarching set of institutions providing a multitude of public services and lifelong social security for all citizens. A Swedish welfare proponent from the early years of welfare systems in Nordic countries, Assar Lindbeck, has become famous for saying that the Nordic welfare society is one of the triumphs of Western civilization, since it takes care of people "from the womb to the tomb."

Earlier in this chapter I credited the Marthas with beginning to promote a notion of nationwide welfare for families decades before the state in Finland made a systematic plan for social development (see also Pietilä, 2001). The Marthas developed a unique and original method for alleviation of poverty at a time when there were no resources for building up public institutions for a welfare system. Has this female version of the welfare society been good for women? Is their nonstate or pre-state method a workable way of combating poverty as it now appears in many countries of the global South?

Long-term welfare researcher Anneli Anttonen (1994) argues that "women's path from private to public, from daughters and wives to workers and full citizens has gone through the welfare state. In countries where there does not exist any established social service state, women's role has remained more traditional" (27). Because of the welfare society, in Nordic countries, women and men have "three citizenships," for in addition to political citizenship, both social and economic provisions are considered types of citizenship rights, basic entitlements held by virtue of being a member of the community.

In present international discussions about the eradication of poverty, the argument instead is that a country first should gain adequate wealth, only then turning to the problem of providing social and economic well-being to its people. In Finland, the process took a different path: the gradual construction of the welfare system in all its dimensions was the strategy for ensuring economic growth and then became the guarantee for its continuation. For example, free public education was not something that was provided after wealth was created; it was part of the process that created economic wealth and supported the struggle for political rights.

With constant economic growth it was possible to conduct the process in a balanced and controlled way, meaning that a mutually beneficial interplay between economic growth and improvement of people's well-being took place. For women, Finland's emerging welfare system provided free education from the beginning, equal access to health and other social services, and finally also day care services and increasing public care services for the elderly, which made it possible even for women with children to participate in the labor market and gain economic independence (Pietilä, 2001).

The leading welfare researcher in Finland, Raija Julkunen, views the birth of a modern state in the Nordic countries and its development to a welfare state as a historical process in which happiness, welfare, needs, and rights have received increasing legitimacy in the public political arena. As part of this same process and despite their remaining political subordination, women have acquired power and strength (Julkunen, 1990).

Julkunen points out:

> As welfare state citizens, clients, users and professionals women have been integrated into the public sphere. Simultaneously, the rigid classical liberal distinction between public and private has faded. Because women do not have a strong market position or strong corporate organizations at their command, they are compelled to realise their interests through the state. . . . Women's life strategies and collective emancipatory struggles—at least in the Nordic countries—need the state.

In this mutually supportive way, says Julkunen, "the caring state can be considered a particularly feminist achievement. With the state, women redistribute the caring tasks belonging to the private life circle." In all the Nordic countries, the state is the mechanism for the redistribution of wealth, rights, and utilities. Globally, it is evident that if the state does not perform this function, there is no other conceivable mechanism for it. The market will never operate for the elimination of disparities and for equalization; it operates in just the opposite direction (Pietilä, 2001).

Yet no matter how woman-friendly the state, the welfare society has not yet been able to eliminate women's gendered disadvantages in the fields of employment, income, and power. Such universal problems as gender segregation of the labor market, masculine hegemony in economic policies,

business practices, and even defining common meanings in culture concern Finnish feminists, too. In spite of the advanced status of women and
the relatively high level of gender equality, violence against women in all
its forms continues to be a painful problem in Finland. In this respect
there are big differences between the Nordic countries, the frequency of
violence being highest in Finland.

After all, Raija Julkunen takes the welfare society as a particular expression of the society's gender perspective, but at the same time her words
can be taken also as criticism and even warning of possible, unwanted
consequences of the welfare society:

> The usual indicators of gender gaps or the participation of women in the
> labour force, education and political institutions place them in the van-
> guard of developed nations. *In the Nordic societies women have, to an excep-
> tional degree, been integrated into male society. Women's and men's status as
> citizens has become more similar than perhaps in any other country in the
> world.* (Julkunen, 1992:1; italics added)

We can question whether the latter features are a positive or negative
outcome. They would possibly have been avoided if women had had more
feminist consciousness.

In recent decades, these issues have been engaged as transnational questions. What do neoliberalism, the welfare state, and national security have
to do with gender equality? The way that feminists approach and use
transnational institutions and treaties indicates how they answer the preceding questions.

The Public Policies for Equality Today

The Finnish Equality Act of 1987 applied only to employment relations
and provided compensation for discrimination that was shown to have
already occurred, but offered no means to prevent discrimination based
on gender before it occurred. It could deal only with the issues of waged
work, differences of salaries, promotions and applications for posts, and
the like.

In many countries, the fields occupied mainly by women are poorly
paid, whereas those where most employees are men are much better paid.
Statistically the average salaries of women in Finland have stagnated at the

level of about 80 percent of men's salaries. The different training and qualifications required in various professional fields is often used as an explanation and excuse for persistent disparities. With good reason, women ask,
why is caring for a machine, be it a car, computer, or paper mill, always
better paid than caring for human beings in schools, hospitals, day care
centers, and old-age homes?

Another cause of work-related inequalities is gender segregation in the
labor market. The Nordic recipe for alleviating such segregation has been
affirmative action plans. Women have been encouraged to seek jobs in traditionally male fields to get better pay, while it is believed that the way to
raise salaries in low-paying fields is to attract more men into these fields.
Incentives have been given to employers for hiring men in traditionally
female fields and women in the male-dominated ones. However, these
efforts have shown very little success.

These strategies are based on the assumption that only the work that is
popular among men is valuable. These measures to break gender segregation may also be unfair to young people if they lead them to choose professions in which they are not genuinely interested. Young women are still
persistently seeking to enter the professions they find interesting and
motivating, for instance, nursing, teaching, social work, and catering, in
spite of lower earnings in these fields.

Public equality policies in Finland have primarily aimed at opening
avenues for women to gain status and positions equal with men, including
corresponding wages. This policy inevitably leads to constant competition
by women with men on male terms, and thus it only strengthens masculine values and norms. Women try to prove that they are as ambitious,
strenuous, efficient, and competitive as those men who are doing well.
Thus, the vital values in good human society such as caring and compas-
sion, empathy and caution, emotional intelligence, economizing and managing skills, dexterity and practicality, intuition and sensitivity are pushed
aside and ignored. In this way, the supreme capabilities and gifts emanating from women's culture are forgotten and lost. This is very detrimental
to women and the whole culture, literally and symbolically.

Transformational feminist politics should resist the excessive valuation
of jobs according to their commercial profitability. On these premises the
most essential work within human society—such as caring and nursing in
various forms—will tend not to be paid for at all, as has been the case in
the past when women took care of these functions entirely within households. In Nordic welfare societies, these functions largely have been trans-

ferred into public society and constitute a huge part of the labor market employing mainly women. Thus, a significant part of unpaid work within households has now become paid work for women in the public "households," but the wages paid are very unfair.

The essential caring, nursing, and education functions of life should be considered as part of public entitlements, to use the concept of feminist economist Amartya Sen. The salaries and terms in these fields of labor should be defined by democratically elected decision makers on social grounds. They have to take into consideration the human qualifications and responsibilities needed in these tasks and do justice to people performing this work.

The political decision makers have to face seriously these concerns with gender justice and premises for welfare societies. From the human point of view, service and caring work in the society is indispensable and cannot be measured by productivity and economic profit. The purely legal and labor force centered equality policies are blind to these kinds of basic social and human factors. Such policies are not acceptable if they lead to detrimental consequences for women and for the society as a whole.

Thoughts about Women's Empowerment for Change

From a narrow, formalistic point of view, women's equality with men is an end in itself. Naturally, equality in status and treatment is a basic right; it is the right to not be discriminated against on any grounds. But according to my feminist understanding, equality is a precondition for making change. One of the shortcomings in Finnish gender equality is that women have the right to speak but not to be heard and taken into consideration. It is much more difficult for a woman than a man to be published and be recognized in public fields, to be heard culturally and politically. This is especially true if a woman speaks in "another voice," in her own voice.

The Beijing Platform for Action (PfA) declares as its purpose being "an agenda for women's empowerment" (United Nations, 1996, paragraph 1). According to the PfA, women's empowerment "aims at removing all the obstacles to women's active participation in all spheres of public and private life through a full and equal share in economic, social, cultural and political decision-making. This means that the principle of shared power and responsibility should be established between women and men at home, in the workplace and in the wider national and international communities" (PfA, paragraph 1).

The issue is not only about words and concepts. It is also about perceptions and understandings concerning the relationships of men and women and their respective status in society and culture. It is about recognizing and admitting that men also have gender, which profoundly influences their thinking, attitudes, and behavior. Within the last ten years this new perception and way of thinking have become part of the UN culture. At the UN level and in the Beijing PfA the gender perspective has very much replaced traditional equality thinking as such, with the aim of eliminating obstacles to women's empowerment.

Through this gender lens, equality is no longer only a technical and statistical matter. It should imply gender mainstreaming and an understanding that the views, values, and experiences of both women and men should be equally heard and recognized in society, especially because they may be basically different. Only then can women and men equally and democratically make their impact on society. Thus, the equal participation and impact of women in society becomes not only their legitimate right but also a social and political necessity for achieving more balanced and sustainable national development (Pietilä and Vickers, 1990, 140).

The equality movement and formal equality policies say very little about *the alternatives to our presently unequal culture and society*. Prevailing equality thinking is legalistic, statistical, and technical and therefore does not have much dynamism and potential to make change. By contrast, the empowerment of women as a concept already brings potential alternatives into the picture. But if women do not have any vision and ideas for how they would like to change society, they will not be able to truly benefit from empowerment.

The challenge the transnational feminist movement faces—in my view—is to say what difference we would want to make if women were to have equal power to influence decisions, to define the meanings in culture and the priorities in society, economy, and culture. I can think of at least a few examples where women have been asking for alternatives for ages.

One is that *women's unpaid work* in households and neighborhoods be recognized and counted as an indispensable contribution to society. This idea has been discussed among women for at least a hundred years. In Finland in the 1920s, Laura Harmaja, a pioneering woman economist, was already asking for the unpaid work and production in households to be assessed, counted, and included in the gross national product. A recommendation for counting this work has been adopted by each of the four UN world conferences on women since 1975. But economists and politicians continue to ignore this issue and make policies as if no work for the well-being of nations and peoples had ever been done in the homes and households anywhere.

Another issue on which women have been campaigning for ages is *peace and elimination of violence in all its forms.* Violence against women, that is, male violence in its endless number of forms at the interpersonal level, has been recognized as an obstacle for peace in the UN documents since the Nairobi conference in 1985. We all know too well how little women's claims, struggles, and efforts for another kind of culture in this respect have been heard and taken into consideration. We have dramatically experienced that again in recent years, as conflicts inside and between states have led to rape and atrocities against women. Women's yearning for peace has been expressed also in their worldwide interest in and support for the United Nations as first and foremost an organization for peace.

Hundreds of books have been written about the efforts and campaigns of women to make global changes, yet the results have been slow and meager. However, the history of Finland and the experiences of women transnationally also speak to the power of joining women's rights and socioeconomic development in a common agenda for change. We have tools in hand in the form of papers and programs, such as the Beijing PfA and even Resolution 1325 of the UN Security Council, that feminists can use to press governments for commitments to the empowerment of women. The necessity today is, as it was for the Marthas of generations past, to pick up the tools and get to work to make governments accountable for implementation of their resolutions.

BIBLIOGRAPHY

Anttonen, Anneli. 1994. "Welfare Pluralism or Woman-Friendly Welfare Politics?" In Anneli Anttonen, eds., *Women and the Welfare State: Politics, Professions and Practices.* Department of Social Policy, University of Jyväskylä, working paper no. 87/1994
————. 1998. "Vocabularies of Citizenship and Gender: Finland." *Critical Social Policy* 183:355–375.

————. 2001. "The Female Working Citizen: Social Rights, Work and Mother-hood in Finland." *Kvinder, køn & forskning,* 2, no. 1: 33–44.

Haavio-Mannila, Elina, and Torild Skard. 1985. *Unfinished Democracy: Women in Nordic Politics.* Oxford: Pergamon Press.

Haltia, Manja. 1949. *Marttatoiminta 1899–1949* (The work of the Marthas, 1899–1949). Helsinki: Marttaliitto.

Holli, Anne Maria, Terhi Saarikoski, and Elina Sana, eds. 2002. *Tasa-arvopolitiikan haasteet* (Challenges to equality policies). Helsinki: WSOY.

Jallinoja, Riitta. 1983. *Suomalaisen naisasialiikkeen taistelukaudet* (The battle periods of the Finnish women's movement). Juva: WSOY.

Julkunen, Raija. 1990. "Women in the Welfare State." In Merja Manninen and Päivi Setälä, eds., *The Lady with the Bow: The Story of Finnish Women,* 140–160. Helsinki: Otava Publishers.

————. 1992. "The Nordic Countries—Women-Friendly Societies?" Presentation at the conference "The CSCE Process: Supporting Women in Their Efforts to Develop a Just Society." Helsinki, June 4–5.

————. 1994. "Suomalainen sukupuolisota?" (The Finnish gender war). In Sara Heinämaa and Sari Näre, eds., *Pahan tyttäret. Sukupuolitettu pelko, viha ja valta,* 17–33. Helsinki: Gaudeamus.

Koskelainen, Liisa. 1999. *Marttaa ja vähän Mariaakin. Marttajärjestön toiminta 1950–1999* (About Marthas and a little about Marys: The work of Marthas in 1950–1999). Helsinki: Otava.

Marakowitz, Ellen. 1996. "Gender and National Identity in Finland: An Exploration into Women's Political Agency." *Women's Studies International Forum* 19:55–63.

Olin, Ulla. 1979. "Case for Women as Co-managers: The Family as a General Model of Human Social Organization and Its Implications for Women's Role in Public Life." In Irene Tinker and Michele Bo Bramsen, eds., *Women and World Development.* Washington, D.C.: Overseas Development Council.

Pietilä, Hilkka. 1995 (as revised 2003). "Women in Policy- and Decision-Making: Does It Make a Difference?" Paper presented at the INSTRAW seminar, Huairou, China, September 1995.

————. 2001. "Eradicating Poverty by Building a Welfare Society: Finland as a Case Study." In *Cooperation South,* 79–96. UNDP, no 2.

————. 2002b. *Engendering the Global Agenda. The Story of Women and the United Nations.* Development dossier by UN/NGLS, Geneva.

————. 2002. "Onko tasa-arvosta muutoksen välineeksi?" (Is equality a means for change?). In Anne Maria Holli, Terhi Saarikoski, and Elina Sana, eds., *Tasa-arvopolitiikan haasteet* (Challenges to equality policies), 221–239. Helsinki: WSOY.

Pietilä, Hilkka, and Jean Vickers. 1990. *Making Women Matter: The Role of the United Nations.* London: Zed Books.

United Nations. 1996. Platform for Action and the Beijing Declaration. Fourth World Conference on Women, Beijing, China, 4–15 September 1995. New York: United Nations.

———. 1999. *1999 World Survey on the Role of Women in Development: Globalization, Gender and Work.* New York: United Nations.

Part III

Activism in Transnational Space

8

Regional Women's Activism
African Women's Networks and the African Union

Melinda Adams

Transnational women's activism is not always global in scope; sometimes it is regional in character. In fact, regional women's networks are increasingly playing an important role in diffusing norms and strategies on a range of women's and gender issues. Regional networks are actively promoting women's human rights, women's economic empowerment, gender mainstreaming in domestic and international policy and institutions, women's representation in decision making, and the inclusion of women in peace and conflict resolution initiatives. In Africa, in particular, regional networks are playing an important role in diffusing gender norms across national boundaries and even setting global standards on certain women's and gender issues.

Regional networks are institutions that facilitate exchanges among activists and organizations within a particular geographic region (i.e., Africa, Latin America, or Asia). Exchanges may take place in face-to-face encounters or "virtually," via e-mail or other communications technology. Regional networks are, of course, international, since they span state boundaries. Nevertheless, in this chapter, I distinguish regional from international networks based on whether the focus is on bringing together women's organizations *within* or *across* geographic regions. Regional networks, as defined here, are those that are "organized by and for women" in that particular geographic context; they may accept external funding, but they formulate their own policy objectives (Basu 2000, 74–75). Though frequently linked to broader global movements, regional networks operate primarily within a bounded geographic context. The Encuentros

(Encounters), a series of intraregional meetings that have brought together a wide array of Latin American activists, analyzed by Alvarez et al. (2003), are the best-known case of regional activism. Though the *Encuentros* are unique to Latin America, regional activism also exists in Africa, Europe, Asia, and elsewhere.

This chapter examines regional networking as a distinct form of transnational women's activism. It proceeds in four parts. It begins by briefly examining regional networking in Africa during the terminal colonial and immediate post-colonial periods. It argues that the rise of single-party states curtailed autonomous regional networking in the 1970s and early 1980s. The chapter then addresses the revitalization of regional networking that began in the mid-1980s and continues today. Both domestic and international factors fueled this development. The chapter then turns to a case study—African women's networks' lobbying of the African Union—to examine how a specific regional initiative has successfully influenced policy. The chapter concludes by drawing from the specific case to speculate on the applicability of regional networking to other issues and contexts.

Regional Women's Networks in Africa

First Wave of Regional Activism (1950s–1970s)

Regional networking among African women's organizations is not a new phenomenon. As early the late 1950s and early 1960s, women came together at the subregional and regional levels to discuss common problems, share experiences, and strategize about potential solutions to these problems.[1] More than three hundred African women came together in Lomé, Togo, in July 1958, for example, to participate in the Regional Seminar of the World Union of Catholic Women's Organizations. Representatives from ten African countries and territories discussed topics such as education, bride price, and the civic role of African women.[2] After organizing regional seminars on women and public life in Bangkok, Thailand, in 1957 and in Bogotá, Colombia, in 1959, the United Nations organized an African Seminar on the Participation of Women in Public Life in Addis Ababa, Ethiopia, in 1960. The goal of the meeting was "to bring together women from the countries and territories of Africa to consider the implications of civic rights and increased participation of women of Africa in public life."[3] Representatives from thirty-one African countries and territories participated in the Addis Ababa seminar.[4] Margaret Kenyatta, daughter of Kenya's first president, Jomo Kenyatta, organized seminars that brought together Kenyan women's organizations in 1962 and 1963 and an East African Women's Seminar in 1964 that brought together representatives from Uganda, Tanzania, and Kenya (Snyder and Tadesse 1995). Women from socialist-oriented countries, including Egypt, Ghana, Guinea, and Tanganyika, came together in Bamako, Mali, and later in Dar es Salaam, Tanzania, in 1962 to establish the All Africa Women's Conference (AAWC; Snyder and Tadesse 1995). The AAWC was the only regional organization to participate in the drafting of the Convention on the Elimination of All Forms of Discrimination against Women (CEDAW; Tripp 2005; Zwingel 2004). The Pan-African Women's Organization (PAWO) was also established in 1962. This brief list of regional initiatives demonstrates that women were coming together across national boundaries in the terminal colonial and immediate postcolonial eras.

The rise of the single-party state throughout Africa demonstrated that opportunities for regional networking were conditioned by state-society relations. Specifically, as the relative political openness of the immediate postcolonial era gave way to single-party states, opportunities for representatives of autonomous organizations to network across national borders diminished. In the vast majority of African states, party and state organizations dominated the field of women's activism from the late 1960s through the 1980s. States strongly "encouraged" and sometimes even compelled autonomous women's organizations to join these state- and party-sponsored umbrella bodies.

Though official state and party delegations increasingly dominated regional and international meetings, some regional networking continued during this period. In 1975, the UN Economic Commission in Africa (ECA) founded the African Training and Research Center for Women (ATRCW), the first UN-affiliated regional institution devoted to women's issues. The ATRCW served as a model for the formation of similar regional bodies in other world regions. It organized numerous meetings at the regional level, including those held in Nouakchott, Mauritania, in 1977; in Lusaka, Zambia, in 1979; and in Arusha, Tanzania, in 1984. These meetings focused primarily on development issues, including integrating women into development, promoting women's cooperatives, developing small-scale industries, training rural women to take on leadership positions, and establishing national mechanisms for integrating women in development projects. Though regional linkages continued to exist, there were relatively few opportunities for representatives of autonomous organizations to come together across national boundaries during this period.

Second Wave of Regional Activism (1980s–2000s)

Changes in both international and domestic political contexts in the 1980s and 1990s facilitated the rise of autonomous organizations and the revitalization of regional networks. The second wave of regional organizing began in the mid-1980s and continues today. Economic crisis and the structural adjustment programs and other neoliberal economic reforms that followed it contributed to the retreat of the state. These developments ceded space and critical tasks to nonstate actors, encouraging the growth of autonomous organizations. Political developments, including the demise of single-party states, a return to multipartyism, and political liberalization more generally, further promoted the formation of national and regional women's associations and networks. New laws on association created a legal environment more auspicious for nongovernmental organizations. The weakening of state-sponsored women's associations opened space for the creation of autonomous organizations. These developments were the flip side of those that occurred in the 1960s and 1970s. Changes in the domestic economic and political environments facilitated the formation of autonomous organizations and provided openings for the emergence of new regional initiatives.

At the same time, regional and international developments were also critical to the rise of autonomous women's activism. UN world conferences, particularly the 1985 Nairobi conference and the 1995 Beijing conference, spurred national and regional networking across the continent. For African women's organizations, the Nairobi conference was a watershed, sparking the development of new organizations, linkages, and ways of mobilizing. Just as the 1975 Mexico City conference spurred regional activism in Latin America, and the 1980 Copenhagen conference added impetus to European women's activism, so too did the 1985 Nairobi conference stimulate the formation of new national and regional organizations throughout Africa. For example, Women in Law and Development in Africa (WiLDAF), an organization that seeks to link law and development to empower women, traces its origins to the UN World Conference on Women in Nairobi in 1985 (Hodgson 2003; Foster 1995). Similarly, FEMNET, a network developed to share information, experiences, and

ideas among African women's organizations, emerged from NGO participation the UN Decade on Women (1975–1985), especially the African
regional preparatory meeting held in Arusha, Tanzania, in 1984 and the
Nairobi conference in 1985 (Radloff 1999).

Beijing and, perhaps even more important, the preparatory process
leading up to the Fourth World Conference on Women (FWCW) gave further impetus to the development of regional networks. Many of these networks were established between 1985 and 1995; therefore, they "cut their
teeth" preparing for the FWCW.[5] The Beijing process spurred nascent networks to organize national, subregional, and regional meetings to prepare
for official meetings at Dakar and Beijing. WiLDAF, for example, began
preparing for Beijing by organizing a series of subregional conferences. At
meetings held in East, West, and Southern Africa, participants from each
subregion selected a target issue, choosing armed conflict, structural
adjustment, and violence against women, respectively. Following these
subregional meetings, WiLDAF sent representatives to the regional NGO
forum in Dakar in November 1994. It concluded its preparations by organizing a Pan-African Preparatory Meeting that brought together members
from the three subregions. Commenting on the FWCW, a WiLDAF publi-
cation notes: "For us, Beijing was the dawn of a new era. It was a platform
for a takeoff that will help us in coordinating the process of integrating
African women into the process of development" (Foster 1995, i).
WiLDAF's and other networks' success in organizing for Beijing inspired
greater activism in the region after the world conference concluded. Networks transferred the institutional learning they acquired while preparing
for Beijing to new issues and arenas.

The official Beijing preparatory process similarly consisted of various
levels of activism, beginning with the grassroots, moving to national and
subregional levels, and culminating in the Dakar and Beijing conferences
at the regional and international levels, respectively. Following local and
national meetings, five subregional conferences—in East, Southern, Central, North, and West Africa—brought together representatives from the
various subregions to discuss issues of particular relevance to women in
each area. The regional preparatory process culminated in the Fifth
African Regional Conference on Women in Dakar, Senegal, in 1994. It was
here that delegates finalized and approved the African Platform for Action.
The norms embedded in the African Platform for Action and later the
Beijing Platform for Action continue to inform activists' work. Networks
focusing on gender parity draw on the Dakar and Beijing platforms' com-

mitment to a minimum of 30 percent women in decision-making positions. Organizations focusing on women's human rights similarly draw on and build from the commitments made in these and other regional and international documents. In contrast to previous world conferences on women, the process leading up to Beijing changed the institutional landscape of women's activism in Africa, sparking the formation of networks at the subregional and regional levels.

As the profile of nonstate actors grew, so too did their access to regional meetings. Beginning in the mid-1980s, national delegations to regional and international conferences no longer consisted solely of state and party representatives. Representatives of autonomous organizations increasingly participated in NGO forums that shadowed official conferences. The Sixth African Regional Conference on Women held in Addis Ababa, Ethiopia, in 1999 was the first regional intergovernmental conference to bring together both national delegates and NGO representatives, enabling nonstate actors to participate fully in the official conference proceedings.

Contemporary regional women's networks are quite diverse. Examples of African regional women's networks include the African Women's Development and Communication Network (FEMNET), the Forum for African Women Educationalists (FAWE), Women in Law and Development in Africa (WiLDAF), Gender in Africa Information Network, the Association of African Women for Research and Development (AAWORD), ABANTU for Development, Akina Mama wa Afrika, the Association for Women in Development (AWID), and Femmes Africa Solidarité (FAS), among many others (Radloff 1999; Tripp 2005). Many of these are issue-based networks focusing on topics such as women's human rights, violence against women, women's representation in decision-making positions, HIV/AIDS, conflict resolution, and women's economic empowerment. Different networks seek to bring together different groups of actors (e.g., grassroots associations, academics, activists, and/or policymakers) and are located in distinct organizational settings (e.g., NGOs, universities, other research bodies, or government agencies). Some networks are highly institutionalized, with officers, newsletters, Web sites, and regular meetings, whereas others are more amorphous, coming together for a specific campaign and then dispersing until another issue brings them together. Many regional networks have their headquarters in Africa, though some, either for strategic reasons or because African expatriates initiated them, are located in Europe or elsewhere.[6] Thus, to talk about regional women's networks in Africa is to discuss a broad and diverse institutional field.

In some ways, African regional networks are similar to those in other world regions. Alvarez et al. (2003) argue that regional meetings in Latin America have encouraged the formation of issue-specific networks focusing on women's health, reproductive rights, violence against women, and women's political representation. Similar issue-based networks have emerged in Africa. In addition, similar domestic and international developments facilitated the growth of regional networks. As in Africa, democratic transitions, neoliberal economic reforms, and preparations for UN conferences contributed to the formation of regional networks in Latin America.

Still, there are important differences. Regional activism is a more recent development in Africa than in Latin America or Europe, in part because political openings came later in Africa than in other world regions. Many Latin American countries experienced democratic transitions in the 1980s. In contrast, political liberalization did not occur in Africa until the 1990s. The timing and location of UN conferences also affected world regions differently. The 1975 Mexico City conference sparked regional activism in Latin America, while the 1980 Copenhagen conference played a similar role in mobilizing women in Europe. Delegates from Africa participated in both these meetings; however, it was the 1985 Nairobi conference that first changed the institutional landscape in Africa. Furthermore, while activists in Latin America have been meeting in informal, intraregional Encuentros since 1981, there is no similar process in Africa. As described by Alvarez et al. (2002), the Encuentros have served as spaces where activists from all over Latin America converge to discuss the current state of feminism and women's activism in the region. The Encuentros served not only as forums to debate women's and gender issues and discuss various advocacy strategies but also as venues to discuss fundamental questions like who is a feminist, what should be the relationship between feminism and the state, and who has the right to participate in these meetings. In contrast, African regional networks have directed greater attention toward policy advocacy and less to normative questions about the composition and nature of the "movement."

Finally, although many women's and gender issues span regional boundaries, some are particularly salient in certain regions and locales. Peace building and conflict resolution have been particularly critical issues in Africa, where many of the world's contemporary conflicts exist. Women's organizations have taken the lead in promoting peace and conflict resolution. The Mano River Women's Peace Network (MARWOP-

NET), for example, worked to bring leaders from Liberia, Sierra Leone, and Guinea to the negotiation table, promoting peace in this war-torn region of West Africa. The United Nations recognized MARWOPNET's contributions to peace in the subregion, awarding the organization the 2003 UN Human Rights Prize. Women's organizations have been active in peace-building initiatives in the Great Lakes region, Rwanda, Somalia, and Sudan. In October 2000, African women's networks successfully lobbied for the adoption of UN Security Council Resolution 1325. The resolution calls on states to increase the number of women in decision-making positions, incorporate women into peace negotiations, protect the human rights of women and girls, and integrate a gender perspective into peace processes.

Recently, African women's organizations have also taken the lead on the issue of women's political representation. The 1997 Southern African Development Community (SADC) "Declaration on Gender and Development," for example, commits signatories to achieving at least 30 percent representation of women in decision-making positions by 2005. The African Union has attained gender parity in its commission and has established a gender quota for national delegations to the Pan-African Parliament. African organizations have been among the most active in fifty-fifty gender equity campaigns, which call for women to occupy at least half the seats in parliament. Specifically, organizations in South Africa, Namibia, Uganda, Kenya, and Sierra Leone have mobilized to achieve gender parity in legislative representation (Tripp 2005). African networks have also called particular attention to the gender dimensions of the HIV/AIDS pandemic and to the exclusion of women from development. How has the rise of regional women's networking affected the rules and practices of African polities? The next section addresses this question through a case study of African women's networks' campaign to engender the African Union.

African Women's Networks and the African Union

The African Union (AU), the successor to the Organization of African Unity (OAU), was launched in July 2002. Modeled after the European Union (EU), the AU seeks to promote unity among African countries and peoples, political and economic integration, peace, and respect for democracy and human rights.[7] One of the most remarkable aspects of the AU is its progressive stance toward gender issues. It has achieved gender parity in its executive arm, the AU Commission, a feat unmatched by any other regional or international organization. Women, in contrast, constitute just 28 percent of the EU Commission (seven out of twenty-five).[8] In addition, a woman—Gertrude Mongella, who gained international acclaim as the chair of the 1995 Beijing conference—heads the newly inaugurated Pan-African Parliament (PAP). A gender quota ensures that state delegations to the PAP include at least one woman. In 2003, the AU passed the Protocol on the Rights of Women in Africa, which prohibits female genital cutting, sets a minimum age of marriage of eighteen, and is the first international document to guarantee a woman's right to an abortion in the cases of rape, incest, or to save the life of the mother.[9] Finally, in 2004, the AU Assembly adopted the Solemn Declaration on Gender Equality in Africa, which among other things calls on state parties to sign and ratify the Protocol on the Rights of Women in Africa and to submit annual reports on progress made in terms of gender mainstreaming. It also requests that the AU write an annual report on the implementation of gender policies.[10]

These developments demonstrate the AU's growing commitment to gender equity. This commitment, however, was not an inevitable development, nor was it born overnight. African women's networks mobilized and fought to achieve these gender equity provisions. Drawing on and building from norms embedded in regional and international documents—including the Dakar and Beijing Platforms for Action and CEDAW—regional women's networks lobbied member states and the OAU/AU throughout the transition process. They pressured states and OAU/AU bureaucrats to incorporate gender equity and mainstreaming policies into AU structures and procedures. The lobbying efforts of African women's networks played a critical role in securing these commitments to promoting gender equity within the newly established Union.

To understand how women's networks were able to attain these gender commitments, one must understand the dynamics that led to formation of the AU. Decisions taken at four pan-African summits led to its creation. In 1999, the OAU held an Extraordinary Session in Sitre, Libya, where it decided to establish the AU. The Lomé Summit in 2000 led to the adoption of the Constitutive Act of the African Union, and the Lusaka Summit in 2001 provided a road map for the transition from the OAU to the AU. Officially established in May 2001 when the Constitutive Act entered into force, the AU was launched at the Durban Summit in July 2002.[11] There are currently fifty-three member states.[12]

Modeled after the European Union, key institutions of the African Union include the Assembly, the Executive Council, the Pan-African Parliament (PAP), and the Commission. The Assembly, which meets at least once a year, is the "supreme organ of the Union" and is composed of heads of state and government or their appointed representatives. The Executive Council is composed of ministers of foreign affairs; it meets at least twice a year. The Commission, located in Addis Ababa, Ethiopia, consists of ten members. It is the secretariat of the AU and is responsible for day-to-day affairs. The PAP, the legislative wing of the AU launched in March 2004, is composed of five-member delegations from each member state. Additional AU institutions include the Permanent Representative Council; the Peace and Security Council (PSC); the Specialized Technical Committee; the Economic, Social and Cultural Council; and the financial institutions. In addition, a court of justice is in the process of formation.

The AU seeks, among other things, to promote "greater unity and solidarity between the African countries and the peoples of Africa," "to accelerate the political and socio-economic integration of the continent," and to encourage "peace, security, and stability on the continent."[13] Though similar to the OAU's mandate, the AU's objectives are even more far-reaching. Distinguishing the AU from the OAU, Maria Nzomo (2003) asserts that the AU's defining feature is that it seeks to unite both governments and peoples. To this end, the AU has taken steps to create a Pan-African Parliament (PAP), which aims to give greater voice to African citizens. The PAP Protocol was adopted at the Fifth Extraordinary Session of the Assembly of the Heads of State and Government in Sitre, Libya, on March 2, 2001, and it entered into force on December 14, 2003. To date, the PAP has met twice: it held its inaugural session in March 2004 in Addis Ababa, Ethiopia, and its second session in September 2004 in Midrand, South Africa. During a five-year interim phase, the PAP serves only as an advisory and consultative body. Governments select PAP delegates from among national parliamentarians. After this interim period, the PAP is envisioned to evolve into an institution with full legislative powers with directly elected pan-African parliamentarians.

The AU has also created and strengthened mechanisms that enable NGOs and other civil society actors to influence the AU policy process. Established in 1998 by the OAU and the UN Economic Commission for Africa (UNECA), the African Women's Committee on Peace and Development (AWCPD), for example, provided an institutional mechanism linking African governments, intergovernmental organizations, and

NGOs. Specifically, the AWCPD sought to increase the participation of African women in peace and development processes in the region. Throughout the transition from the OAU to the AU, the AWCPD actively lobbied for the greater inclusion of women in the new organization. Despite its key location linking the OAU/AU and women's organizations, the AWCPD has not been as effective as activists had hoped. Describing the limitations of AWCPD, Mary Wandia, a staff member at FEMNET, indicated that it has "worked more from without than within the OAU," due to insufficient human and financial resources.[14] The AU has recognized as much. In July 2003, at the Third Ordinary Session of the Executive Council in Maputo, Mozambique, an AU delegation highlighted the need "to associate women from the broad spectrum of society in the activities of the African Union" and "deplored the circumstances which paralyzed the operations of the African Women's Committee for Peace and Development" (Wandia 2003).[15] Senegal, in particular, urged the AU Commission to reactivate the committee and review its mandate, structure, and membership. Recently the AWCPD was transformed into the AU Women's Committee, which will serve as an advisory body to the AU Commission. It is hoped that its access to AU commissioners will enhance its influence.

Though the AWCPD has not been as strong as civil societal groups would have liked, it pressed, alongside regional women's networks, for the greater inclusion of women in the African Union. In March 2001 at the Fifth Extraordinary Assembly of Heads of States and Governments in Sirte, Libya, regional women's organizations, led by the AWCPD and Femmes Africa Solidarité (FAS), initiated a campaign for gender parity and mainstreaming within the AU. Representatives from these organizations lobbied key members of the Executive Council to push for greater inclusion of women in the transition process, initiating a consultative process that brought together the AWCPD, the UNECA, subregional economic communities, and other stakeholders to discuss the incorporation of women's and gender issues in the AU.[16] The OAU also organized the meeting "Gender Mainstreaming in the African Union" in May 2002 in Addis Ababa, which brought together representatives of these various institutions. The AWCPD also initiated its own consultation process, bringing together women's organizations from across the continent to discuss "strategies to ensure women's full participation and representation in the transition process, and subsequently within the AU."[17] This led to the development of the Pan-African Networks,[18] which have met on several subsequent occasions to press for gender equity and gender mainstreaming within the AU.

The AU has taken a number of pathbreaking steps on women's and gender issues. Femmes Africa Solidarité (FAS), an organization active in regional lobbying networks, published a press release immediately following the Durban Summit in 2002 stating:

> With the closing of the African Union summit in Durban this week, it is evident that among improvements the African Union will enjoy over its predecessor, the OAU, is a significant commitment to the inclusion of women in the new pan-African body. This historical progress on the part of Africa's leaders was clearly the outcome of work carried out by participants of the Consultation on Gender Mainstreaming and the Effective Participation of Women within the African Union, which took place 28–30 June in Durban, just prior to the opening of the AU Summit. The Consultation resulted in a set of recommendations that was forwarded to members of the AU to ensure that women's issues and voices be included in AU policies, programmes, and structures, including NEPAD [New Partnership for Africa's Development] and the CSSDCA [Conference on Security, Stability, Development and Co-operation in Africa].[19]

Throughout the transition from the OAU to the AU, African women's networks actively lobbied both the AU and individual member states to address a broad range of women's and gender issues. These networks lobbied to advance gender mainstreaming within the AU, to gain a commitment to gender parity in decision-making positions, and to advance women's rights through the Protocol to the African Charter on Human and Peoples' Rights Relating to the Rights of Women in Africa. Meetings of representatives of African women's organizations and networks resulted in several documents—the Durban Declaration, the Dakar Strategy, and the Maputo Declaration—that advance specific policy recommendations.[20] Over time, the network has grown, and the number of organizations participating in the meetings has increased dramatically. While eleven and twelve organizations signed the Durban Declaration and Dakar Strategy, respectively, forty-three organizations signed the Maputo Declaration.[21] In Addis Ababa in 2004, African women's networks drafted the document "African Women's Contributions to the Declaration on Mainstreaming Gender in the African Union," which celebrates their achievements and puts forward additional recommendations. The case study demonstrates that campaigns organized by regional networks to "engender" regional institutions can be effective. They have brought women into the process and established norms to which states can be held accountable.

It is important to recognize, however, that the AU is, in some ways, a special case. The transformation of the OAU into the AU provided women's organizations with a critical opening. Institutions are notoriously sticky and difficult to change; thus, the OAU's decision to create a new institution rather than merely tinker with the existing one provided women's groups with greater leverage as they advocated for substantial changes to gender policies. The Durban Declaration on Mainstreaming Gender and Women's Effective Participation in the African Union acknowledges as much, stating that signatories were "convinced that African women must seize the opportunity provided by the historical moment of the launching of the African Union to ensure their full and effective participation in its operationalisation."[22] Similarly, a report on the proceedings of the women's pre-summit meeting in Maputo notes that the shift from the OAU to the AU "provided the opportunity for women's organisations and networks to meet and discuss the pertinent issues facing gender and women on the Continent and to develop strategies and recommendations to address these issues within the newly formed structures."[23]

This is also true at the national level. Scholars studying campaigns to mainstream gender and to increase women's political representation in African states have argued that regime change provides opportunities for women to overhaul the political system, challenge patriarchal structures, and increase women's representation (Britton 2002; Goetz and Hassim 2003; Seidman 2001; Tripp 2004). Women in states undergoing regime change have often been able to draw on authority established during national liberation struggles to push for the inclusion of gender equity provisions in new institutions. Women's networks have been able to draw on successes achieved at Nairobi and Beijing to push for change at the regional and subregional level. Still, preexisting institutions, both formal and informal, influenced the development of the AU, and women's organizations were fighting an uphill battle to implement such wide-reaching changes.

Having looked at women's organizations' interactions with the African Union in general, a closer examination of two specific campaigns—one to adopt the Protocol to the African Charter on Human and Peoples' Rights on the Rights of Women in Africa, and another to achieve gender equity in

AU institutions—demonstrates the potential of regional networks to promote gender equity. The chapter will now turn to examine these cases.

Protocol to the African Charter on Human and Peoples' Rights on the Rights of Women in Africa

The Protocol to the African Charter on Human and Peoples' Rights on the Rights of Women in Africa was adopted by the Assembly of Heads of State and Government of the African Union on July 11, 2003, in Maputo, Mozambique. It supplements the 1981 African Charter on Human and Peoples' Rights and will enter into force thirty days after the deposit of the fifteenth instrument of ratification. As of August 2005, twelve countries— Cape Verde, Comoros, Djibouti, Libya, Lesotho, Mali, Malawi, Namibia, Nigeria, Rwanda, South Africa, and Senegal—had ratified the protocol.[24]

The adoption of the protocol was the culmination of a long process. The OAU's adoption of the Protocol on the Rights and Welfare of the Child in 1990 first sparked interest among activists in promoting a protocol that would specifically refer to women's rights. The 1993 World Conference on Human Rights in Vienna, Austria, brought worldwide attention to women's human rights, placing pressure on African states to recognize and to protect women's rights. The process of drafting a protocol began in March 1995, when Women in Law and Development in Africa (WiLDAF) organized the seminar "The African Charter on Human and Peoples' Rights and the Human Rights of Women in Africa" in Lomé, Togo. Forty-four participants, representing seventeen countries, came together at the seminar to discuss the need to make the African Charter "more responsive" to women's rights.[25] After discussing various potential strategies, including an amendment to the African Charter, an optional protocol, and an additional protocol, participants decided to pursue an additional protocol.

The African Commission on Human and Peoples' Rights (ACHPR) presented this recommendation to the OAU at the Thirty-first Ordinary Session of the Assembly of Heads of State and Government in Addis Ababa, Ethiopia, in June 1995. The Assembly supported the recommendation and called on the ACHPR to produce a draft text.[26] The ACHPR appointed a working group of commissioners, NGO representatives, and other experts to begin drafting the document. This group met for the first time in January 1998 in Banjul, the Gambia. It came together two additional times—in Dakar, Senegal, in June 1999 and in Kigali, Rwanda, in October 1999—before completing a draft protocol. At its twenty-sixth session in Kigali, the ACHPR examined and adopted this draft protocol and passed it on to the OAU Commission.

The commission submitted the draft protocol to two meetings of experts in Addis Ababa: one in November 2001, and a second in March 2003.[27] At the ministerial meeting of March 27 and 28, 2003, ministers approved the draft protocol and passed it on to the Executive Council and finally to the AU Assembly. After eight years of deliberation, the AU Assembly adopted the protocol at the Maputo Summit in July 2003.

African women's organizations were active in the process from its inception to its adoption. They initiated the process of drafting an additional protocol, influenced the language and content of the document, kept the protocol on the OAU's and later the AU's agenda even as states' support for it waned, and placed pressure on states to adopt and ratify it. One important arm of these advocacy efforts was a series of meetings organized by women's networks "to discuss how best to act strategically as women in advancing gender mainstreaming within AU structures."[28] At these meetings and in the documents that came out of them, African women's networks advanced a number of specific recommendations on the draft protocol.

A pre-summit meeting in Durban, South Africa, in June 2002, for example, resulted in the Durban Declaration, which advanced four recommendations directly related to the draft protocol. Signatories called on the AU to take appropriate measures to ensure the effective participation of government experts—including women—in the Second Experts' Meeting on the Protocol. Second, they recommended that the AU take the necessary steps to ensure that appropriate ministers are able to participate effectively in the ministerial meeting that followed the experts' meeting. They also asked the AU to ensure that the protocol conformed to existing regional and international standards on women's human rights. Finally, they called for the "expedient adoption, ratification and enforcement of the Draft Protocol."[29] Signatories presented their recommendations at the First Ordinary Session of the Assembly of Heads of State and Governments in Durban.

Following the Durban Summit, NGOs continued to place pressure on the AU and individual states to adopt a protocol acceptable to activists. The organizations and networks that participated in the Durban meeting put together a proposal for implementing the Durban Declaration.

WiLDAF and the African Centre for Democracy and Human Rights Studies (ACDHRS) were the NGOs in charge of working on the "enactment,
enforcement and dissemination" of the draft protocol.[30] Strategies
included letter-writing campaigns, lobbying, organizing press conferences
and other forms of public outreach, and pursuing linkages with international organizations.[31]

Yet, despite the inauguration of the AU, the movement toward adopting
a protocol came to a standstill in 2002. The AU was forced to postpone
experts' and ministerial meetings twice due to a lack of a quorum, which
activists interpreted as evidence of states' weak commitment to women's
human rights. African women's networks forged links with international
human rights organizations. In January 2003, Equality Now, an international human rights organization with a regional office in Nairobi, Kenya,
organized a meeting of African women's rights activists to strategize on
how to overcome this impasse. Participants sought "to facilitate a collective review of the draft and coordinated advocacy for the adoption of a
text that would truly advance the rights of African women in international
law."[32] This effort led to the development of a consensus text. It also led to
revitalized efforts to lobby AU officials to schedule the second experts' and
ministerial meetings and to pressure representatives of national ministries
of justice and gender to attend the meetings. A sufficient number of representatives attended both March 2003 meetings, enabling the process to
move forward. In this case, international human rights organizations—
Equality Now and Amnesty International—reinforced regional women's
networks, placing additional pressure on the AU to move forward on the
protocol.

In April 2003, African women's networks met again and drafted "The
Dakar Strategy on Mainstreaming Gender and Women's Effective Participation in the African Union." This follow-up to the Durban Declaration
advanced two additional recommendations on the Draft Protocol on the
Rights of Women in Africa.[33] The Dakar Strategy called on the AU to
adopt the protocol and to establish a mechanism for ratification. It also
asked member states to consider withdrawing their reservations to the
draft text to strengthen the final document. These recommendations were
reiterated in the Maputo Declaration of July 2003, which came out of the
pre-summit meeting of women's organizations and networks.

The final protocol is the culmination of an eight-year process that
brought together state and societal actors. Its drafting illustrates an
increasingly open process that encouraged dialogue between government

representatives, AU officials, and NGOs and other nonstate actors. The women's organizations active in the process assert that they had a causal impact on the final document, arguing that the Protocol on the Rights of Women would not be as strong as it is today without the input of nongovernmental actors. Reviewing the process, a representative of Equality Now noted that the "concerted lobbying of African governments by nongovernmental organizations (NGOs) and networks all over Africa on a consensus text resulted in significant gains to the original draft."[34]

Following the adoption of the protocol, Sara Longwe, of the FEMNET, stated: "Congratulations to all the African women for the adoption, by the Maputo AU Summit, of the Protocol on Women's Rights to the African Charter on Human and People's Rights!!!!! Let us celebrate the Protocol and share the full text through our websites, newsletters, meetings, art— *and* vigorously and relentlessly agitate for the Protocol's ratification and implementation by every State. Power to the sisterhood!"[35] Similarly, the FAS Web site states that "FAS's advocacy programme resulted in . . . the adoption of the Protocol on the Rights of Women in Africa to the African Charter on Human and People's Rights."[36] African women's organizations have expressed a sense of ownership in the achievement.

The final document is impressive. As noted earlier, the protocol takes a number of pathbreaking steps in the protection of women's rights on the continent. It prohibits female genital cutting and other harmful practices, sets a minimum age of marriage at eighteen, and indicates that women have "the right to choose any method of contraception."[37] It is also the first international document to specify explicitly a woman's right to an abortion "in cases of sexual assault, rape, and incest, and where the continued pregnancy endangers the mental and physical health of the mother or the life of the mother or the foetus."[38] In addition, it explicitly endorses affirmative action to promote the equal representation of women in decision-making spheres.[39]

Considering the composition of the AU Assembly, its adoption of the protocol is significant. Commenting on the Protocol, L. Muthoni Wanyeki, FEMNET executive director, notes: "That it was passed, by what is essentially a bunch of older African men, whose commitment to those rights can only be called questionable, given what goes on in their own states, is nothing short of momentous."[40] Jakkie Cilliers, a representative of the South African–based Institute for Security Studies, similarly observed: "It is one of the most remarkable texts, I think. The text is very impressive. This will really be a gigantic step forward."[41] As these comments indicate, the AU, on its own, was not necessarily committed to advancing women's rights. The lobbying efforts of regional women's networks kept the protocol on the agenda during the long, eight-year process. Moreover, women's networks lobbied the AU and individual member states to ensure that the final document was strongly worded. Though the jury is still out on whether and when the document will enter into force and, perhaps more important, be enforced, it is an important achievement that at the very minimum provides activists with standards to which they can hold signatories accountable. The existence of new laws protecting women's human rights will not immediately or inevitably change behavior on the ground, but it does reinforce norms and set standards. Activists can use these standards to place pressure on national governments to eliminate discriminatory national laws, to establish gender quotas, and to protect the rights of women.

Since the adoption of the protocol, African women's networks have turned their attention to campaigns urging African states to ratify it. Ratification is significant because it is only after the protocol enters into force that states will be held accountable to their commitments. According to the protocol, state parties are required to submit periodic reports to the ACHPR on the steps taken to implement the protocol, to integrate its principles into their constitutions and other domestic legislation, and to eliminate discriminatory laws and practices. To pressure states to ratify the document, African women's networks have initiated an online petition campaign. They have also employed new strategies to encourage widespread participation in the campaign. Recognizing that Africans have greater access to mobile phones than to the Internet, African women's networks have initiated a phone campaign.[42] Citizens can sign a petition in support of the campaign urging African states to ratify the protocol by sending a text message from their mobile phones. This is just one example of the kinds of innovative strategies that regional women's networks are employing to advance their work.

The regional nature of the campaign was significant. As noted previously, the protocol addresses a number of culturally sensitive issues, including female genital cutting, abortion, and polygamy. These are the very kinds of issues that have generally posed problems for transnational activists. Indigenous supporters of these practices attack the legitimacy of activists by labeling them "Western," "foreign," or "feminist." The regional basis of the campaign helps to remove the sting from these critiques. Thus, the success of this initiative can be partially attributed to the fact that it was organized and led by African women's organizations and networks. African activists knew how to frame debates in ways that were palatable to grassroots populations. They discussed such practices as female genital cutting and polygamy without disparaging indigenous traditions and religious beliefs.

Another factor that contributed to the success of the campaign was the fluidity of the developing AU institutional structure. The fact that the AU was a new institution facilitated African women's networks lobbying efforts. Activists were able to push for a more substantial document given that the AU was looking for ways to differentiate itself from its predecessor. In addition, the AU, unlike the OAU, envisions itself as an organization that links both states and peoples across the continent. This focus on a more inclusive process has opened the way for joint civil society–state initiatives. Were these factors also influential in the gender parity campaign? The following section examines a second case study: African women's networks' lobbying for greater gender balance in AU institutions.

Gender Parity in AU Institutions

African women's networks have also successfully lobbied for greater gender equity in AU institutions. Specifically, their efforts helped to realize gender parity within the AU Commission. The ten-member commission is the secretariat of the AU, which runs the day-to-day affairs of the Union. Two commissioners are elected from each of five subregions (North, East, West, Central, and Southern). In 2002, women's organizations lobbied successfully for a gender parity provision that stipulates that one representative from each region must be a woman.[43] It was not, however, a foregone conclusion that this rhetorical commitment would be put into practice. Seeking to improve the regional representation of the organization, several AU representatives sought to decrease the number of women commissioners. Women, however, held their ground and were able to preserve parity in the commission (Tripp 2005).

Gender parity in the AU Commission officially moved from a rhetorical commitment to reality at the July 2003 African Union summit in Maputo, Mozambique, where the Assembly elected five female commissioners: Julia Dolly Joiner of Gambia (Political Affairs); Bience Philomina Gawanas of Namibia (Social Affairs); Saida Agrebi of Tunisia (Human Resources and Science and Technology); Elisabeth Tankeu of Cameroon

(Trade and Industry); and Rosebud Kurwijila of Tanzania (Rural Economy and Agriculture).[44] All these women are influential figures in their respective countries. Joiner, Gawanas, Kurwijila, and Tankeu have all served in high-level government posts, Joiner as head of the Gambian Civil Service, Gawanas as ombudswoman to the government of Namibia, Kurwijila as Tanzania's minister of agriculture, and Tankeu as Cameroon's minister of planning and territorial management. Gawanas and Kurwijila have also worked in universities. Gawanas was a lecturer in law at the University of Namibia, where she specialized in human rights and gender law, and Kurwijila lectured at the Sokoine University in Tanzania in the agriculture department. Agrebi heads the Tunisian Mother's Association.

Activists have drawn on gender equity norms embedded in a number of regional and international documents to legitimate their claims. The Kampala Action Plan, adopted at the 1993 Regional Conference on Peace and Development in Kampala, Uganda, for example, promotes women's political representation in all representative bodies (Tripp 2005). The Dakar and Beijing Platforms for Action both call for a minimum of 30 percent women in decision-making positions. As stated earlier, the 1997 SADC "Declaration on Gender and Development" calls for all SADC member states to ensure that at least 30 percent of the seats in national legislatures are held by women by 2005.

The AWCPD played a key role in ensuring that gender equity and mainstreaming issues were placed on the AU agenda from the very beginning (Tripp 2005). Activists reached out to male politicians, seeking the support of strategic allies throughout the transition process. In fact, a number of key male leaders expressed support for the gender parity proposal. In response to the AU's commitment to gender parity in the commission, Nigerian president Olusegun Obasanjo stated: "We are doing better than Beijing!"[45] A deputy minister noted at the 2003 Maputo Summit: "When we move, we move."[46] Similarly, a journalist commenting on these developments wrote: "African leaders, determined to put their critics to shame, have also scored a world-first regarding gender representation in the AU. For, nowhere else in the world—whether at the national, continental, or even global level—has such a decision been taken, that the top echelons of an inter-governmental organisation shall have a 50% representation of women and men."[47]

One reason for the dramatic increase in gender representation in the AU is that compared with the European Union or the United Nations, it is a relatively weak institution. In general, the strength of an institution is inversely related to gender representation, that is, the more powerful the institution, the fewer the women. Another factor contributing to the AU's commitment to gender equity is linked to the institution's identity. Africa is frequently portrayed as backward and as lagging behind other world regions. By taking the lead on gender equity, the AU gains symbolic political capital. It is able to portray itself as a world leader, more advanced than even Europe.

As in the case of the Protocol on the Rights of Women in Africa, lobbying efforts of African women's organizations contributed to this outcome. African women's networks addressed the issue of women's participation in AU decision-making organs at the series of workshops. The recommendations, made by key regional, subregional, and national organizations at the Durban, Dakar, and Maputo summits, influenced AU policy.

On the issue of women's participation in the structures of the AU, the Durban Declaration offered a vague recommendation calling on the AU to "guarantee a gender balance in all the organs of the African Union within a reasonable timeframe."[48] By the time African women's networks signed the Dakar Strategy in April 2003, they devoted an entire section to the participation of African women in the organs of the AU. Recommendations were far more specific, calling for at least two female representatives in each country's five-member delegation, the effective participation of women in the Peace and Security Council's Panel of the Wise, gender parity in the Economic, Social and Cultural Council (ECOSOCC), and the establishment of the Specialized Technical Committee on Gender.[49] The Maputo Declaration advanced similar recommendations relating to women's participation in the AU.

Activists encountered resistance from some male politicians. At the July 2003 Maputo Summit, for example, a "male lobby" attempted to change the agreement made at the Durban Summit that required that five out of the ten AU commissioners be women.[50] Still, the lobby failed to overturn to the gender equity provision. The South African foreign minister, Nkosazana Dlamini-Zuma, "pushed hard to keep the principle."[51] Key political supporters fought to maintain the gender equity provision in the lead-up to the 2003 Maputo Summit, ensuring that gender representation was not sacrificed in favor of greater regional representativeness. Equally important to the success of the initiative were lobbying efforts organized by regional women's organizations. Explaining the positive outcome of lobbying efforts, one activist wrote: "As in any key milestone to engender African institutions and processes, a powerful lobby, structured links, and critical interventions have been at play for these achievements to be realized."[52] Given that men dominate both the Executive Council and the Assembly, women's organizations succeeded in this campaign because they formed strategic linkages with influential politicians.

Despite this positive outcome, activists are quick to point out that the commission is just one of several AU institutions, and that women remain severely underrepresented in many areas. There are no female representatives in the Assembly. Moreover, there are only a handful of female foreign affairs ministers; thus, women have only a nominal presence on the Executive Council.[53] Women's activists view gender parity in the commission as a beginning rather than an end and are continuing to advocate for gender balance in *all* AU institutions.

The very same networks that advocated for gender parity in the AU Commission have now turned their focus to the Pan-African Parliament. Citing the quota's failure to meet the minimum 30 percent women in decision-making laid out in the Dakar and Beijing Platforms for Action, they are calling for 50 percent women PAP representatives and lobbying for an amendment to the PAP Protocol that stipulates that at least two out of each country's five delegates be women. Currently, the protocol establishing the Pan-African Parliament stipulates that just one out of each state's five-member delegation (i.e., 20 percent) must be a woman.[54] In the interim period, governments select PAP delegates from members of national parliaments. Eventually PAP delegates are to be directly elected by African citizens. In addition to targeting the AU, activists have also focused their attention on individual member states. They have taken a multilevel approach and are pressuring states to uphold their regional and international commitments to increasing women's participation in decision-making spheres. Members of the SADC are especially vulnerable to this kind of pressure, since they have committed to achieve a minimum of 30 percent women in decision-making positions by 2005. PAP's current gender requirement (one out of five, or 20 percent) falls below this threshold. South Africa has taken the lead in this area; its National Assembly resolved to send three women to the PAP, far surpassing SADC's 30 percent target.[55] Non-SADC countries are also vulnerable to this kind of pressure, since the vast majority have signed the Dakar and Beijing Platforms for Action, both of which identify women's participation in decision making as a critical area. Margaret Keck and Kathryn Sikkink's (1998) boomerang model emphasizes how transnational activism influences domestic policy. Activists draw on transnational human rights and gender equity norms to change domestic laws and practices. This case study demonstrates that the boomerang model can operate in complex ways. It does not always operate from a higher (transnational) level to a lower (domestic) level of activism. It can also originate at a lower (subregional) level and move to a higher (regional) level. Activists from SADC countries, for example, have pressured their states to honor the 30 percent gender quota at the AU level by appointing at least two women to their respective PAP delegations.

As in the case of the Protocol on the Rights of Women, advocacy organizations express a sense of ownership over the achievement. The gender parity provision was not a top-down initiative imposed by AU officials. Instead, it was the result of an intense lobbying campaign organized by national, subregional, and regional women's networks. It reflects the demands of women's groups on the ground. In a January 2004 document, Femmes Africa Solidarité, for example, indicates that one of its primary achievements in the past year was that "FAS advocacy resulted in gender parity in the African Union, with the election of five women commissioners out of ten in July 2003."[56]

Regional women's networks achieved gender parity in the AU Commission, yet they continue to fight for gender equity in other AU institutions. The Assembly and the Executive Council are relatively impervious to gender quotas. While gender quotas have been critiqued for producing "second-class" or tokenized participation, they remain one of the most effective means of quickly increasing women's participation in decision-making spheres.

As in the case of the Protocol on the Rights of Women, African women's networks mobilized to influence AU policies. In this case, the fact that the OAU was in the process of becoming the AU was particularly important. The development of a new institution, with new rules and procedures, gave women's organizations a crucial opening. It allowed them to shape the development of a new institution rather than engage in the long process of changing existing policies. Calls for gender balance are controversial in that they directly threaten the position of men, who, until now, have dominated all AU bodies. Gender equity, however, is less culturally sensitive than female genital cutting or polygamy. In fact, the regional campaign for gender balance in the AU drew from global initiatives, like the 50/50 by 2005: Get the Balance Right campaign launched in New York in June 2000. The regional nature of the campaign was important because the target of the campaign was a regional institution, yet the campaign also drew legitimacy and strength from global initiatives.

Conclusions

The two case studies demonstrate that African women's networks had a causal impact on AU policy. They shaped the nature of the Protocol on the Rights of Women and secured a commitment to gender equity in the AU Commission. They achieved these pathbreaking commitments by drawing on established gender norms, mobilizing throughout the OAU/AU transition process, and employing a two-prong approach of lobbying both the AU and individual member states. To attain these commitments, African women's networks formed critical alliances with high-level politicians sympathetic to their cause and collaborated with international women's organizations and human rights groups. The regional nature of the campaign was critical, particularly in the case of the Protocol on the Rights of Women, which addressed a number of highly sensitive issues. The fact that these campaigns occurred during a transition from the OAU to the AU provided greater leverage for activists, but regional activism can be successful in a more fixed institutional environment as well.

The chapter has emphasized that transnational activism is not always international in scope. It occurs at the subregional, regional, and international levels. The subregional and regional arenas are important middle rungs linking the local and the global. The classic boomerang model emphasizes how activists can draw on international norms to change domestic policy and practices. This chapter demonstrates that activists can call on subregional commitments (e.g., SADC's gender quota) to influence regional policies (e.g., AU quotas). The various levels of transnational activism interrelate in complex ways

The selected case—African women's networks' lobbying of the African Union—may be particularly well suited to regionally organized campaigns; nevertheless, the lessons drawn from the specific case studies are relevant to other kinds of campaigns. In addition to focusing specifically on regional issues, these networks can mobilize to influence national, subregional, and international policies. Regional networks facilitated African women's organizations' efforts to influence which issues got on the international agenda. At Beijing, African women's networks mobilized to ensure that their issues and concerns were on the agenda. Networks can also mobilize to effect change in a particular state. Regional networks, for example, have organized to overturn the conviction of Amina Lawal, who was convicted of adultery and sentenced to stoning in northern Nigeria. In short, regional networking is not limited to regional issues. Networks can mobilize to shape policy in a variety of arenas.

Regional networks span state boundaries, exist beyond the reach of any single government, and call upon the experiences of activists in various domestic contexts. At the same time, they are rooted in the African context, providing legitimacy and hindering critics' ability to label activists "Western" or "foreign." In short, regional networks occupy an important middle rung between the local and the global. They are well placed to avoid both the Scylla of localism and the Charybdis of international domination.

NOTES

1. Here, "regional" refers to the entire African continent, and "subregional" refers to regions within Africa, e.g., East, West, North, and Southern Africa.

2. Participants hailed from Togo, Ghana, Ivory Coast, Nigeria, Congo-Brazzaville, Dahomey, Belgian Congo, Guinea, Upper Volta, and Cameroon. National Catholic Welfare Conference, Office for UN Affairs, ed., *African Women Speak: Regional Seminar of World Union of Catholic Women's Organizations, Lomé, Togo, July 1958* (New York: World Horizon Reports, 1960).

3. See ST/TAO/HR/9, United Nations, "1960 Seminar on Participation of Women in Public Life, Addis Ababa, 12 to 23 December" (New York: United Nations, 1961), 1.

4. The thirty-one countries and territories include Basutoland, Bechuanaland, and Swaziland, Cameroons, Republic of Cameroun, Comoros, Congo (Brazzaville), Ethiopia, Federation of Rhodesia and Nyasaland, Federation of Nigeria, Gabon, Gambia, Ghana, Ivory Coast, Kenya, Liberia, Madagascar, Mali, Islamic Republic of Mauritania, Mauritius and Dependencies, Morocco, Mozambique, Niger, Seychelles, Sierra Leone, Sudan, Tanganyika, Togo, Tunisia, Uganda, United Arab Republic, Upper Volta, and Zanzibar.

5. A list of the years in which regional organizations and networks were founded indicates that this was a particularly fecund period for the establishment of such institutions: ABANTU for Development (1991); the African Centre for Constructive Resolution of Disputes (ACCORD) (1992); the African Leadership Forum (ALF) (1988); the African Women's Development and Communication Network (FEMNET) (1988); Akina Mama wa Afrika (1985); the African regional office of Equality Now (1992); the Federation of African Women in Education (FAWE) (1992); Femmes Africa Solidarité (1996); the Forum for Community Development (FDC) (1990); and Women in Law and Development in Africa

(WiLDAF) (1990). All these organizations have been active in recent regional initiatives.

6. Femmes Africa Solidarité, a regional women's organization created in 1996, chose to locate its headquarters in Geneva, Switzerland, for strategic reasons. Its Web site states: "FAS established its Secretariat in Geneva in order to facilitate its efforts in resource mobilization and to maximize the visibility of African women's initiatives at the international level. See Femmes Africa Solidarité, http://www.fas-ngo.org/en/presentation/index.htm.

7. See Article 3 of the Constitutive Act of the African Union, http://www .au2002.gov.za/docs/key_oau/au_act.htm, accessed September 14, 2004.

8. European Commission, http://europa.eu.int/comm/commission_barroso/ index_en.htm, accessed December 6, 2004.

9. See Protocol to the African Charter on Human and Peoples' Rights on the Rights of Women in Africa, http://www.achpr.org/english/_info/women_en.html, accessed on September 14, 2004.

10. See Solemn Declaration on Gender Equality in Africa, http://www.africa-union.org/AU%20summit%202004/Assm/Assembly%20Declaration%20_III_%2 0final.pdf, accessed on September 14, 2004.

11. See Organization of the African Unity, Constitutive Act of the African Union, July 2000. The OAU adopted the Constitutive Act at the Thirty-sixth Ordinary Session of Heads of State and Government in Lomé, Togo on July 11, 2000. It entered into force on May 26, 2001.

12. Nearly all North and sub-Saharan African states are members of the AU. A notable exception is Morocco, which withdrew from the OAU in 1984 when OAU admitted the Saharawi Arab Democratic Republic.

13. See African Union, "African Union in a Nutshell," http://www.africa-union.org/home/Welcome.htm.

14. Mary Wandia, "African Union and NEPAD: Briefing Paper on the Challenges and Opportunities for African Women," African Women's Development Fund Briefing Paper, http://awdf.org/lib/pdf/femnetpaper.pdf, 1.

15. EX/CL/Draft/Rpt(III), Executive Council, Draft Report of the Third Ordinary Session of the Executive Council, Maputo, Mozambique, July 6–8, 2003, http://www.au2003.gov.mz/maputodocs/ecrep.pdf.

16. See CM/Rpt (LXXIII), Council of Ministers, Seventy-third Ordinary Session/Eight Ordinary Session of the African Economic Community, February 24–26, 2001, Tripoli, Libya, Decision on Women and Gender.

17. Femmes Africa Solidarité, Draft Project Proposal: Mainstreaming Gender in the African Union, 3.

18. Organizations participating in the campaign include Abantu for Development, African Centre for Constructive Resolution of Disputes (ACCORD), the African Centre for Democracy and Human Rights Studies (ACDHRS), the African

Leadership Forum (ALF), African Women's Development and Communication Network (FEMNET), Akina Mama wa Afrika, Equality Now, the Federation of African Women in Education (FAWE), Femme Africa Solidarité (FAS), the Forum for Community Development (FDC), and Women in Law and Development in Africa (WiLDAF).

19. *Femmes Africa Solidarité,* "Historical Move towards Gender Equality in Africa," July 15, 2002, http://www.womenwagingpeace.net/content/articles/0230a .html.

20. The documents came out of three meetings: "Mainstreaming African Women's Vision and Effective Participation in the African Union" held in Durban, South Africa, from June 28 to 30, 2002; "Mainstreaming Gender and Women's Effective Participation in the African Union," held in Dakar, Senegal, from April 24 to 26; and the "Women's Pre-Summit Meeting on Gender Mainstreaming and the Effective Participation of Women in the African Union, held in Maputo, Mozambique, from June 23 to 24, 2003 respectively.

21. Signatories to the Durban Declaration on Mainstreaming Gender and Women's Effective Participation in the African Union include the African Centre for Constructive Resolution of Disputes (ACCORD); African Centre for Democracy and Human Rights Studies (ACDHRS); African Commission on Human and Peoples' Rights (ACHPR); Africa Leadership Forum (ALF); African Women's Committee on Peace and Development (AWCPD); African Women's Development and Communication Network (FEMNET); Commission on Gender Equality—South Africa (CGE); Comité National Femmes et Developpement—DRC (CONAFED); Femmes Africa Solidarité (FAS); OAU Women, Gender and Development Division; and Women in Law and Development in Africa (WiLDAF). Signatories to the Dakar Strategy on Mainstreaming Gender and Women's Effective Participation in the African Union include ABANTU for Development; ACCORD; ACDHRS; ALF; AWCPD; FEMNET; Equality Now-Africa Office; FAS; FCD; International Alert; SAFER Africa; and WiLDAF. Signatories to the Maputo Declaration on Gender Mainstreaming and the Effective Participation of Women in the African Union include ABANTU; African Gender Institute, University of Cape Town; ACCORD; African Union Women; Gender and Development Directorate; AWCPD; FEMNET; Akina Mana wa Afrika; Associacao das Mulhers Empresarias; Associacaon das Mulhers Juristas de Mozambique; Association Nationale de Soutien au Enfants em Difficulte et em Institution (ANSEDI); Association Tunisienne des Meres; Center for Human Rights, University of Pretoria; Center for Reproductive Rights; Commissao African dos Direitos Humnos e dos Povos; Commission on Gender Equality South Africa; Development Bank of South Africa; Economic Commission of Africa; African Center for Gender and Development; Embassy of Finland, Maputo; Equality Now Africa Regional Office; FAS; Forum do ONG Femininas de Norte Provincia da Zambezia; FAWE; Forum Mulher; Fundacao

para Desenvolvimento da Communidade (FDC); Gabinete Juridico da Mulher Pemba, Mozambique; Ministerio de Coordinacao da Accao Social, Mozambique; Ministerio de Saude, Mozambique; Modeste, Societe Civile du Congo DRC et OPDAL; Muleidi, Office for the Status of Women, Northern Cape; RSA; PACFA; SADC Gender Unit; SADC Parliamentarians; South African High Commission; Southern African Research and Documentation Centre (SARDC); UNDP; UNFPA; UNHCR; Uniao Geral das Cooperatives (UGC); WLSA Mozambique; WWGG; Women and Law in Southern Africa (WiLSA); Women's Caucus Assembleia da Republica da Mozambique; and WiLDAF.

22. Durban Declaration on Mainstreaming Gender and Women's Effective Participation in the African Union, http://www.africaneducationdecade.org/pages/Durban%20Declaration%20.htm.

23. Foundation for Community Development, Report on the Proceedings, http://www.fdc.org.mz/auwps/docs.

24. See African Union, "List of Countries which have Signed, Ratified/Acceded to the Protocol to the African Charter on Human and People's Rights on the Rights of Women in Africa, http://www.africa-union.org/Official_documents/Treaties_%20Conventions_%20Protocols/List/Protocol%20on%20the%20Rights%20of%20Women.pdf, Accessed August 9, 2005.

25. WiLDAF, "The African Charter on Human and Peoples' Rights and the Additional Protocol on Women's Rights," WiLDAF News http://site.mweb.co.zw/wildaf/news5.html.

26. See Resolution AHG/Res240(XXXI). At the Thirty-fourth Ordinary Session of the Assembly of Heads of State in Government in Ouagadougou, Burkina Faso, in June 1998, the Assembly called on the commission to complete a draft protocol. See Decision AHG/Dec.126(XXIV).

27. The meetings brought together representatives from the ACHPR, regional NGOs, and international observers. See "The African Charter on Human and Peoples' Rights and the Additional Protocol on Women's Rights," WiLDAF News, http://sitemweb.co/zw/wildaf/news5.html.

28. Foundation for Community Development, Aide Memoire, http://www.fdc.org.mz/aups/docs/aide_mem.htm.

29. Durban Declaration, http://www.africaneducationdecade.org/pages/Durban%20Declation%20.htm.

30. Nepad-Forum, Follow-up to Durban Consultation, http://www.lists.kabissa.org/archives/nepad-forum/msg00055.html.

31. Femmes Africa Solidarité, Draft Project Proposal: Mainstreaming Gender in the African Union, 5.

32. Equality Now, "African Union Adopts Protocol on the Rights of African Women: Right to Abortion Articulated for the First Time in International Law," July 14, 2003, http://www.hrea.org/lists/women-rights/markup/msg00205.html.

33. Dakar Strategy, http://www.wildaf-ao.org.

34. Equality Now, "African Union Adopts Protocol on the Rights of African Women: Right to Abortion Articulated for the First Time in International Law," July 14, 2003, http://www.hrea.org/lists/women-rights/markup/msg00205.html.

35. Nepad-Forum, July 17, 2003, http://www.lists.kabissa.org/archives/nepad-forum/msg00070.html.

36. Femmes Africa Solidarité, http://www.fasngo.org/en/presentation/index.htm.

37. See Protocol to the African Charter on Human and Peoples' Rights on the Rights of Women in Africa, Articles 5, 6, and 14, respectively, http://www.achpr .org/Protocol_Women-_Maputo_final03.pdf.

38. Protocol to the African Charter on Human and Peoples' Rights on the Rights of Women in Africa, Article 14, section 2, paragraph c.

39. Protocol to the African Charter on Human and Peoples' Rights on the Rights of Women in Africa, Article 9.

40. L. Muthoni Wanyeki, "Ssssh . . . African Women Have Human Rights," Global News Wire—Asia Africa Intelligence Wire, July 21, 2003.

41. Fienie Grobler, "Women Challenge African Traditions at AU summit," July 8, 2003.

42. See "Africa Mobile Phone Users Rally for Women's Rights," *Pambazuka.*

43. Article 6 of the Statutes, Rule 39 of the Rules of Procedure of the Assembly.

44. Men head the remaining commissions: Peace and Security, Infrastructure and Energy, and Economic. Men also serve as the chairperson and deputy chairperson.

45. Femmes Africa Solidarité, "Historical Move towards Gender Equality in Africa," July 15, 2002, http://www.womenwagingpeace.net/content/articles/0230a .html.

46. Farah Khan, "Gender Dinosaurs at AU Conference," Inter Press Service News Agency, July 9, 2003.

47. Tom Mbakwe, "Good News for All Women of Africa," *New African,* London, September 2002.

48. Durban Declaration, http://www.africaneducationdecade.org/pages/Durban%20Delcaration%20.htm.

49. Dakar Strategy, www.wildaf-ao.org.

50. Farah Khan, "Gender Dinosaurs at AU Conference," Inter Press Service News Agency, July 9, 2003.

51. Ibid.

52. Pamela Mhlanga, "Gender Parity in Decision-Making—Are African Institutions Coming of Age?" *The GAD Exchange: A Gender and Development Newsletter for Southern Africa,* 30, August–October 2003, http://www.sardc.net/Widsaa/Gad/ Iss30/genderparity.htm.

53. Baleka Mbete, "The Pan-African Parliament: An Opportunity for African

Women" (paper presented at the Regional Strategy Meeting on Women's Political Participation and Gender Mainstreaming in AU and NEPAD, Nairobi, October 27–31, 2003), 14.

54. Women's networks have already taken up this issue. Baleka Mbete, in her discussion of the Pan-African Parliament, argues that women's organizations in SADC countries should invoke SADC's Declaration on Gender Equality, which commits signatories to a target of 30 percent women in decision-making structures, and push for at least two women on each delegation. She also notes that the South African National Assembly adopted a resolution to include three women on its PAP delegation. Women in other states can lobby for similar resolutions. See Mbete, "The Pan-African Parliament," 14–15.

55. Ibid., 15.

56. Femmes Africa Solidarité, Aide Memoire Gender, Peace and Development Centre Review Meeting, January 28, 2004, 2.

Bibliography

African Union Commission. 2004. "The Road to Gender Equality in Africa: An Overview." Addis Ababa.

Alvarez, Sonia E. 2000. "Translating the Global Effects of Transnational Organizing on Local Feminist Discourses and Practices in Latin America." *Meridians: Feminism, Race, Transnationalism* 1, no. 1: 29–67.

Alvarez, Sonia, Elisabeth Jay Friedman, Ericka Beckman, Maylei Blackwell, Norma Stoltz Chinchilla, Nathalie Lebon, Marysa Navarro, and Marcela Rios Tobar. 2003. "Encountering Latin American and Caribbean Feminisms." *Signs: Journal of Women in Culture and Society* 28:537–579.

Basu, Amrita. 2000. "Globalization of the Local/Localization of the Global: Mapping Transnational Women's Movements." *Meridians: Feminism, Race, Transnationalism* 1, no. 1: 68–84.

Britton, Hannah E. 2002. "Coalition Building, Election Rules, and Party Politics: South African Women's Path to Parliament." *Africa Today* 49, no. 4: 33–67.

Cilliers, Jackie. 2003. "From Durban to Maputo: A Review of 2003 Summit of the African Union." Institute for Security Studies, ISS Paper 76.

"Directory of Information Centres." 1999. *Women's Information Services and Networks: A Global Source Book*, 58–71. Amsterdam: Royal Tropical Institute.

Foster, Joana, ed. 1995. "The Power of Women: A Report of WiLDAF's Preparation for and Participation in the 4th World Conference on Women." Harare, Zimbabwe: WiLDAF.

Githaiga, Grace. 2003. "Report: Regional Strategy Meeting on Women's Political

Participation and Gender Mainstreaming in the African Union and Its Specialized Mechanisms." Nairobi, October.

Goetz, Anne Marie, and Shireen Hassim, eds. 2003. *No Shortcuts to Power: African Women in Politics and Policymaking.* London: Zed Books.

Hodgson, Dorothy L. 2003. "Women's Rights as Human Rights: Women in Law and Development in Africa (WiLDAF)." *Africa Today* 49, no. 2: 3–26.

Keck, Margaret, and Kathryn Sikkink. 1998. *Activists beyond Borders: Advocacy Networks in International Politics.* Ithaca, N.Y.: Cornell University Press.

Maboreke, Mary. 2003. "The Quota System within the African Union." Paper presented at the International Institute for Democracy and Electoral Assistance (IDEA)/Electoral Institute of Southern Africa (EISA)/Southern African Development Community (SADC) Parliamentary Forum Conference, The Implementation of Quotas: African Experiences, Pretoria, November 11–12.

Mbete, Baleka. 2003. "The Pan-African Parliament: An Opportunity for African Women." Paper presented at the Regional Strategy Meeting on Women's Political Participation and Gender Mainstreaming in AU and NEPAD. Nairobi, October 27–31.

National Catholic Welfare Conference, Office for UN Affairs, ed. 1960. *African Women Speak: Regional Seminar of World Union of Catholic Women's Organizations, Lomé, Togo, July 1958.* New York: World Horizon Reports.

Nzomo, Maria. 2003. "From OAU to AU and NEPAD: Regional Integration Processes in Africa and African Women." Keynote address presented at the Regional Strategy Meeting on Women's Political Participation and Gender Mainstreaming in AU and NEPAD. Nairobi, October 27–31.

Radloff, Jennifer. 1999. "Celebrating the Power, Diversity, and Strength of African Women's Networks." In Sarah Cummings, Henk van Dam, and Minke Valk, eds., *Women's Information Services and Networks: A Global Sourcebook,* 31–40. Amsterdam: Royal Tropical Institute.

Seidman, Gay. 2001. "'Strategic' Challenges to Gender Inequality: The South African Gender Commission." *Ethnography* 2:219–241.

Snyder, Margaret C., and Mary Tadesse. 1995. *African Women and Development: A History.* London: Zed Books.

Tripp, Aili Mari. 2004. "The Changing Face of Africa's Legislatures: Women and Quotas." In Julie Ballington, ed., *The Implementation of Quotas: African Experiences,* 72–77. Stockholm: International Institute for Democracy and Electoral Assistance, in collaboration with the Electoral Institute of Southern Africa and the Southern African Development Community Parliamentary Forum.

———. 2005. "Regional Networking as Transnational Feminism: African Experiences." *Feminist Africa,* no. 4. Available at www.feministafrica.org/2level/html.

Valk, Minke, Henk van Dam, and Sarah Cummings. 1999. "Women's Information Centres and Networks: A Global Perspective." In Sarah Cummings, Henk van

Dam, and Minke Valk, eds., *Women's Information Services and Networks: A Global Sourcebook,* 21–29. Amsterdam: Royal Tropical Institute.

Wandia, Mary. 2003. "African Union and NEPAD: Briefing Paper on the Challenges and Opportunities for African Women." African Women's Development Fund Briefing Paper, http://awdf.org/lib/pdf/femnetpaper.pdf.

Zwingel, Susanne. 2004. "Making Women Matter: Global Norms and Local Struggles on Gender Equality." Unpublished paper.

9

Measuring Feminist Mobilization

Cross-National Convergences and Transnational Networks in Western Europe

Dorothy E. McBride and Amy G. Mazur

The recent shift of feminist activism to the transnational arena challenges researchers to measure the complexities of feminist politics at local, national, and international levels of mobilization across diverse cultural settings. In this chapter, we respond to this challenge. We offer a conceptual approach grounded in comparative research on women's movements, social movements, and feminism to assess feminist mobilization in Western Europe. This approach is intended to yield valid and reliable comparative findings. Although a test of the proposed measure could eventually be made in any setting, this chapter uses qualitative data from a cross-national study of women's movements and women's policy offices conducted by the Research Network on Gender Politics and the State (RNGS).[1] With these findings, we offer propositions about feminist mobilization and transnational advocacy networks in Western Europe. Thus, in addition to proposing a more meaningful way of studying feminist action, this chapter contributes to discussions of whether there are regional patterns in feminist mobilization—a by-product, some argue, of the globalization of feminism—and whether transnational advocacy networks have an impact on the unfolding of feminist mobilization within nation-states.

The chapter consists of two sections. The first describes the operational definition of *feminist mobilization* based on comparative women's movement scholarship and the research imperatives of the RNGS project. The components of the concept are *forms* of activism, feminist *discourse and framing*, and state-based women's policy *agencies.* The second section provides a preliminary assessment of the hypothesis of regional convergence of feminist mobilization across Western European countries. This assessment examines a selection of thirty-four policy debates from the RNGS study, in Austria, Belgium, France, Germany, Great Britain, the Netherlands, and Sweden, across three different issues—abortion, prostitution, and political representation. We find that although there are some similarities in the *forms* of activism among the seven countries, there is a significant divergence of feminist *frames* advanced by women's policy agencies (WPAs) and women's movement actors (WMAs) across the three policy areas. In addition, there appears to be no relation between the presence of transnational advocacy networks and cross-national patterns in feminist mobilization. Finally, there is little evidence of a trend toward cross-national convergence of feminist activism since the 1970s. These preliminary findings suggest that, at least for Western Europe, the type of policy issue may matter more than regional dynamics in understanding feminist mobilization in the context of an increasingly multilevel transnational world. In the conclusion we suggest some explanations for these preliminary findings.

Feminist Mobilization inside and outside of the State

The concept of feminist mobilization includes the full range of individual, formal, and informal women's movement actors that are agents for mobilization outside of the state, state agencies that have been explicitly established to promote women's rights, and the feminist frames that are forwarded by these state-based and society-based actors. Given the developments in feminist activism that brings together state and nonstate activities, it is only through a definition that incorporates different forms of women's movement actors, women's policy agencies, and their use of feminist discourse that researchers can systematically study feminist mobilization.

In addition, feminist mobilization is more a *construct* than a single concept. As such, the research definition comprises several conceptual components, each of which is rigorously defined and related to all the other components. We begin with the assumption that feminist movements are subsets of women's movements; all feminists are part of the women's movement, but not all women's movements are feminist. There is some disagreement in the literature about this point. Some use the terms interchangeably, referring to all women's movements as feminist (Bull, Diamond, and Marsh 2000; Ferree and Hess 2000; Mansbridge 1996; Weldon 2002; Mazur 2002; Kaplan 1992; Lovenduski 1987; Katzenstein and Mueller 1987). Others see the two as different based on their aims. For Beckwith (2000), for example, women's movement aims involve women and women's issues but differ from feminist movements in that they do not necessarily involve challenges to patriarchy. Agreeing with Beckwith and with Ferree and Mueller (2004), the RNGS researchers identify women's movements and feminist movements in terms of the ideas they present.

Comparative Criteria

Mapping this multidimensional notion of feminist mobilization requires comparative research involving researchers working in different cultural and scientific traditions. This raises the problem of comparable nominal and operational definitions. There are two choices. First, researchers can agree to accept each author's use of key terms in their research. Using this approach, for example, the actual ideas labeled feminist will be those the researcher identifies as feminist in each study. This avoids the imposition of a single view of feminism, developed in one context, on other cultures; the disadvantage, however, is that it makes it impossible to come to empirically verified conclusions, limiting theory-building. The second choice is to develop a nominal and operational definition to guide data collection and to classify and compare the findings of the researchers. The advantage with this option is that it permits cross-national analysis; the disadvantage is that all researchers must agree and understand the concept (which can be difficult to achieve), and there is little guidance from the literature. We have selected the second option, which involves answering these controversial questions: What, empirically, are women's movements? Are all women's movements feminist? If not, what is the difference? Are women's policy agencies different from women's movements?

To serve the requirements of the comparative method, where cases are used to sort through rival explanations (Collier 1993; Ragin 1987), working research definitions of key concepts must meet the following criteria: (1) They must include both nominal and operational elements, directing the researcher to observations that distinguish phenomena that represent the concept from those that do not. The nominal definition is the key to the operational definition. The conceptual leap from words to operations, however, should be minimal. (2) The observations that are produced must be *valid*, that is, coincide with experienced scholars' understanding of the concept (Kaplan 1992). (3) The operationalizations and measurements must also be *reliable*, applied in similar ways with similar results by a variety of researchers. To be useful for cross-national research, both nominal and operational definitions must direct researchers to pertinent observations in different national contexts. At the same time, the problem of conceptual stretching must be reduced, while recognizing the need to find a balance between the flexibility of the definition and the potential range of cases (Sartori 1970; Collier and Mahon 1993). This is a midrange theory-building effort; thus we set criteria for a study of most similar cases, where commonalities are used as controls to explain for variation, rather than a most different research design (Collier 1993). (4) For purposes of longitudinal analysis, the definition must take into account changes in phenomena of interest over time, a key aspect of this study's operational definition of feminist mobilization.

In the following section we lay out the conceptual path to conducting comparative research on feminist mobilization. First, we describe women's movements as actors that present a particular discourse developed by women. Second, we set out the elements that distinguish women's movement discourse and then show how feminist discourse builds on this base. The final component of feminist mobilization involves the women's policy agencies and their relation to movement activism.

Women's Movements

The RNGS research definition of women's movements has two components: a particular discourse and forms of activism of women who articulate this discourse in public life. In this chapter, as in the project, the focus of research is these women's movement actors and their discourse—terms that are empirically grounded—rather than women's movements as collective entities. In this section we describe the derivation of this approach in terms of women's movement and social movement literature.

There is no consensus about the definition of women's movements for comparative purposes (Beckwith 2000; Molyneux 1998). And, although a group of social movement scholars encourage more comparative studies (e.g., McAdam, McCarthy, and Zald 1996; Meyer, Whittier, and Robnett 2002), they have yet to offer a research definition that meets the four criteria for comparative study (Stetson and Mazur 2003). To understand the problem and move forward, it has been necessary to examine the basic assumptions underlying definitions of movements encountered in the literature. Such definitional assumptions are revealed in the *definiens*—the expression that immediately follows the *definiendum*—"the women's/social movement is. . . ." Many definitions in the literature are based on the assumption that a social movement fundamentally is a specific form of collective behavior—either institutions, ordinary people, groups, social networks, or nonelites—and that women's movements are subcategories of social movements. Such explicit definitions offer some ease in meeting the criterion of reliability due to the ease of operationalization, but they lack validity: most scholars agree that social movements and women's movements comprise more than one form or set of actors.

Other scholars conceptualize movements as processes and interactions. For example, Whittier (2002) describes movements as "shifting clusters of organizations networks, communities and activist individuals" (289), as well as a "vast array of actions undertaken by individuals and small groups in everyday life" (291). Adding such complexity to the nominal definition increases validity yet compounds the difficulties in finding a reliable operational definition.

Still another approach is to focus on ideas as central to the identity and identification of movements. Mansbridge's 1996 description is illustrative:

> The entity—"women's movement" . . . is neither an aggregation of organizations nor an aggregation of individual members but a discourse. It is a set of changing, contested aspirations and understandings that provide conscious goals, cognitive backing, and emotional support for each individual's evolving feminist identity. . . . The "movement" is made up of women figuring out and telling one another what they think makes sense, and what they think can explain and help crack the gender domination that they feel and are beginning to understand. (27–28)

While many scholars point to the content of ideas as essential to defining a movement, the Mansbridge approach—seeing the movement only as a discourse—has neither validity nor reliability.

This assessment of the usefulness of definitions from the social movement and women's movement literature led RNGS researchers to unpack the concept into its component parts. This deconstruction produced workable definitions that meet the research definition criteria and form the basis for the study of feminist mobilization. Using Mansbridge, we began with the assumption that the movement is first defined by its ideas—the discourse developed by women. The second component incorporates those actors who develop and articulate the discourse. Jenson (1996) offers some insight about the relation between actors and ideas in the movement, especially in public life. She defines politics as comprising "actors' efforts to carve out a constituency for themselves by mobilizing support for their preferred formulation of their own collective identity and for the enumeration of their interests, which follows from that collective identity" (74). For Jenson, politics entails two kinds of representation: *of the self as a collective identity* and *of interests:*

> Representation of self—that is, a collective identity—involves, among other things, naming oneself since only an actor with a name is recognizable to others. A second type, familiar from the language of liberal democracy, is the representation of interests—a process which, since the emergence of the modern state, has included presentation to the state through more or less stable organizations. (74)

Jenson's conceptual map to the women's movement in France distinguishes between the process of establishing discourses about collective identities and their interests from the actors who present this discourse in public life. Rochon (1998) has a similar approach, by situating social movements in the context of *critical communities*—thinkers who develop new values:

> Movement leaders take an active role in choosing, bundling together, and shaping the ideas of one or more critical communities in such a way as to maximize the chances of movement success. . . . Movements are formed by the melding of a critical discourse to collective action. Movement strategies and action are aimed at achieving change in both the political and social arenas. (48)

According to Rochon's definition, movements exist in the relation between the community that produces the discourse and the groups and organizations that advocate them. As Prügl (2001) asserts, movements have a "capacity to produce agents" (10).

There is widespread agreement on workable research definitions for these "agents" or women's movement actors. The vast majority of empirical studies of movements look at organizations, both informal and formal, which contest social norms and public policies. The most controversial issues in operationalizing the concept *women's movement actors* are (1) whether individuals without organizational affiliations can be part of the movement and (2) whether men articulating women's movement discourse are women's movement actors. With respect to the first issue, it is conventional for social movement and women's movement scholars to include a wide variety of actors—individuals, informal networks, and formal organizations—as part of both social and women's movements. As for the second issue, many RNGS members have been reluctant to exclude men who articulated women's movement discourse from the study of women's movement activism. They realized, however, that if men were included then it would become impossible to distinguish those in political parties, government offices, and media who were persuaded by activism to support movement goals from the movement actors themselves. To resolve the matter, we agreed with Ferree and Mueller (2004), who define the women's movement as *women organizing as women.*[2] Thus men using women's movement discourse can be considered *allies.*

To summarize: First, Mansbridge's definition suggests a definiens for women's movement in terms of a set of discourses, beliefs, opinions, and identities about women as women. Second, Jenson and Rochon point to the movement actors in the spaces between the ideas and the action. Ferree and Mueller define these actors to be women organizing *as* women. Putting these pieces together, for RNGS, women's movements comprise a particular discourse, represented in public life by women activists as individuals and organizations.

Women's Movement and Feminist Discourse

Key to identifying women's movement actors and the subset of feminist women's movement actors is to define the distinguishing features of their discourse. Women's movement and feminist discourses created by and about women find their genesis in what Tolleson-Rinehart (1992) calls *gender consciousness:*

> The recognition that one's relation to the political world is at least partly shaped by being female or male. This recognition is followed by identification with others in the "group" of one's sex, positive affect toward the group, and a feeling of interdependence with the group's fortunes. It is suffused with *politics* when women's fortunes are assessed relative to those of other

"groups" in society, women's particular contributions to politics and policy are weighed, and political orientations are constructed according to what the individual believes to be in the group's interest or expressive of the group's special point of view." 32)

The ideas, aspirations, beliefs, and opinions in dynamic interaction that compose all women's movement discourse are based on recognition of the special meaning of one's sex group and identification with others in the same group.

Following from these discussions, RNGS agreed to the following elements of women's movement discourse to identify all women's movement actors: (1) It expresses explicit *identity with women as a group*, a form of explicit gender consciousness (Tolleson-Rinehart 1992). (2) The language is *explicitly gendered*, referring to women as distinct from men. Gendered references include the following: images of women and what they are like; how women are different from men; how women are different from each other; the ways gender differences shape identities (see Katzenstein 1995). (3) The ideas are expressed in terms of *representing women as women* in public life (Ferree and Mueller 2004). To be identified as women's movement discourse, all three of these elements must be present: identity with women as a group, explicitly gendered language about women, and representation of women as women in public life.

As a subcategory of women's movements, feminist movements share these elements of women's movement discourse along with specific feminist ideas: These include (1) the belief that there is something wrong with the treatment and status of women and goals that will *advance the status of women;* and (2) views that explicitly or implicitly *challenge gender hierarchies and forms of women's subordination.* To be considered feminist, therefore, discourse must include all of these elements: express identity with women; be explicitly gendered; represent women; seek to improve the status of women; challenge gender hierarchies.

To summarize: Feminist actors are women's movement actors distinguished by a particular kind of discourse. While all feminist discourse is based on gender consciousness, many women with gender consciousness would not be considered (and would not consider themselves) feminists. Women's movement actors (all of whom are women) form a variety of relationships—interacting and organizing collectively as well as participating individually. What matters is the discourse used by the actors. When women's movement actors use core ideas of feminism, they are feminist women's movement actors, or, for short, feminist movement actors. Taken together in a particular social context (e.g., community, region, institution, nation-state, internationally) at a particular time, these actors and their ideas may be referred to as a women's movement or feminist movement, depending on the discourse.

Feminism inside the State: Women's Policy Agencies

Women's policy agencies are formal organizations that may espouse women's movement, even feminist movement, discourse. As the RNGS studies and other research on state feminism have shown, these relatively new government bodies have played important roles in advancing feminist perspectives and goals in setting government agendas, policy content, and the implementation of public policies (Stetson and Mazur (1995; Mazur 2002; Sawer 1990; Rai 2003). More recently, women's policy agencies have been important players in the development of transnational feminist policy networks at subnational, national, and extranational levels (e.g., True and Mintrom 2001; Woodward 2003; Rai 2003; Weldon 2002). As such, they are an integral part of the process of feminist mobilization under consideration here.

The status of women's policy agencies as formal and official bodies that are part of the state's apparatus distinguishes them from other organizations that present such discourse, that is, women's movement actors. Women's movement actors are not official state agencies; in this they share the characteristics of social movement organizations as being, by definition, *nonstate* structures.[3] Similarly, individuals who hold positions in women's policy agencies are not women's movement actors. While they may express feminist ideas and may be or have been participants in the women's movement organizations, having a position in a women's policy agency precludes them from being considered part of the women's movement. This distinction allows us to compare feminist activism by the women's movement actors and feminist activism of women's policy agencies, or state feminism.

Feminist Mobilization in Western Europe: Preliminary RNGS Findings

Based on the working research definitions of women's movement, feminism, and women's policy agencies, we examine patterns of feminist mobilization and the potential for transnational feminism in a sample of issues and countries in Western Europe. Many scholars assert that there is an increasing convergence of feminism through the globalization process (e.g., True and Mintrom 2001; Keck and Sikkink 1998; Ferree and Mueller 2004; Moghadam 2000; Rai 2003; Naples and Desai 2002; Inglehart and Norris 2003). If so, it is likely to be based in growing agreement among women's movement actors cross-nationally. If such a convergence is under way, it may be evident in findings from the RNGS study, which includes case studies within a number of nation-states over more than thirty years. The units of comparison are distinct policy debates that have led to an authoritative state action. They represent the most important policy actions on an issue since the 1970s.[4] In this chapter, we assess the potential for transnational feminist mobilization based on evidence from thirty-four policy debates on abortion, prostitution, and political representation in the 1970s, 1980s, and 1990s in Austria, Belgium, France, Germany, Great Britain, Netherlands, and Sweden. These cases represent about one-quarter of the cases that will be available when the project is complete.[5]

For this preliminary examination of feminist mobilization, the thirty-four cases provide an opportunity to generate propositions, regarding regional convergence and transnational feminism. We examine the following questions:

1. How does feminist mobilization—forms of women's movement activism, expression of feminist ideas, and women's policy agencies activities and feminism—vary according to issues? Is feminist mobilization different on some issues than others? To what extent is there cross-national agreement on feminist ideas?

2. How has feminist mobilization changed since the 1970s? Is there evidence of a growing cross-national convergence on feminist discourse?

3. To what extent are women's movement actors involved with transnational advocacy networks? Has that involvement increased since the 1970s?

To measure feminist mobilization, we use the following framework:

Women's Movement Actors (WMA) are those who present women's movement discourse in public life. As actors they may take several forms.[6] *Individuals* are single persons who do not claim to represent any organized or collective entity. Individuals may be located in women's movement organizations or other forms of organizations such as parliament, media, and universities. *Women's movement organizations* are those whose primary mission is to promote women's movement ideas, aspirations, and identities. These may be informal or formal, freestanding or inside another organization.

Informal movement organizations are collective actions through loosely organized means, without written rules and policies, such as demonstrations, coalitions, networks, consciousness-raising groups, and publics. *Formal movement organizations* are group activities driven by written rules and policies, such as lobbying organizations, professional organizations, and political parties. *Freestanding movement organizations* are either informal or formal organizations not located within another organization. *Organizations inside a non-WMA* are either informal or formal women's movement organizations located inside another organization not part of the movement; in this study the most common example of this is the women's section of a political party.

For this study we examine the ways women's movement actors define issues and their policy goals. To be considered *feminist,* discourse must include all of the following elements: identify with women; be explicitly gendered; represent women; seek to improve the status of women; and challenge gender hierarchies. As reflective of *feminist discourse,* we examine frames presented by women's movement actors in the debate. Whereas discourses are "systems of meaning that provide a way of seeing and interpreting information, categorize individuals and events, and justify power relations" (Whittier 2002, 302), frames are the ways movement actors define specific social problems to persuade others—especially state actors—to address those problems. Frames have two components: a definition of a problem, and a suggestion—often a substantive policy proposal—for fixing it (McCarthy, Smith, and Zald 1996). Based on these frames, we can identify those actors who are presenting feminist perspectives from other women's movement actors. The present organization of the data does not allow us to link a specific frame or discourse to a particular WMA form. We are able to determine which debates included feminist frames presented by at least one women's movement actor.

WPA activity involves any agency formally established by government statute or decree charged with addressing women's status and rights or promoting sex-based equality which expresses a position in the policy debate.

A *QUAWPA* is an agency attached to government institutions or political process that functions like a WPA (charged with furthering women's rights and status) but without a formal governmental directive of establishment.[7]

Feminist WPA frames are the feminist definitions and policy goals offered by a WPA or a QUAWPA in the policy debate.

It is important to note that the feminist labels assigned in this analysis to a given women's movement actor or women's policy agency are debate specific. That is, WPAs and WMAs that offer a feminist frame in a certain debate may not espouse feminist positions at all times, or even be identified, or be self-identified, with feminism as a comprehensive ideology. Similarly, those who do not present feminist discourse in one debate may do so in other contexts. Essentially, this is an ideational study of policy-making. Such a debate- or frame-specific approach allows researchers to get around the thorny problem of labeling actors feminist who do not think of themselves as feminists, a problem that often impedes the analysis of feminist mobilization in a comparative perspective.

Table 9.1 shows how each policy debate is coded on these dimensions for two debates.

Feminist Mobilization across the Issues

There are sixteen cases of abortion policy debates in the sample, and women's movement actors made demands in all. As Table 9.2 shows, their activism took various forms. The most common, in twelve, or 75 percent, of the debates, were informal networks, often associated with the autonomous movement activists. Women's sections of political parties (mostly left-wing parties) presented demands in only five, or 31 percent. Individuals, usually members of Parliament (MPs), spoke for movement goals in half (eight) of the debates, and formal women's movement organizations were active in seven.

Feminist frames were articulated in all debates, and one of two (or both) major themes were found in all but one debate. Abortion was considered a matter of women's self-determination and choice in ten out of

TABLE 9.1
Examples of Classification of Policy Debates

| Debate Nat'l | Dates | Forms | Examples of Classification of Policy Debates | | | |
| | | | WMA | WPA/ | WPA | Trans |
		of WMA	Frames	QUAWPA	Frames	Network
Germany AB1 Legalization of abortion	1969-74	Informal Formal Individuals Party sect	Women should have" legal right to abortion; part of women freeing themselves and self-determination regarding their bodies and their lives; "my belly belongs to me"	NO WPA	NA	NO
France PT3 Penal Code reform of nists pimping and solicitation	1991-92	Formal	Against any form of regulation; prostitution is a result of patriarchy in society; prosecute clients and pimp	DMWR	Prostitution was a form of sexual exploitation of women and were against state regulation of prostitution	YES; French femi- involved in TAN
Austria 3	1994-99	Individual Mps Party sections	Link party financing to force parties to increase women's representation	Ministry for Women's Affairs	NONE	NO

TABLE 9.2
Patterns of WMA Forms by Issue

Form	Abortion 16 debates	Prostitution 8 debates	Political Representation 8 debates
Formal organizations	7 44%	8 100%	4 50%
Informal organizations	12 75%	1 12%	3 38%
Women's section of political party	5 31%	0	4 50%
Individuals in parliament, media, universities	8 50%	2 25%	5 62%

sixteen debates. Similarly, abortion exemplified the need for women to control their bodies in ten debates. "My belly belongs to me," "master of one's womb," and "boss of my own body" were popular feminist slogans. Less frequently, WMAs made connections between abortion and women's emancipation and a general notion of "women's rights." Only in Germany, however, did discourse center abortion rights as a challenge to patriarchy. All these actors supported policies that would decriminalize and then maintain legal abortion.

Feminism was not expressed inside the state as often as outside during the abortion debates. Of the sixteen debates, there were seven WPAs and QUAWPAs (quasi WPAs, usually women's sections of leftist parties) that took a position on abortion reform, and only four (just one WPA) of these expressed a feminist frame in the debate. Their feminist goals were similar to those of the WMAs: the need for women to have self-determination and make the decision on whether to obtain an abortion.

In considering reform of prostitution laws, our sample includes nine cases. WMAs were active in all but one of the cases; in all, formal free-standing organizations led the way, with minimal participation by informal organizations (1) and individuals (2) (see Table 9.2). Women's sections of parties did not take a position on prostitution debates in any country. Some WMAs in all countries presented feminist demands, but there was little agreement cross-nationally on the issue. One discourse focused on prostitution as sex work and the failure to provide equal rights as sex discrimination, envisioning support for prostitutes as achieving gender equality. Another discourse defined prostitution as sex work, but more in terms of rights to work than gender equality and thus did not meet the definition of feminist discourse. The third represented a starkly different view of prostitution from the rest—as the product of patriarchal society and a form of sexual slavery. These discourses tended to be the same in all debates in each country, and none pertained to more than one country. WPAs took part in six of the debates and presented feminist definitions—the sexual slavery discourse—in three (all in France). Again, these patterns vary according to the country where the debate occurred and show little cross-national agreement.

Of the nine policy debates related to political representation, WMAs offered claims in eight. There was no clear pattern of WMA forms associated with the issue, however (see Table 9.2). Individuals, in parliament, parties, and academia, spoke out in five of the debates where WMAs participated. Party sections and formal women's movement organizations presented demands in half the cases. There were informal organizations active in three. In all debates where WMAs participated, at least one of them presented feminist frames. All these frames involved reasons for wanting more women in politics. Promoting gender equality in democracies was the call in three cases, while improving the status of women was the purpose proposed in two cases. Three were more assertive by explicitly defining the issue as a challenge to male-dominated politics and society. There was some cross-national agreement on each of these feminist perspectives, but none predominated.

Again, state activists lagged behind those outside the state. Five WPAs and one QUAWPA expressed opinions about representation proposals, and all but one (a WPA) saw the issue in feminist terms, similar to the discourse expressed by the WMAs: promoting gender equality, challenging the old boys' network, creating a balance of power between women and men. They did not mention improving women's position as a factor that justified increasing representation of women in politics.

To compare the findings according to issues being debated we find that, while women's movement actors are involved in all abortion and nearly all prostitution and political representation debates, the forms of activism vary by issue. Informal, autonomous forms are much more likely to be involved in abortion debates (75 percent), less likely on political representation (38 percent), and nearly absent on prostitution issues. For prostitution, formal women's movement organizations are especially active (100 percent) but are moderately active on the other issues as well (44 percent and 50 percent). Women's sections of party organizations are most likely to participate in political representation debates and to abstain entirely on prostitution issues. Individuals in parliament, parties, and academia are the most visible WMAs on political representation questions.

While the forms of activism vary across the issues, the feminist content of the frames varies even more. The abortion issue shows evidence of a European feminist viewpoint: there was agreement in 93 percent of the debates on a definition of the issue either in terms of self-determination or in terms of women's control of the abortion decision and their bodies. There was a feminist frame in eight of the nine political representation debates, and three of these found agreement cross-nationally, however, with much less frequency than in the abortion debates. In one-third of the debates actors claimed that greater political representation for women would combat male domination. In 22 percent, WMAs justified promoting more women in politics for gender equality or to improve women's status. There was no agreement cross-nationally on feminist views of prostitution.

Whereas there has been a greater cross-national similarity among WMA feminist frames in the abortion debates, there has been more convergence among WPAs with respect to political representation. WPAs and QUAWPAs were active in 67 percent of the debates, and 67 percent of these presented feminist frames. WPAs and QUAWPAs were almost as active on abortion debates (63 percent), but only 30 percent of them expressed feminist positions. Half of the active WPAs (in 67 percent of the debates) on the abortion issue presented feminist ideas. Three of the non-feminist WPAs were in one country, however.

The following propositions are suggested by these comparisons of feminist mobilization by the three issue areas:

1. WMA activists are engaged with policy debates regardless of the issue being debated.
2. The form of WMA activism varies by issue: Informal autonomous organizations are most active on abortion debates; formal organizations dominate in prostitution debates; women's sections of political parties participate most in political representation debates.
3. Cross-national convergence on feminist discourse varies by issue: greatest in abortion debates and least in prostitution debates. There is some agreement on political representation issues.
4. State feminism through WPAs and QUAWPAs is greatest on the political representation issue and least on abortion, with variation by country on the prostitution debates.

Feminist Mobilization over Time

In this section we compare feminist mobilization across three decades using the four indicators of feminist mobilization outlined earlier in the chapter. Scrutinizing the data by decade allows us to consider whether there are trends toward regional patterns of feminist mobilization over the past thirty years. As can be seen from Table 9.3, there are distinct variations cross-nationally in the forms of women's movement activism across the time periods. As might be expected, there has been a decline in informal forms associated with the autonomous movements' heyday in the 1970s. This has been replaced by more activism from formal women's movement organizations, defined here as those established with written rules and policies. Involvement of individual WM actors has increased; many of these work from bases in parliament, media, and universities, where numbers of women have increased over the period. Activism from women's sections of political parties grew in the 1980s and has since declined. Because many of these are associated with left-wing parties, this may coincide with a shift in activism from the party organization to the government. Alternatively, it might support the assertion by some activists that as governments establish WPAs to comply with EU directives and requirements of the Convention on the Elimination of All Forms of Discrimination against Women (CEDAW), these agencies, especially in left-wing governments, take policy leadership roles formerly held by party sections. In France, for example, the women's section of the Socialist Party, a powerful and important feminist actor in the 1970s, became far less prevalent following the years of the Ministry of Women' Rights under the Socialist government in the 1980s; this ministry was largely built, by Socialist Party feminist Yvette Roudy, from the women's section of the party (Mazur 1995).

Have there been changes in the degree of cross-national convergence in feminist frames over the last thirty years of the twentieth century as well? At first glance, the pattern is in the opposite direction: there was more agreement on feminist views in the 1970s than the 1990s. These findings cannot be separated, however, from the pattern of issues. Three-fifths of the debates in the 1970s were about abortion, compared with 40 percent in the 1980s and 27 percent in the 1990s. There was only one prostitution debate in the 1970s, whereas 45 percent of the debates in the 1990s were about prostitution or trafficking. Thus, it can be expected that, since abortion generates more transnational feminist agreement than prostitution,

TABLE 9.3
Forms of WMAs in Debates by Decade

Form	1970s 13 debates	1980s 10 debates	1990s 11 debates
Formal organizations	7 54%	3 30%	9 81%
Informal organizations	9 69%	4 40%	2 18%
Women's sections of political party	2 15%	4 40%	3 27%
Individuals in parliament, media, universities	6 46%	5 50%	7 63%

the 1970s showed more European feminism than the 1990s. This finding is most likely due to the issue variation rather than any influence from factors associated with temporal change.

Patterns of WPA and QUAWPA activism are evident across the decades, as Table 9.4 shows. There has been an increase in the proportion of debates taking place where a formal state agency has the opportunity to get involved, and they have been involved at greater and greater rates over the years. This has coincided with a decrease in QUAWPA activism as the state takes over. However, state feminism has declined. Agencies are active in debates, but in the 1990s they offered a feminist view of the issue in only 18 percent of them. The heyday of state feminism for these cases was the 1980s, when WPAs promoted feminist claims in 50 percent of the debates. It is likely that the decline of state feminism may be associated with an increase in the success of the center and right parties in the 1990s. RNGS studies to date have shown that left-wing governments are more likely to promote state feminism, especially when the women's movement actors are also close to the left (Stetson 2001; Outshoorn 2004).

Based on this longitudinal comparison, we offer the following propositions:

1. There are cross-national patterns in the forms of women's movement activism. Mobilization through autonomous/informal organizations has declined, replaced by activism through formal organizations and individual advocates inside parliaments, media, and universities.

TABLE 9.4
WPAs and QUAWPAs

WPA/QUAWPA in Debates	1970s 13 debates	1980s 10 debates	1990s 11 debates
NO WPA/ QUAWPA	3 23%	0 0%	0 0%
WPA Participated	4 30%	6 60%	8 73%
WPA did not participate	3 23%	4 40%	3 28%
QUAWPA participated	3 23%	1 1 0%	0 0%
WPA Feminist goals	1 8%	5 50%	2 18%
QUAWPA Feminist goals	3 23%	1 10	Not Applicable

Women's sections of political parties were active in the 1980s but have since declined.

2. There is no variation in the cross-national convergence of feminist frames over time apart from that associated with the prevalence of particular issues on public agendas. When abortion policy is under review, there is more transnational agreement, while country-specific feminist discourse on prostitution persists over time.

3. Women's policy agencies have increased since the 1970s, whereas QUAWPA activism in parties has declined. State feminism grew in the 1980s but has declined in the 1990s. The explanation for these patterns may be associated with the fortunes of left-wing parties, which are more likely to support feminist positions from within the state.

Transnational Advocacy Networks

Of the thirty-four debates analyzed here, researchers reported that WM activists were influenced by or connected with transnational actors in only nine. These tended to vary by issue. There were no such connections in the abortion debates. The political representation debates showed the importance of international organizations, especially the United Nations international women's conferences and resolutions. In activism related to prostitution, WM activists were connected to NGO-type transnational advocacy networks. We do not have information on whether these networks expressed feminist discourse. The connections did not always coincide with feminist frames from women's movement activists in the policy debates.

Conclusions

This chapter has presented a new approach to measuring feminist mobilization in comparative and transnational perspective. This operational definition of women's movements clearly delineates actors from ideas, making it possible to treat feminist activism as a subcategory of women's movement activism. It first measures mobilization in terms of forms of action, and then maps the content and place of feminist ideas transmitted by these actors in policy debates. It also brings the crucial state feminist element of mobilization into the mix. This multidimensional definition of feminist mobilization builds in a cumulative fashion from previous research on women's movements and feminism to address some of the major conceptual gaps in that work, and in doing so strengthens this area of research. Thus it offers a systematic and valid analysis of women's movement activism and feminist discourse that withstands the challenges of cross-national and transnational applications. The examination of the sample of policy debates from the RNGS study presented here suggests the usefulness of the approach for exploring and understanding the state of feminist mobilization in Western postindustrial democracies.

The findings suggest the importance of examining propositions about women's movements and feminist mobilization across issues as well as cross-nationally. Although the sample is small, there is strong evidence that development of regional feminism in Europe must be explored issue by issue. In this study, the most variation was found between frames on abortion debates and prostitution debates. Over the last thirty years, feminist frames have remained remarkably similar. With respect to prostitution, however, the data show important disagreements among European women's movement actors across countries. Outshoorn (2004) documents that conflict over the meaning of prostitution to women is a feature within as well as between nation-states.

In mapping feminist mobilization issue by issue, it is important to consider the relationship among the issue constituencies and the dominant issue frames in the political arena. Issues may affect women as constituents in different ways. For example, women form a homogeneous constituency across nations for abortion debates. Dominant issue frames in most political arenas recognize abortion as a medical procedure, and all women may be potential clients and women are the only clients. There is less room for interpretation with respect to the meaning of a reproductive rights issue to women. The prostitution constituency, however, has much greater diversity among women, with prostituted women closely affected and many other women only remotely involved. Such divided constituency is ground for divided gendered perspectives. Why one or the other of the two competing feminist frames—prostitution as oppression versus prostitution as work—becomes dominant in one country and not another is likely to pertain to a particular mix of social definitions of sexuality, work, and state powers and how these social meanings are transposed into the institutions and organization of prostitution.

It remains to be seen whether the concept of feminist mobilization as developed to study postindustrial democracies is portable outside the Western context. Given the boom in research on women's movements and feminism outside the West, as many of the chapters in this volume attest, it should not be difficult to test the soundness of this approach in other countries and regions of the world. Features of the approach make this extension promising. By focusing on the basic elements of women's movement and feminist discourse, it allows for a variety of content in issue frames advanced in political arenas. The distinguishing features of feminism—the challenge to gender hierarchies—may be adaptable to the particular hierarchies found in non-Western contexts. Further, the ideational approach does not identify any particular individual or group as "feminist," a label that might come with adverse historical baggage. At the same time, one should remain skeptical and mindful of barriers to the use of this approach. It is grounded in institutions and practices of democracy and is likely to be useful only where democratization has made some inroads. Further, in nondemocratic systems, women's policy agencies may be instruments of hierarchy and control, rather than responses to movement demands. In such situations, WPAs may need to be completely discounted as legitimate sites of feminist mobilization.

We have used the new measure to address the issue of transnational feminism. The contributions of this chapter in this regard are, however, mitigated. First and foremost, a relatively small sample of RNGS debates has been used, thirty-four out of the nearly one hundred debates from Western European countries (other debates in the project cover the United States, Canada, Australia, and Japan). Therefore, the findings can be presented and used only in the form of propositions to be investigated when the project is complete and, ultimately, by other researchers using different issues and countries. Still, we see that national feminist mobilization, at least in Western Europe, has, at best, common characteristics in terms of women's movement forms and women's policy agency involvement, while convergence in feminist discourses is apparent only in certain issue areas. This convergence, moreover, according to these preliminary findings, does not seem to occur as a result of feminist transnational advocacy networks.

Despite their tentative nature, these findings are evidence of the significance of nation-state studies of feminist politics to understanding emerging transnational processes being examined in this book. Does transnational feminism exist apart from the women's actors in national politics? Do transnational feminist advocacy networks develop from the basis of cross-national agreement (e.g., on abortion or political representation) or as a way to extend a national position where there is little cross-national agreement, for example, on prostitution politics? At the very least, national-level dynamics may very well be a powerful intervening variable when looking at the new politics of transnational feminism.

APPENDIX

Coverage of RNGS Policy Debates
Overall: 34/140

Abortion (16/32):
Austria
    AUAB1: Social Democratic Party draft liberalization 1970–1972
    AUAB2: People's Initiative (antiabortion) and
        National Council reaffirmation of legal abortion 1975–1978
    AU AB3: Regulation of mifegyne: abortion pill 1998–1999
Belgium
    BELAB1: State Commission for Ethical Problems 1974–1976
    BELAB2: Detiège bill to suspend prosecutions 1981–1982
    BELAB3: Reform of abortion law 1986–1990
France
    FRAAB1: Reaffirmation of legal abortion in the first trimester 1979
Germany
    DEUAB1: Legalization of abortion 1969–1974
    DEUAB2: Post-unification liberalization 1990–1992
    DEUAB3: Restoration of limited abortion law 1993–1995
Great Britain
    GBRAB1: White bill and Lane Committee 1970–1972
    GBRAB2: Corrie bill to restrict abortions 1975–1979
    GBRAB3: Human Fertilisation and Embryology Act: upper limit ...1987–1990
The Netherlands
    NLDAB1: First cabinet proposal for limited reform 1971–1972
    NLDAB2: Reform of abortion law 1977–1981
    NLDAB3: Implementation of statute to register/license
        abortion facilities 1981–1984

Prostitution (9/36):

Austria
AUTPT1: Penal Code amendment on pimping 1984
AUTPT2: Vienna's prostitution law 1991
AUTPT3: Social insurance for private enterprise 1997
France
FRAPT1: Prostitute rights and law enforcement 1972–1975
FRAPT2: Public health/AIDS 1989–1990
FRAPT3: Penal Code reform of pimping and solicitation 1991–1992
Netherlands
NLDPT1: Bill 18202 repeal of brothel ban 1983
NLDPT2: Bill on the trafficking of persons .1989–1993
NLDPT3: Bill 25417 on repeal of brothel ban 1997–2000

Political Representation (9/33):
Austria
AUTPR1: Cabinet access 1975–1979
AUTPR2: Equal treatment for civil servants .1981–1992
AUTPR3: Gendering public party finances 1994–1999
Netherlands
NLDPR1: Social Democratic Party 1966–1977
NLDRPR2: Equality Policy Plan 1981–1985
NLDRPR3: Corporatism 1989–1997
Sweden
SWEPR1: More women in politics 1967–1972
SWEPR2: Quotas for appointed positions 1985–1987
SWEPR3: Establishment of a women's party .1991–1994

By Decade:
(Debates that spanned two decades were placed
in decade where most of debate took place)

1970s (13)
AUTAB1: Social Democratic Party Draft Liberalization 1970–1972
AUAB2: People's Initiative (antiabortion) and
    National Council reaffirmation of legal abortion 1975–1978
AUTPR1: Cabinet access 1975–1979
BELAB1: State Commission for Ethical Problems 1974–1976
DEUAB1: Legalization of abortion 1969–1974
FRAPT1: Prostitute rights and law enforcement 1972–1975
FRAAB1: Reaffirmation of legal abortion in the first trimester 1979
GBRAB1: White bill and Lane Committee 1970–1972
GBRAB2: Corrie bill to restrict abortions 1975–1979

NLDPR1: Social Democratic Party 1966–1977
NLDAB1 : First cabinet proposal for limited reform 1971–1972
NLDAB2: Reform of abortion law 1977–1981
SWEPR1: More women in politics 1967–1972

1980s (10)

AUTPT1: Penal Code amendment on pimping 1984
AUTPR2: Equal treatment for civil servants 1981–1992
BELAB2: Detiège bill to suspend prosecutions 1981–1982
BELAB3: Reform of abortion law 1986–1990
FRAPT2: Public health/AIDS 1989–1990
GBRAB3: Human Fertilisation and Embryology 1987–1990
NLDPR2: Equality Policy Plan 1981–1985
NLDPT1: Bill 18202 repeal of brothel ban 1983
NLDAB3:Implementation of statute to
    register/license abortion facilities 1981–1984
SWEPR2: Quotas for appointed positions 1985–1987

1990s (11)

AUTPT2: Vienna's prostitution law 1991
AUTPT3: Social insurance for private enterprise 1997
AUTPR3: Gendering public party finances 1994–1999
AUT/AB3: Regulation of mifegyne: abortion pill 1998–1999
DEUAB2: Post-unification liberalization 1990–1992
DEUAB3: Restoration of limited abortion law 1993–1995
FRAPT3: Penal Code reform of pimping and solicitation 1991–1992
NLDPR3: Corporatism 1989–1997
NLDPT2: Bill on the trafficking of persons 1989–1993
NLDPT3: Bill 25417 on repeal of brothel ban 1997–2000
SWEPR3: Establishment of a women's party 1991–1994

Notes

This material is based on work supported by the National Science Foundation under grant 0084580. Any opinions, findings, and conclusions or recommendations expressed in this material are those of the authors and do not necessarily reflect the views of the NSF. The European Science Foundation also provided support for meetings at which the RNGS network developed the conceptual framework used in this chapter. The authors acknowledge and thank the following RNGS researchers who collected, but did not analyze, the data presented here: Joyce Outshoorn (Netherlands); Jean Robinson (France); Lynn Kamenitsa (Germany); Regina Koepl (Austria); Birgit Sauer (Austria); Jantine Oldersma (Netherlands); Diane Sainsbury (Sweden); and Karen Celis (Belgium).

1. RNGS has designed and is completing a research project that examines if, how, and why women's policy offices, through their relations with women's movements, make postindustrial democracies more democratic and the state more feminist. The research explores the interface between women's movements and women's policy machineries from the late 1960s to 2001 in individual policy debates on five key issues: job training, abortion, prostitution, political representation, and an issue of national significance in each country. Fifteen teams in fourteen countries and at the European Union level have been collecting data on 140 policy debates since 1997. Project findings are presented qualitatively in five edited volumes, one for each issue area—Mazur 2001b; Stetson 2001; Outshoorn 2004; Lovenduski et al. 2005; and Haussman and Sauer 2006—and quantitatively in an electronic data set to be made available in 2007. For more project details, see http://libarts.wsu.edu/polisci/rngs/.

2. Beyond this idea, our use of the concept differs from that of Ferree and Mueller, who consider women organizing as women toward any goal as the women's movement. Our definition requires a particular gender-conscious discourse as outlined here.

3. Individuals can, however, be women's movement actors inside state organizations by retaining their connections with outside actors (Ferree and Mueller 2004).

4. Debates in each country were selected from the universe of policy debates based on these criteria: (1) debates take place in public arenas such as the legislature, courts, news media, political party conferences, or electoral campaigns; (2) debates occur in periods when a women's policy agency was in existence; (3) debates represent the range of discussions on the issue in the country in the period under study (see later discussion); (4) debates end with an official state decision, including, for instance, legislation, an executive order, a court ruling, or a government policy proposal. The time frame for each debate on an issue may vary from country to country depending on when the debates appeared on the public agenda.

5. Not all issues are covered in each country. It is important to note that the selection of cases analyzed for this chapter is based on the stage of completion of the study, not theoretical criteria. Here we have the cases where data collection is complete. In the larger study, there are three policy debates in each country for each issue area, selected according to a common set of criteria agreed upon by the network. For more on the RNGS case selection criteria, see Mazur 2001b; Stetson 2001; or the current project description on the RNGS home page. The Appendix presents a detailed list of cases by country, issue area, and time period.

6. Rucht (1996) refers to a similar typology of "mobilizing agents."

7. In this study QUAWPAs are all attached to political parties. When a women's section of a party is classified as a QUAWPA. it is not considered a WMA.

BIBLIOGRAPHY

Banaszak, Lee Ann, Karen Beckwith, and Dieter Rucht. 2003. *Women's Movements Facings a Reconfigured State.* New York: Cambridge University Press.

Beckwith, Karen. 2000. "Beyond Compare? Women's Movements in Comparative Perspective." *European Journal of Political Research* 37:431–468.

Bull, Anna, Hanna Diamond, and Rosalind Marsh, eds. 2000. "Introduction." In A. Bull, H. Diamond, and R. Marsh, eds., *Feminisms and Women's Movements in Contemporary Europe*, 1–18. New York: St. Martin's Press.

Collier, David. 1993. "The Comparative Method." In A.W. Finifter, ed., *Political Science: The State of the Discipline II*, 105–119. Washington D.C.: American Political Science Association.

Collier, David, and James E. Mahon. 1993. "Conceptual 'Stretching' Revisited: Adapting Categories in Comparative Analysis." *American Political Science Review* 87:845–855.

Ferree, Myra Marx, and Beth Hess. 2000. *Controversy and Coalition: The New Feminist Movement across Four Decades of Change.* 3rd ed. New York: Routledge.

Ferree, Myra Marx, and Patricia Yancey Martin, eds. 1995. *Feminist Organizations.* Philadelphia: Temple University Press.

Ferree, Myra Marx, and Carol McClurg Mueller. 2004. "Feminism and the Women's Movement: A Global Perspective." In David A. Snow, Sarah A. Soule, and Hanspeter Kriesi, eds., *The Blackwell Companion to Social Movements.* Oxford: Blackwell.

Haussman, Melissa, and Birgit Sauer, eds. 2006. *Gendering the State in the Age of Globalization: Women's Movements and State Feminism in Post-Industrial Democracies.* Boulder, Colo.: Rowman Littlefield.

Inglehart, Ronald, and Pippa Norris. 2003. *Rising Tide: Gender Equality and Cultural Change around the World.* Cambridge: Cambridge University Press.

Jenson, Jane. 1996. "Representations of Difference: The Varieties of French Feminism." In M. Threlfall, ed., *Mapping the Women's Movement: Feminist Politics and Social Transformation in the North*, 73–114. London: Verso.

Kaplan, Gisela. 1992. *Contemporary Western European Feminism.* London: Allen and Unwin.

Katzenstein, Mary Fainsod. 1995. "Discursive Politics and Feminist Activism in the Catholic Church." In Myra Marx Ferree and Patricia Yancey Martin, eds., *Feminist Organizations*, 35–52. Philadelphia: Temple University Press

———. 1998. *Faithful and Fearless: Moving Feminist Protest Inside the Church and Military.* Princeton, N.J.: Princeton University Press.

Katzenstein, Mary Fainsod, and Carol McClurg Mueller, eds. 1987. *The Women's Movements of the United States and Western Europe: Consciousness, Political Opportunity, and Public Policy.* Philadelphia: Temple University Press.

Keck, Margaret E., and Kathryn Sikkink. 1998. *Activists beyond Borders: Advocacy Networks in International Politics.* Ithaca, N.Y.: Cornell University Press.

Lovenduski, Joni. 1987. *Women and European Politics: Contemporary Feminism and Public Policy.* London: Wheatsheaf.

Lovenduski, Joni, Petra Meier, Diane Sainsbury, Marila Guadagnini, and Claudie Baudino, eds. 2005. *Feminism and the Political Representation of Women in Europe and North America.* Cambridge: Cambridge University Press.

Mansbridge, Jane. 1996. "What Is the Feminist Movement?" In Myra Marx Ferree and Patricia Yancey Martin, eds., *Feminist Organizations: Harvest of the New Women's Movement,* 27–33. Philadelphia: Temple University Press.

Mazur, Amy G. 1995. "Strong State and Symbolic Reform: The Ministère des Droits de la Femme in France." In Dorothy McBride Stetson and Amy G. Mazur, eds., *Comparative State Feminism,* 76–94. Thousand Oaks, Calif.: Sage.

———. 2001a. "Drawing Lessons from the French Parity Movement." *Contemporary French Civilization* 24:201–220.

———, ed. 2001b. *State Feminism, Women's Movements, and Job Training: Making Democracies Work in the Global Economy.* New York: Routledge.

———. 2002. *Theorizing Feminist Policy.* Oxford: Oxford University Press.

McAdam, Doug, John D. McCarthy, and Mayer N. Zald, eds. 1996. *Comparative Perspectives on Social Movements: Political Opportunities, Mobilizing Structures, and Cultural Framings.* Cambridge: Cambridge University Press.

McCarthy, John, Jackie Smith, and Mayer N. Zald. 1996. "Accessing Public, Media, Electoral, and Governmental Agendas." In D. McAdam, J. D. McCarthy, and M. N. Zald, eds.,291–311. *Comparative Perspectives on Social Movements: Political Opportunities, Mobilizing Structures, and Cultural Framings.* Cambridge: Cambridge University Press.

Meyer, David S., Nancy Whittier, and Belinda Robnett, eds. 2002. *Social Movements: Identity, Culture, and the State.* Oxford: Oxford University Press.

Moghadam, Valentine M. 2000. "Transnational Feminist Networks: Collective Action in an Era of Globalization." *International Sociology* 15:57–85.

Molyneux, Maxine. 1998. "Analyzing Women's Movements." In Cecile Jackson and Ruth Pearson, eds., *Feminist Visions of Development: Gender, Analysis and Policy,* 65–88. London: Routledge.

Naples, Nancy A., and Manisha Desai, eds. 2002. *Women's Activism and Globalization: Linking Local Struggles and Transnational Politics.* New York: Routledge.

Outshoorn, Joyce, ed. 2004. *The Politics of Prostitution: Women's Movements, Democratic States, and the Globalisation of Sex Commerce.* Cambridge: Cambridge University Press.

Prügl, Elizabeth. 2001. "Globalized Patriarchy: Elements of an Institutionalist Theory." Presented at the Minnesota International Relations Colloquium, Minneapolis, February 5.

Ragin, Charles. 1987. *The Comparative Method: Moving beyond Qualitative and Quantitative Strategies.* Berkeley: University of California Press.

Rai, Shirin M., ed. 2003. *Mainstreaming Gender, Democratizing the State? Institutional Mechanisms for the Advancement of Women.* Manchester: Manchester University Press.

Rochon, Thomas R. 1998. *Culture Moves: Ideas, Activism, and Changing Values.* Princeton, N.J.: Princeton University Press.

Rucht, Dieter. 1996. "The Impact of National Contexts on Social Movement Structures: A Cross-Movement and Cross-National Comparison." In D. McAdam, J. D. McCarthy, and M. N. Zald, eds., *Comparative Perspectives on Social Movements: Political Opportunities, Mobilizing Structures, and Cultural Framings,* 185–204. Cambridge: Cambridge University Press.

Santoro, Wayne A., and Gail M. McGuire. 1997. "Social Movement Insiders: The Impact of Institutional Activists on Affirmative Action and Comparable Worth Politics." *Social Problems* 44:503–519.

Sartori, Giovanni. 1970. "Concept Misformation in Comparative Politics." *American Political Science Review* 64:1033–1053.

Sawer, Marian. 1990. *Sisters in Suits: Women and Public Policy in Australia.* Sydney: Allen and Unwin.

Stetson, Dorothy McBride, ed. 2001. *Abortion Politics, Women's Movements and the Democratic State: A Comparative Study of State Feminism.* Oxford: Oxford University Press.

Stetson, Dorothy McBride, and Amy Mazur, eds. 1995. *Comparative State Feminism.* Thousand Oaks, Calif.: Sage.

———. 2003. "Reconceptualizing the Women's Movement in Comparative Perspective: Discourse, Actors and the State," Paper presented at the annual conference of the International Studies Association, Portland, Oregon, February 25–March 1.

Tarrow, Sidney. 1994. *Power in Movement: Social Movements, Collective Action and Politics.* Cambridge: Cambridge University Press.

Tolleson-Rinehart, Sue. 1992. *Gender Consciousness in Politics.* New York: Routledge.

True, Jacqui, and Michael Mintrom. 2001. "Transnational Networks and Policy Diffusion: The Case of Gender Mainstreaming." *International Studies Quarterly* 45:27–57.

Weldon, S. Laurel. 2002. *Protest, Policy and the Problem of Violence against Women: A Cross-National Comparison.* Pittsburgh: University of Pittsburgh Press.

Whittier, Nancy. 2002. "Meaning and Structure in Social Movements." In D. Meyer, N. Whittier, and B. Robnett, eds., *Social Movements: Identity, Culture and the State,* 289–308. Oxford: Oxford University Press.

Woodward, Alison. 2003. "European Gender Mainstreaming: Promises and Pitfalls of Transformative Policy." *Review of Policy Research* 20:65–88.

10

Transnational Feminist NGOs on the Web
Networks and Identities in the Global North and South

Myra Marx Ferree and Tetyana Pudrovska

Although in many countries the women's movement became less visible on the streets in the 1990s, the past decade has also witnessed an unprecedented proliferation of spaces and places in which feminist groups act and feminist discourses circulate (Alvarez 1999). Rather than only in local demonstrations or explicitly feminist small groups, the commitment to changing gender relations has been expressed increasingly in "transnational advocacy networks" (Keck and Sikkink 1998). Such networks bring together policymakers, experts, nongovernmental organizations, and concerned citizen-activists around shared principles and values across national boundaries. In today's wired world, these networks may be not only face-to-face (actual) but also virtual, that is, relying on the Internet for communication among widely dispersed memberships. Discourses about gender equality circulate internationally by means of both actual and virtual networks, and organizations based in many different parts of the world participate in forming such transnational channels for discussion and influence. At both a national and an international level, feminist networks have been involved in framing policy questions and raising social concerns.

In this chapter, we look at the nature of the virtual linkages among transnational women's NGOs and the patterns of sharing revealed in their online discourses. We are particularly interested in the identities that such organizations construct for themselves on their own Web pages by means of the links they make to other organizations and the language they use in describing themselves and their goals and activities. Unlike media coverage of movements, Web pages are an unmediated self-presentation by an organization, and the terms it chooses to describe itself and the links it displays are signs of what identity it presents to the world. Like media coverage, a Web page is public information, an important means of reaching those not already part of the movement and creating a public presence. Thus it is an ideal location to find the public identity of a movement organization. Our question is how and to what extent such Web-circulated identities vary among transnational women's organizations as a consequence of where they are located in the physical world.

We expect that both the local and the global dimensions of organizing matter to group identity. Feminist scholars have argued that women's geographic location is an important aspect of their transnational organizing (Basu 2001; Alvarez 1998). The needs, interests, and perspectives of women reflect the social conditions and political concerns that are part of their national and local context. Yet the flexibility of time and space in online networks fosters collective authorship and allows feminist activists across the globe to collaborate effectively in creating, interpreting, and disseminating information and discourses (Sampaio and Aragon 1997).

Social movement researchers have also emphasized the importance of the World Wide Web as a tool for effectively becoming present and acting in a transnational arena (Schulz 1998; Diani 2000; Garrido and Halavais 2003). Although what we call "techno-optimists" highlight the potential of the Web for transcending geographic limits and the successful use of the Internet by social movement participants, such as Zapatista insurgents and activists in Seattle World Trade Organization (WTO) protests, the "techno-pessimists" stress the continued relevance of resource and skill differences to creating a "digital divide" at a global level. This study considers the implications of both perspectives by examining how the geographic location of transnational feminist groups relates to their self-presentations in virtual space.

Using a sample of thirty transnational feminist organizations, this study treats both the hyperlinks and the linguistic choices of groups on their Web pages as aspects of feminist public identity in virtual space. We first ask how the online networking that connects the global North and South figures into self-presented identities, then whether the ways that transnational groups frame the concepts "women," "gender," and "feminist" differ depending on their geographic location. Finally, we ask to what extent the Web-based organizing represented in these pages transcends and reflects differences between parts of the world in actual space.

Women's NGOs and Institutionalized Global Discourse

One of the defining features of transnational NGOs is the ongoing discursive work they perform at a global level (Gamson 1992). Discourses, or ways of framing the terms of discussion, are always used to legitimate social goals and authorize political action. Discursive politics is "the effort to reinterpret, reformulate, rethink, and rewrite the norms and practices of society and the state" (Katzenstein 1998:17). Keck and Sikkink (1998:192) name "discursive change, or establishing prescriptive status of norms," among the main criteria of the effectiveness of transnational advocacy networks because activists "try not only to influence policy outcomes but to transform the terms and nature of the debate" (Keck and Sikkink 1998:3).

The discussion of women's rights certainly has been transformed by transnational discourses about human rights, development, empowerment, and gendered violence. Transnational feminist mobilization has been successful in placing gender issues on the global agenda in diverse contexts, from the Vienna Conference on Human Rights to the World Social Forum in Brazil. Such frames as "women's rights are human rights" (Keck and Sikkink 1998), "women as resources for development" (Berkovich 1999), and "birth control through women's education and empowerment" (Ferree and Gamson 1999) have become widely familiar. These frames signify a process of mutual accommodation between radical feminist demands for transformation of gender relations and the dominant institutional discourses of individual rights, human capital, and personal self-fulfillment (Walby 2002; Khagram, Riker, and Sikkink 2002).

Such globally circulating discourses are deployed by local activists as resources to influence nation-states and to create space for women to demand greater recognition (Ferree and Mueller 2004). The broadest and most generally applicable discourses of transnational gender politics are expressed in the Beijing Platform for Action and the Convention on the Elimination of All Forms of Violence against Women (CEDAW). These normative statements institutionally anchor a newly hegemonic and largely liberal discursive opportunity structure. As well as these global discourses, there are more regional or local concerns that matter to women, and these have often surfaced in conflicts at the transnational level about defining "women's issues." For example, peace has sometimes been defined as a women's issue, especially in parts of the world where religious or ethnic conflict is endemic. Organizations based in the global South have been especially active in pressing for attention to the specificity of indigenous women's perspectives and the intertwining of women's needs with questions of power and inequality based on race, class, and nation (Snyder, this volume). Framing women in relation to men, children, and families and/or as independent persons with claims to individual rights also creates controversy among women's movement organizations in different parts of the world (Ertürk, this volume). When movement organizations bring their discourses online, they demonstrate their own collective identity, participate in spreading values and understandings that matter to them, and potentially create communities of discourse that share their norms. Thus recognizing the differences as well as the similarities within the global discourses about gender and women is important for understanding feminism.

Though feminist international discourses travel from global arenas to regional contexts, providing local activists with leverage to challenge gender relations in their own countries, it is up to an organization to decide how radical it is ready to be in its discursive work. Organizations choose either to support institutionally anchored discourses (to be resonant with them) in order to make policy more effective or to be "radical" by challenging common frames in the hopes of eventually changing the discourse itself (Ferree 2003). The term "feminist" is generally seen as a radical frame for wanting change in the position of women. Internationally, "I'm not a feminist, but . . ." is a common way to endorse the resonant aspects of specific women's movement claims while distancing oneself from this radical identity.

In this study we use the words "woman(-en)," "gender," and "feminist(s)" as linguistic indicators of groups' self-constructed identities on the Web by analyzing the connotations of meanings of three pivotal words: "woman(-en)," "feminist(s)," and "gender." We are particularly interested in how radical or resonant with dominant discourses organizations choose to be in their framing of these key words, and how global and local elements interact in the discourses of transnational women's groups. On the one hand, we focus on the appropriation of the global discourses of women's individual rights and gender equality by Northern and Southern nongovernmental organizations (NGOs). On the other hand, we examine how particularistic discourses influence the global feminist arena and to what extent organizations in the North appropriate discourses of development and social justice associated with the global South.

Power Inequalities and Networking on the Web

According to Khagram, Riker, and Sikkink (2002:11), the characteristic form of relations in the nongovernmental sector is neither authority nor market "but rather the informal and horizontal network." Transnational feminist NGOs tend to operate in network and coalition form (Keck and Sikkink 1998; Ferree and Hess 2000). Rather than centralized organizations completely dominating the articulation of issues and strategies, feminist groups have built up dynamic networks of coalitions, with many interlocking lines of communication and cooperation (Ferree and Hess 2000). Transnational advocacy networks (TANs) are composed of organizations connected to advance shared interests, which may or may not have any grassroots mobilization behind them (Sikkink 1993). The power differences that are visible on the Web are not those between leaders and members within a single organization but among the organizations that are part of the Web-based network. There are different expectations for how significant these differences would be.

A *techno-optimist* expects that communication technologies will tend to eliminate inequalities and hierarchies of the real world. Techno-optimists suggest that globalization of mass media promotes empathy with distant, different others and allows group solidarity to be maintained despite great distances (Miller 1992; Diani 2000). Computer-mediated communication can make the very existence of transnational networks possible by improving the effectiveness of transnational interaction (Diani 2000). The Internet disseminates information rapidly and globally at low cost via electronic newsletters and linkages to useful Web sites (Sampaio and Aragon 1997). The Internet thus is seen by a techno-optimist as a medium for discussing political concerns in such a way that new forms of democracy emerge and contribute to the transformation of the late modern society (Sassi 2001). Because of the lack of institutional and cultural norms in cyberspace, Vogt and Chen (2001) find the Internet similar to other unconventional forms of "free space" that the women's movement has used to create new identities and consciousness.

By contrast, a *techno-pessimist* regards cyberspace as an extension of real space, where the unequal distribution of power and resources is reproduced (Kole 1998). Cyber-pessimists reject the idea of neutrality and impartiality of technology and argue that the Internet presents problems for transnational feminism, such as profound disparities in economic, social, and cultural resources that restrict access to the new technologies for women in the global South (Sampaio and Aragon 1997; Scott 2001). Not only resource differences but also differences in willingness to listen to those who are "other" may reproduce exclusions and inequalities in cyberspace. Techno-pessimists expect the choice of language and the prestige of Web sites to reflect real-world inequalities of influence and access to power.

Both optimists and pessimists take organizations to be key players in cyberspace. NGOs are crucial to articulating the so-called social movement webs—the elaborate connections among feminists located in diverse social and political spaces. In producing publications, organizing conferences, and establishing electronic networks, NGOs function as "the key nodal points through which the spatially dispersed and organizationally fragmented feminist field remains discursively articulated" (Alvarez 1999:185). Transnational NGOs by definition bring women from different countries together to create a platform of solidarity that crosses national boundaries. Through the process of networking, transnational feminist NGOs in different regions learn from others' successes. They learn to utilize the opportunities and ideas that transnational organizing provides (Sperling, Ferree, and Risman 2001).

Networks of NGOs contribute to the formation of global civil society "by providing an infrastructure that facilitates transnational communication and action, by cultivating transnational identities, and by developing a global public discourse" (Smith 1998:93). Social movement webs are a virtual space in which organizational identities are constructed and used to relate local interests and identities to global institutions and organizations. The links offered on a Web site need not reflect any actual interorganizational cooperation to be significant as indicators of how groups want to be seen. On the one hand, groups that are highly selected *by* others have high status in the network, and the links thus created also contribute to their visibility in search engines such as Google that count links as signs of importance and relevance. On the other hand, those groups that post many links *to* other transnational organizations also are thereby advertising their international orientation as part of their own identity. Both links to and links from an organization's Web site are therefore indicators of the identity of the group in the overall transnational feminist network of which it is a part. Thus our network analysis of the hyperlinks between the Web sites of women's organizations within and across the North-South divide intends to suggest how the Web works to promote transnational organizing, and to what extent the prestige and identity of groups in cyberspace are reflections of differences in their global geographic locations in the physical world.

Data and Methods

We selected thirty organizations (ten based in the United States, ten based in Europe, and ten based in the Third World) by disproportional stratified random sampling from the population of international women's organizations whose URLs are given in the *Yearbook of International Organizations* 2002–2003 (sampled groups are listed in the Appendix). These groups are counted by the *Yearbook* as being both international and "women's" organizations, but they are not necessarily self-described as feminist, nor do they have to include any particular feminist language or goals to be included in our sample, since our goal was to see the extent of variation in just such factors. The country given in the *Yearbook* as the site of the headquarters of the organization is taken as its global location.

We downloaded the Web sites using TeleportPro, with the limit on the program being set to include up to 10,000 levels within each Web site. The analysis is conducted primarily on pooled Web sites: ten Web sites of Europe-based groups were merged into one file, ten Web sites of U.S.-based groups were merged into the second file, and ten Web sites of third world–based organizations were merged into the third file. These three pooled files are analyzed and contrasted in this study.

Representations of Identity in Network Hyperlinks

Assuming that the hyperlinks an organization provides to other feminist groups reflect its choice of how and with whom it wants to be seen, we consider such networking on the Web as signaling group identity. Groups for which outreach to other parts of the world is important will have more links to groups outside their own region, and those for whom a regional identity is more important will have more intraregional ties. While these links may not accurately reflect patterns of actual social relations on the ground or even the prevalence of online communication, they are how a group presents its position in the world to others (Park and Thelwall 2003; Jackson 1997). To analyze the hyperlink structure of the transnational feminist web, we extracted all links on each Web site from the downloaded

HTML files using the program Essay11 and imported them to MS Access, where the outward links were separated from internal links ("within-sample" hyperlinks). The pooled number of hyperlinks among the three groups of Web sites was calculated using MS Excel. In this chapter we focus exclusively on the within-sample links of our organizations, thus equating the potential network sizes for all groups.

We then calculated the density and centralization of this network. A transnational network is inherently composed of relationships and therefore lends itself to social network analysis (Wasserman and Faust 1999; Marsden 1990; Wellman 1983). The measure of network density indicates how many of the ties exist of those that are theoretically possible. The measure of centralization for the whole network indicates the relative proportion of incoming and outgoing ties for a particular group relative to the others in the network (Wasserman and Faust 1999).[1] Within the network, we consider the number of incoming ties (links that other organization make to it) to be an indicator of a group's *prestige* and the number of outgoing ties (links to other groups on its own Web site) to be an indicator of the extent to which *outreach* is an important part of a group's identity.

Representation of Identity in Word Choices

The identity of each group is also expressed by the frequency and context in which the pivotal words "woman(-en)," "feminist(s)," and "gender" are used on its Web site. "Woman/women" is taken as a neutral word that acquires different shades of meaning depending on its semantic environment. A more "conservative" version of woman/women would anchor this word in relation to "family, man, child," and a more "liberal" reading would place it in relation to "individual, rights, equality." Either or both of these contexts may be locally resonant. By contrast, "feminist(s)" is a more controversial word that suggests a more radical identity. Inclusion or exclusion of the word "feminist" is likely to be a conscious decision on the part of the organization and so can be regarded as a critical element of the Web-based identity of organizations that choose to use it.

The word "gender" has two related social contexts "off-line" that may influence how it is used to construct a group's online identity. On the one hand, it has gained "official" transnational status after the Beijing conference, and its usage can indicate a group's identification with the transnational Platform for Action in which it figures prominently and controversially. This would make it a top-down, policy-focused word. On the other hand, "gender" is a term of academic feminist discourse, developed in English-language theoretical writing, and may also indicate a discourse about women that is institutionally anchored in universities and conferences. Both the off-line worlds of academic theory and UN-centered policymaking are transnational contexts, so we consider the word "gender" to be a more transnational word. We ask whether it is especially used by organizations in the North or tied more closely to their concerns in the words with which it is associated.

Using TextAnalyst software for quantitative content analysis, we identified all lexical words appearing in the same sentence with "woman(-en)," "feminist(s)," and "gender" for the three pooled groups of Web sites. Same-sentence locations are what are defined here as "collocations" for the analysis. When words occur in recurrent collocations, it shows "the associations and connotations they have, and therefore the assumptions that they embody" (Stubbs 1996:172). Thus such word clusters provide a context within which the meanings of "woman(-en)," "feminist(s)," and "gender" can be disambiguated. We show the top ten collocations and also calculate the relative prominence of certain collocation clusters based on the top fifty collocations.[2]

Results

The estimated network size for the sample of thirty groups is 135, which is the total number of hyperlinks found. Table 10.1 presents the matrix of all links within this sample and allows one to see the pattern of links by and from individual groups. Expressed as a proportion of all the possible links among these thirty groups (30*29), the network density measure of .16 indicates that this network is not particularly dense. In other words, these thirty organizations created only 16 percent of all theoretically possible "within-sample" links. The centralization index of .34 for the network as a whole suggests that the network is decentralized and *not* dominated by one or two exceptionally central actors receiving and/or initiating a disproportionate number of ties. Table 10.1 highlights those groups giving or receiving five or more links as the "more networked" groups.

TABLE 10.1

Hyperlinks among Individual Organizations

Link from: \ Link to:	digilander.libero.it	www.antenna.nl (wecf)	www.apwld.org	www.arrow.org.my	www.awid.org	www.awmc.com	www.awsa.net	www.bpwintl.org	www.cwgl.rutgers.edu	www.dawn.org.fj	www.eawhr.org	www.equalitynow.org	www.fawe.org	www.globalfundforwomen.org	www.ifuw.org	www.isiswomen.org	www.iwdc.org	www.iwtc.org	www.madre.org	www.neww.org	www.oas.org	www.own-europe.org	www.rainbo.org	www.themothersunion.org	www.wave-network.org	www.wedo.org	www.wgnrr.org	www.wilpf.int.ch	www.wluml.org	www.womenlobby.org	Grand Total
digilander.libero.it	■																														0
www.antenna.nl (wecf)		■																							+				+		2
www.apwld.org			■	+					+			+		+												+					5
www.arrow.org.my			+	■	+				+	+				+		+	+	+								+					9
www.awid.org					■					+		+		+		+		+	+							+					7
www.awmc.com						■								+				+													2
www.awsa.net							■																								0
www.bpwintl.org								■																						+	1
www.cwgl.rutgers.edu					+	+	+		■	+		+		+		+		+	+	+			+			+	+	+	+	+	16
www.dawn.org.fj					+					■				+				+									+	+			5
www.eawhr.org											■																				0
www.equalitynow.org												■																		+	1
www.fawe.org													■	+																	1
www.globalfundforwomen.org					+				+			+		■				+	+									+	+		7
www.ifuw.org					+				+						■	+										+					4
www.isiswomen.org		+	+	+					+	+		+		+		■		+								+		+	+	+	12
www.iwdc.org									+	+				+			■	+								+					5
www.iwtc.org					+				+	+		+				+		■	+	+			+			+		+		+	11
www.madre.org									+			+						+	■							+			+		5
www.neww.org					+				+			+	+							■						+				+	6
www.oas.org																					■										0
www.own-europe.org																						■									0
www.rainbo.org									+			+				+		+					■								4
www.themothersunion.org																								■							0
www.wave-network.org									+							+			+						■					+	4
www.wedo.org				+	+				+	+						+			+	+			+			■			+	+	10
www.wgnrr.org					+				+	+																	■				4
www.wilpf.int.ch																										+		■			1
www.wluml.org					+			+	+	+					+				+	+					+	+			■	+	10
www.womenlobby.org					+															+						+				■	3
Grand Total	0	1	2	3	12	1	1	1	13	9	0	9	1	9	1	8	1	10	7	5	0	0	3	0	2	13	3	5	6	9	135

There are differences among these organizations in the prestige they enjoy. Of all the European groups, the European Women's Lobby (EWL), an umbrella group funded by the European Union, is most central but basically due to incoming hyperlinks from other organizations. The EWL has three times more incoming than outgoing links, has only one reciprocal link, with the Network of East-West Women (NEWW), and is primarily Western in scope (for more detail, see Pudrovska and Ferree 2004). For comparison, the most prestigious U.S. organization, the Center for

Women's Global Leadership (CWGL) based at Rutgers University, has a prestige score half again as great as the EWL's (.45 vs .31), and both are more likely to draw links from other organizations than the most prestigious group in the global South, Women Living under Muslim Law (WLUML), at .21. All three of these high-prestige groups were formed as part of the new women's mobilization after the 1970s rather than being survivors from the first wave of feminism (like the Women's International League for Peace and Freedom or the Mother's Union).

For the rest of our analysis we pool our data in the three regions we constructed: the United States (and Canada), Europe (East and West), and the global South. Although we recognize that there is a great deal of diversity within as well as across these three regions (as Table 10.1 indicates), the pooling strategy allows us to compare less organizationally idiosyncratic data. Table 10.2, which presents the network linkages among the pooled groups of Web sites by region, shows that all organizations in all three regions are more likely to link themselves to U.S.-based sites, meaning that these organizations have high prestige in the network. However, U.S.-based Web sites are five times more likely than European-based groups to post a link to a non-Western site, which suggests that outreach to the global South is an important part of their identity. Non-Western organizations in their turn are also six times more likely to post a link to a U.S.-based Web site than to a European site, suggesting that in their eyes at least U.S.-based groups enjoy more prestige than European ones. This reciprocity of regard between the United States and the global South forms a North-South axis of transnational identity.

To a surprising extent, the European organizations stand somewhat outside this axis of connection. They make only four links to non-Western groups themselves, compared with twenty links from U.S. groups to non-Western ones. This is clearly not a matter of resources, as they are not more likely to be poor than U.S. sites or those in the global South. The U.S. sites are central to the network because they are well connected to

TABLE 10.2
Numbers of Network Linkages Shown on Web Sites by Region

Link from:	Link to: US	European	Northwestern	Grand Total
US	27	14	20	61
European	13	8	4	25
Nonwestern	29	5	15	49
Grand Total	69	27	39	135

each other (twenty-seven links), being more linked internally than European (eight links) and non-Western sites (fifteen links) are within their own regions, and also have high prestige, drawing links from groups elsewhere in the world. The U.S. sites also do more outreach outside their own region. They have more links to European sites than non-Western groups do (fourteen compared with five), as well as more links to non-Western sites than European groups do (twenty compared with four). Thus it would not be appropriate to compare an undifferentiated "West" with "the rest," since the U.S. and European patterns differ so markedly. The sample is regrettably too small to see if there are similar differences among the non-Western groups by regions of the world, but this would be an important consideration for further research.

It is striking that European transnational groups do not construct an identity based on looking beyond Europe. These groups are also not seen as partner organizations by those in the global South. This might reflect a focus on the *intra*regional transnationalism that the EU provides in Europe, or also a tendency in Europe for there to be a sharper division between women's organizations and international development groups (that might have some feminist or woman-centered subgroup but would not appear in our sample). How European groups compare in identity on the basis of their framing rather than just their ties to others may help to clarify the meaning of this difference in network position. It is to these framing differences in language choice to which we now turn.

Linguistic Indicators of Identity

Across all three regional groups, as we would expect, the word "women" is used considerably more often than either the word "gender" or the word "feminist(s)" (see Figure 10.1). Again, however, it is the European groups that seem to have a different identity, one that especially eschews the radical concept "feminist." Whereas "women" is used in about one-quarter of all sentences in all three regions, "feminists" is used only in 1.1 percent of all sentences on U.S.-based Web sites, 1 percent on non-Western sites, and 0.2 percent on European sites. European organizations' avoidance of the word "feminist(s)" might indicate their effort to fit into an EU-centered policy-focused discourse about transnationalism rather than embrace a radical social movement identity.

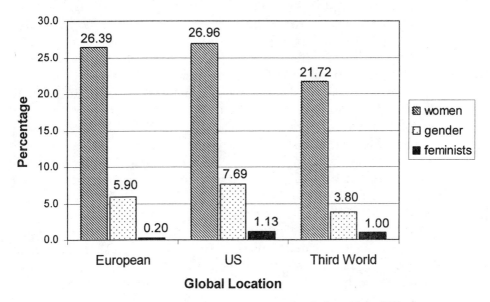

Figure 10.1: Percentages of Sentences that Contain Each of Three Pivotal Words on Websites by Region

Additionally, the word "gender" is used more often than "feminists" and has the highest visibility on U.S.-based Web sites, with 7.7 percent of sentences containing it, followed by European Web sites (5.9 percent of sentences), and Third World–based sites (3.8 percent of sentences). The transnational language of speaking in terms of gender is less pronounced in Europe than in the United States, even though the U.S. government has not endorsed CEDAW and is keeping its distance from the Beijing Platform for Action. The organizations of the global South are even less likely to embrace "gender" as part of their public identity. "Gender" as a term seems to appear more consistently "Western" and to be less embraced in the global South than it is in either Europe or the United States. The relatively frequent use of "gender" on the U.S.-based sites may also be evidence of the importance of English as the native language for all of them, while other sites translate material into English.

A fuller disambiguation of the meanings of these three pivotal terms is made possible by moving from simple comparison of frequencies of use to the collocations that give them contextual meaning. In Table 10.3 we compare the ten top terms used in the same sentences with each of these three concepts by region. In terms of collocations of the pivotal words, on U.S.-based Web sites "rights" is the word most strongly associated with "woman" by a substantial amount (more than 10,000 co-occurrences compared to just over 7,000 for the next most frequent collocation, "development"). "Development" as a term is closely associated not only with "women" but also with "feminists" and "gender." A similar pattern is also seen in the Web sites based in the global South, where women are most prominently tied to "rights." Again, it is the European sites that are different, with a both a regional location (European) and a relational term ("man") being more frequently associated with "women" than "rights" are. It is also striking that in the United States the term "development" figures so centrally in the framing associated with all three pivotal terms, suggesting that a focus on development as well as "international," "human," and "rights" (which also are among the top collocations for all three pivotal words) consistently informs the identity of transnational women's groups based in the United States.

The terms "feminist" and "gender" differ from "women" in all three parts of the world. Uniformly, the term "feminist" relates strongly to the word "movement," and the word "gender" to the word "policy." Thus the term "feminist" is not only a radical concept but one that is more tightly linked with a social movement, and which is also in the United States and the global South more explicitly tied to the concept "political" as well. Although "gender" is associated with both "policy" and "equality" in all three regions, "policy" is one of the top collocations for "women" only in Europe, "development" is missing as a collocation for both "women" and "feminist" only in Europe, and "rights" does not associate with "gender" in Europe either, again suggesting that Europe stands a bit aside from the north-south axis for framing transnational identity. The prominence of "Europe/European" in the top collocations on the Europe-based sites also suggests a distinctive, intraregional identity (organized around gender-equality-policy) that is not seen in the U.S. or global South Web sites.

In this more regionally distinctive European framing, development figures less centrally and policy more centrally in the organizational identity. In the U.S.-based sites, "gender" is more of a theory-centered word, tied strongly to "perspective" and "information," whereas in the European sites

TABLE 10.3
Top Ten Collocations of Pivotal Words (Woman, Feminist, and Gender) by Region

Woman(-en)		U.S.-based sites: Feminist(s)		Gender	
rights	10,349	woman	1,091	women	7,364
development	7,267	**development**	562	**development**	4,967
human	5,880	organization	476	equality	3,509
international	5,013	strategy	356	rights	2,940
violence	4,814	*movement*	351	*policy*	2,264
organization	4,062	international	301	human	2,227
man	3,872	rights	290	international	1,774
information	3,494	social	240	information	1,667
health	3,369	political	188	perspective	1,444
government	3,303	human	157	**violence**	1,313

Woman(-en)		Europe-based sites: Feminist(s)		Gender	
Europe/European	7,348	woman	164	equality	4,580
man	7,017	**violence**	43	women	4,008
violence	3,778	*movement*	39	*policy*	1,783
rights	3,419	peace	36	Europe/European	1,631
international	2,594	international	34	man	1,506
policy	2,500	rights	30	European Union	1,269
action	2,330	health	19	**mainstreaming**	1,243
social	2,191	man	19	social	1,109
member	2,173	national	17	action	857
child	2,014	relation	17	**development**	775

Woman(-en)		Global South sites: Feminist(s)		Gender	
rights	5,211	woman	1,037	women	3,143
international	3,842	*movement*	334	equality	1,285
organization	3,206	social	247	**development**	1,207
health	3,192	**development**	201	*policy*	948
man	3,032	rights	195	rights	811
development	2,647	political	191	social	657
human	2,544	international	180	international	643
information	2,281	activist	169	education	619
action	2,252	organization	118	health	594
violence	2,131	society	103	human	544

its distinctive top ten collocations are with "action" and "mainstreaming," which carry policy connotations. Also, "legislation" and "implementation" are among the top fifty collocates of "gender" in Europe, whereas "justice" and "strategy" appear among the top fifty collocates of "gender" in the other two regions but not in Europe. In the global South, the two distinctive top ten correlates of "gender" are "education" and "health," which suggests the specific issues with which development/equality/policy are conceptually closely related in this particular region.

Another distinction among the top collocations by region is the placement of the term "violence." This word is associated with "women" in all three regions, but more strongly so in both European- and U.S.-based sites. The concern about "violence" is also especially highly associated with "feminism" in Europe and with "gender" in the United States, but with neither of these words in the global South, suggesting that this might be a more "Western" concept. Another way to look at the relative weight given to such linguistic associations across regions is to compute a mean score or compare relative placement among the top fifty rather than merely the top ten collocates of each word. In Table 10.4, which reports scores based on this fuller distribution, we see that "violence" occurs more frequently (has a higher rank/lower number) than "health" in the U.S. and European sites for all three pivotal words, but that "health" has a higher rank (lower number) than "violence" in the global South. Thus although the concept of violence against women as a problem seems to have been embraced by transnational women's organizations in the global South, they continue to give more emphasis to health issues. The relative priority of violence over all other issues is thus something that appears to be "Western." This makes it different than "development," where the priority is shared along a north-south axis in U.S. and global South groups, with Europe being distinctively different.

As Table 10.4 also indicates, the concept "feminist" is a movement- and activist-related term that implies activity and is highly political. Our assumption that this is a challenging, radical word is borne out in its collocations. It is less associated with more conventional, top-down types of politics as captured in the words "government" and "policy," where both "woman" and "gender" are more prominently used in all three regions. The word "political" leans more toward a pattern of collocations that give it a grassroots, movement-like meaning than one that is top-down, suggesting that these NGOs define politics generally as something more than reform-oriented policymaking. "Gender" is thus less associated with being "political" than is "feminist," and the avoidance of the term "feminist" by the Europe-based groups is mirrored also in their lesser use of the concept "political" in relation to all three of the pivot words. It is only on the non-Western sites that the word "feminist" appears as one of the top fifty collocates of "woman" at all, although "woman" is always among the top collocates of feminist and gender.

In the United States, organizations identify themselves more with issues of theory, perspective, analysis, and university settings. Interestingly, as

TABLE 10.4

Selected Relative Ranks (low number = high rank order)
of Collocates of Pivotal Words by Region

Association with the three key words

Relative rankings of selected words	Woman			Feminist			Gender		
	U.S.	South	Europe	U.S.	South	Europe	U.S.	South	Europe
Mean rank: movement-action-activist	28.6	23.3	36.3	10.0	8.6	12.3	40.3	39.3	37.0
Political	19	25	35	9	6	17	42	30	51
Mean rank: policy-government	10.5	14.0	15.0	30.5	24.0	37.5	10.0	12.0	15.0
Information	8	8	27	39	17	13	8	18	33
Theory				13	46	43			
Perspective							9	24	14
Mean rank: man-child-family	20.0	14.0	13.3	46.0	41.3	30.3	39.3	41.6	31.3
Violence	5	10	3	22	39	2	10	13	13
Health	9	4	11	51	21	7	13	9	21
International vs. national	4/14	2/24	5/13	6/25	7/24	5/9	7/21	7/21	34/20
Most frequently named localization (rank)	American (36)	Muslim (28)	European (1)	American (31)	Muslim (40)	European (28)	Africa (38)	Asia (37)	Europe (4)

Table 10.4 also shows, "theory" as a word is consistently associated with "feminist," whereas "gender" is associated with "perspective," and neither "theory" nor "perspective" appears among the top fifty collocates for "woman." "Conference" and "meeting" do figure in as moderately high collocates for all three pivot words, and are not especially tied to "gender." Thus it seems fair to conclude that the transnational meaning that "gender" has acquired is more about formal policymaking than about academic theory, the latter connotation being more significant in the United States, as is the link between "feminism" and "theory." This does not mean that the words do not have such connotations, but rather than these transnational organizations do not make these connotations part of their own professed identities on the Web sites.

As transnational organizations, it is not surprising that these groups use the word "international" more than "national" in relation to all three pivot words, as Table 10.4 shows. Europe again is a bit of an exception. For "gender" "national" actually has a higher rank order than "international," and for "woman" and "feminist" the difference in ranks between these two concepts is smaller than in the other two regions. While "woman" as a term is a more conservative one than either "feminist" or "gender," in that it is more often connected to the words "man," "child," and "family" in all three regions, it is also the case that the familial connotations associated with "woman," "feminist," and "gender" are all higher in Europe than in the other two regions, and even "woman" is framed more strongly in familial terms in Europe than in the United States.

Overall, the patterns of identity among transnational women's organizations that their word choices suggest are consistent with the finding that Europe-based Web sites stand somewhat aside from the main North-South axis. European sites have a more localized and national framing of their identity. This identity also largely eschews the more radical connotations of feminism and frames women as less politically active from the grassroots. Gender and its implications of top-down policymaking joins with the closer connections between the pivot concepts and familial words found in Europe to suggest that these Europe-based transnational organizations present identities that are less challenging to the overall status quo. The organizations based in the United States and in the global South share a discourse in which development and human rights are both very important parts of their identities. However, the ability of the global South to shape the priorities of all groups is also shown to be limited, since their emphasis on health as an issue of greater concern than violence is not mirrored in the organizations based in either region of the West.

Discussion

Our results indicate that these transnational women's organizations have in all regions appropriated institutionally anchored discourses of universal human rights and violence against women into their identities, but they are still somewhat concerned about appearing too radical by embracing the term "feminist." The use of the term "feminist," though relatively rare, is nonetheless strongly associated with movement-centered forms of politics and activism in all three regions. The more popular term "gender" is, by contrast, a more top-down, policy-centered concept of governmental intervention. In Europe, gender equality policy especially means European policy, and is especially strongly linked to the specific approach of "gender mainstreaming," that is, scrutiny of all policymaking for its gender-specific implications, that was adopted as a strategy in the Beijing Platform for Action. For groups based in the United States or the global South, the concept of "mainstreaming" is not one of the top ten (it is number 20 and 22, respectively). In the global South, in particular, education and health are policy issues that rank higher than violence or mainstreaming as terms associated with gender.

Transnational influence on regional policy concerns also figures in the Web identities of U.S.-based and global South–based groups by giving "development" such a prominent association with "women," as well as with "gender" and "feminist." Since the ideas of both development and mainstreaming can be seen as contributions from the global South to the overall transnational discourse about how to attain gender equality formulated in Beijing, this can be counted as a success for the influence of the less powerful. However, the different priority given to health rather than violence as an issue suggests that the ability of the global South to influence the global agenda is limited.

In line with the expectations of the techno-optimists, we find that resource differences are not the main factor explaining relative prestige of these organizations among themselves, as there is a sharp difference between groups based in Europe and those based in the United States. The U.S.-based groups seem to choose to use their resources for outreach more than the European groups do, which not only seems to create more prestige for them from the global South groups in turn, but also appears to lead to a greater sharing of frames along the resultant North-South axis. Transnational groups based in Europe are facing a distinctive and very demanding challenge in the form of the expansion in national members and scope of policy relevance held by the European Union (the so-called widening and deepening of the EU). The EU influence is typically felt through administrative directives and treaties in a top-down way rather than in stirring up grassroots mobilizations, such as the pro-democracy movements in other parts of the world. In such a context, it may not be surprising that the European groups express more concern with regional matters and with top-down policymaking.

Nonetheless, it remains surprising that this inward focus is also one that is expressed in more attention to women in relation to men and families and less of a social movement strategy, both of which could be interpreted as a more conservative outlook, especially in conjunction with the avoidance of the term "feminist" as a self-description. It appears that organizational identities of NGOs that are more actively participating in exchanges of links along the north-south axis could be related to taking up a more challenging and "activist" international discourse. Of course, this is something that would also need to be investigated at the level of the individual organizations and their specific identities.

The findings reported here should thus be seen as merely suggestive of directions for future research. Any examination of identities of organizations really needs a larger and more fully representative sample in order to offer reliable conclusions about how transnational NGOs present themselves. Links to organizations outside even a more inclusive sample would also be important aspects of a group's self-presentation to investigate. Looking at the proportion of the Web site that is in English in relation to the adoption of transnational discourse is another important consideration that this preliminary research could not address. The advantages to a group of sharing the transnational lingua franca of English should not be underestimated, nor the possibilities of linkages that are dominantly organized around a shared non-English language (e.g., Spanish, Russian, or Chinese) and that might give a different picture of the density of ties.

Overall, however, even such a preliminary look at the online community of discourse among transnational women's organizations is helpful. To a large extent, it suggests that optimism about the circulation of discourses and the ability of groups to transcend resource limits is warranted. The emergence of a post–cold war axis of attention between groups based in the global North and South is heartening, as is the mutual recognition implied by concepts like violence and development being so prominent in the discourse of groups based around the world. The finding that groups are still wary of the radical term "feminist" and the activist grassroots stance toward politics associated with it is less cheering for those who fear the loss of a women's movement in the institutionalization of women's issues as policy concerns for governments. The notion of a transnational civil society also receives only limited support, given the relatively low density of the network we found online. Some groups in every region are notably better at doing outreach and have more prestige than others as well, though it is unclear whether their online influence translates to better connections in discursive terms as well. Although there is evidence here of a discourse that circulates transnationally, there are clearly also regional limits to the sharing of identities and links online. How these online communities relate to sharing in the actual world is yet another question that calls for further research.

Overall, our findings show the emergence of innovative and challenging frames in the online transnational discourse that could potentially challenge the dominance of neoliberal ideas. The regional locations and identities of these transnational feminist groups matter even in the realm of the Internet, but the interaction between local and regional focal issues is more complex than any dichotomy between them can encompass. The Web does seem to be a space where meaningful dialogue occurs among multiple, geographically dispersed actors that do not necessarily share common views, history, or experiences (Miller 2000). There are thus grounds for seeing the Web as a new space with potential for becoming a powerful field in its own right, though this potential is far from being fully realized.

APPENDIX. ORGANIZATIONS IN THE SAMPLE

Name (Acronym)	URL	Country in which based and founding year	Total number of sentences on the Web site
African Women's Media Centre (AWMC)	www.awmc.com	Senegal, 1997	8065
Arab Women Solidarity Organization (AWSA)	www.awsanet.org	Egypt, 1982	2856
Asia Pacific Forum on Women, Law, and Development (APWLD)	www.apwld.org	Thailand, 1986	10332
Asian Pacific Resource and Research Centre for Women (ARROW)	www.arrow.org.my	Malaysia, 1993	23510
Association for Women in Development (AWID)	www.awid.org	Canada, 1982	167848
Association of Women of the Mediterranean Region (AWMR)	digilander.libero.it/awmr/int	Cyprus, 1992	2133
Center for Women's Global Leadership (CWGL)	www.cwgl.rutgers.edu	USA, 1989	16774
Development Alternatives with Women for a New Era (DAWN)	www.dawn.org.fj	Fiji, 1984	36752
Equality Now	www.equalitynow.org	USA, 1992	10106

APPENDIX. ORGANIZATIONS IN THE SAMPLE *(Continued)*

Name (Acronym)	URL	Country in which based and founding year	Total number of sentences on the Web site
European Association for Women and Health Research (EAWHR)	www.eawhr.org	Netherlands, 1996	3101
European Women's Lobby (EWL)	www.womenloby.org	Belgium, 1990	85425
Forum for African Women Educationalists (FAWE)	www.fawe.org	Kenya, 1992	27580
Global Fund for Women	www.globalfund forwomen.org	USA, 1987	15241
Inter-American Commission of Women	www.oas.org/CIM	USA, 1928	28264
International Federation of Business and Professional Women (BPWINTL)	www.bpwintl.org	UK, 1930	3562
International Federation of University Women (IFUW)	www.ifuw.org	Switzerland, 1919	27841
International Women's Democracy Center (IWDC)	www.iwdc.org	USA, n/a	4232
International Women's Tribune Centre (IWTC)	www.iwtc.org	USA, 1978	11524
Isis International— Manila (ISIS)	www.isiswomen.org	Philippines, 1974	121131
MADRE	www.madre.org	USA, 1983	20820
The Mother's Union	www.themothers union.org	UK, 1876	18021
Network of East-West Women (NEWW)	www.neww.org	USA, 1990	1191
Older Women's Network—Europe (OWN)	www.own-europe.org	Italy, 1993	4374
Research, Action, and Information Network for the Bodily Integrity of Women (RAINBO)	www.rainbo.org	USA, n/a	2228
Women's Global Network for Reproductive Rights (WGNRR)	www.wgnrr.org	Netherlands, 1978	18562
Women in Europe for a Common Future (WECF)	www.wecf.org	Netherlands, 1992	8713

APPENDIX. ORGANIZATIONS IN THE SAMPLE *(Continued)*

Name (Acronym)	URL	Country in which based and founding year	Total number of sentences on the Web site
Women against Violence Europe (WAVE)	www.wave-network.org	Austria, 1994	8713
Women's Environment and Development Organization (WEDO)	www.wedo.org	USA, 1990	63666
Women's International League for Peace and Freedom (WILPF)	www.wilpf.int.ch	Switzerland, 1915	23828
Women Living under Muslim Laws (WLUML)	www.wluml.org	France, 1985	27093

NOTES

1. The density Δ is calculated using the formula $L/[g(g-1)]$, where L is the total number of ties between actors and g is the total number of actors. This overall centralization index was obtained using the following formula:

$$C_A = \frac{\sum_{i=l}^{g}[C_A(n^\star) - C_A(n_i)]}{\max \sum_{i=l}^{g}[C_A(n^\star) - C_A(n_i)]}$$

where $C_A(n_i)$ is an actor centrality index, and $C_A(n^\star)$ is the largest value of the particular index that occurs across actors in the network (Wasserman and Faust 1999).

2. In the mean score calculations, words omitted from the top fifty were assigned the value of 51, since the ranks become more unreliable as the number of sentences in which the word figures declines. Complete collocation outputs are available upon request.

BIBLIOGRAPHY

Alvarez, Sonia E. 1998. "Latin American Feminisms 'Go Global': Trends of the 1990s and Challenges for the New Millennium." In Sonia E. Alvarez, Evelina Dagnino, and Arturo Escobar, eds., *Cultures of Politics, Politics of Cultures: Revisioning Latin American Social Movements*, 293–324. Boulder, Colo.: Westview Press.

———. 1999. "Advocating Feminism: The Latin American Feminist NGO 'Boom.'" *International Feminist Journal of Politics* 1:181–209.

Basu, Amrita. 2001. "Globalization of the Local/Localization of the Global: Mapping Transnational Women's Movements." *Meridians: Feminism, Race, Transnationalism* 1:68–84.

Berkovich, Nitza. 1999. *From Motherhood to Citizenship: Women's Rights and International Organizations.* Baltimore: Johns Hopkins University Press.

Diani, Mario. 2000. "Social Movement Networks Virtual and Real." *Information, Communication and Society* 3:386–401.

Ferree, Myra Marx. 2003. "Resonance and Radicalism: Feminist Framing in the Abortion Debates of the United States and Germany." *American Journal of Sociology* 109:304–344.

Ferree, Myra Marx, and William Gamson. 1999. "The Gendering of Abortion Discourse: Assessing Global Feminist Influence in the United States and Germany." In Donatella Della Porta, Hanspeter Kriesi, and Dieter Rucht, eds., *Social Movements in a Globalizing World,* 40–56. New York: St. Martins Press.

Ferree, Myra Marx, and Beth B. Hess. 2000. *Controversy and Coalition: The New Feminist Movement across Three Decades of Change.* 3rd. edition. New York: Routledge.

Ferree, Myra Marx, and Carol Mueller. 2004. "Feminism and the Women's Movement: A Global Perspective." In David A. Snow, Sarah A. Soule, and Hanspeter Kriesi, eds., *The Blackwell Companion to Social Movements,* 576–607. Oxford: Blackwell.

Friedman, Susan Stanford. 2001. "Locational Feminism: Gender, Cultural Geographies, and Geopolitical Literacy." In Marianne DeKoven, ed., *Feminist Locations: Global and Local, Theory and Practice,* 13–36. New Brunswick, N.J.: Rutgers University Press.

Gamson, William A. 1992. *Talking Politics.* New York: Cambridge University Press.

Garrido, M., and A. Halavais. 2003. "Mapping Networks of Support for the Zapatista Movement: Applying Social-Networks Analysis to Study Contemporary Social Movements." In M. McCaughy and M. D. Ayers, eds., *Cyberactivism: Online Activism in Theory and Practice,* 165–184. London: Routledge.

Jackson, M. H. 1997. "Assessing the Structure of Communication on the World Wide Web." *Journal of Computer-Mediated Communication* 3(1). http://www.ascusc.org/jcmc/vol3/issue1/jackson.html.

Katzenstein, Mary F. 1998. *Faithful and Fearless: Moving Feminist Protest inside the Church and Military.* Princeton, N.J.: Princeton University Press.

Keck, Margaret E., and Kathryn Sikkink. 1998. *Activists beyond Borders: Advocacy Networks in International Politics.* Ithaca, N.Y.: Cornell University Press.

Khagram, Sanjeev, James V. Riker, and Kathryn Sikkink. 2002. *Restructuring World*

Politics: Transnational Social Movements, Networks, and Norms. Minneapolis: University of Minnesota Press.

Klandermans, Bert. 1997. *The Social Psychology of Protest.* Oxford: Blackwell.

Kole, Ellen. 1998. "Myths and Realities in Internet Discourse: Using Computer Networks for Data Collection and the Beijing World Conference on Women." *Gazette* 60:343–360.

Marsden, Peter V. 1990. "Network Data and Measurement." *Annual Review of Sociology* 16:435–463.

Miller, Byron A. 1992. "Collective Action and Rational Choice: Place, Community, and the Limits to Individual Self-Interest." *Economic Geography* 68:22–42.

———. 2000. *Geography and Social Movements: Comparing Antinuclear Activism in the Boston Area.* Minneapolis: University of Minnesota Press.

Park, Han Woo, and Mike Thelwall. 2003. "Hyperlink Analysis of the World Wide Web: A Review." *Journal of Computer-Mediated Communication* 8 (4). http://www. ascusc.org/jcmc/vol8/issue4/park.html.

Pudrovska, Tetyana, and Myra Marx Ferree. 2004. "Transnational Gender Politics in Cyberspace: The Case of the European Women's Lobby." *Social Politics* 11:117–143.

Sampaio, Anna, and Janni Aragon. 1997. "To Boldly Go (Where No Man Has Gone Before): Women and Politics in Cyberspace." *New Political Science* 41/42:145–167.

Sassi, Sinikka. 2001. "The Transformation of the Public Sphere?" In Barrie Axford and Richard Huggins, eds., *New Media and Politics,* 89–108. London: Sage.

Schulz, Markus S. 1998. "Collective Action across Borders: Opportunity Structures, Network Capacities, and Communicative Praxis in the Age of Advanced Globalization." *Sociological Perspectives* 41:587–616.

Scott, Anne. 2001. "(In)forming Politics: Processes of Feminist Activism in the Information Age." *Women's Studies International Forum* 24:409–421.

Sikkink, Kathryn. 1993. "Human Rights, Principled Issue-Networks, and Sovereignty in Latin America." *International Organizations* 47:411–441.

Smith, Jackie. 1998. "Global Civil Society? Transnational Social Movement Organizations and Social Capital." *American Behavioral Scientist* 42:93–107.

Sperling, Valerie, Myra Marx Ferree, and Barbara Risman. 2001. "Constructing Global Feminism: Transnational Advocacy Networks and Russian Women's Activism." *Signs* 26:1155–1186.

Stubbs, Michael. 1996. *Text and Corpus Analysis: Computer-Assisted Studies of Language and Culture.* Oxford: Blackwell.

Vogt, Christina, and Peiying Chen. 2001. "Feminism and the Internet." *Peace Review* 13:371–374.

Walby, Sylvia. 2002. "Feminism in a Global Era." *Economy and Society* 31:533–557.

Wasserman, Stanley, and Katherine Faust. 1999. *Social Network Analysis: Methods and Applications*. Cambridge: Cambridge University Press.

Wellman, Barry. 1983. "Network Analysis: Some Basic Principles." *Sociological Theory* 1:155–200.

Yearbook of International Organizations: Guide to Global Civil Society Networks. Vol. 3. 2002–2003. Munich: Union of International Associations and K. G. Saur Verlag.

Part IV

Conclusions

11

Human/Women's Rights and Feminist Transversal Politics

Nira Yuval-Davis

Louisa Passerini (2000) talks about the discontinuities and multiple subject positionings of histories. This also includes the histories of the global feminist movement. Nevertheless, if and when we are trying to discover the genealogies of particular norms and practices, the task of constructing an implicit or explicit historical narrative seems unavoidable. And yet, such a task would be taken from particular situated knowledge and imagination (Haraway, 1991; Harding 1991, Stoetzler and Yuval-Davis, 2002), and it may help the reader if I state here that my view of global feminism has grown out of taking part in feminist antiracist and antifundamentalist activism since the 1970s in the context of Israel/Palestine, Britain, and nongovernmental organization (NGO) forums of various UN conferences during the 1990s, as well as in other international gatherings. The impetus to write this chapter has come from a certain sense of discomfort that has been compounded when exchanging views with other feminist activists in the political realities of post–cold war and especially post-9/11 times, the growing disaffection with what activism within the UN framework can achieve, and yet the feeling that acting within alternative global frameworks such as the Global Social Forum[1] and/or the Association of Women in Development (AWID)[2] would not necessarily supply the solution either.

The primary focus of this chapter, however, is not the histories of global feminist activisms during the last fifteen or twenty years (for informative articles on some aspects of these histories, see, for example, Barton, 2004; Bunch et al., 2001; and the concluding chapter of Petchesky, 2004) but certain issues that have been endemic to them and on which I would like to reflect.

Since the 1990s, and definitely since the 1994 UN conference on human rights in Vienna, much of global feminist activism has been constructed in the discourse of rights, under the slogan of "women's rights are human rights" (Bunch, 1990). This discourse of rights has enabled many local, as well as transnational, women's groups to challenge existing customs and legislation that discriminate against women, all around the world. It also helped to transform much of feminist activism from "identity politics" feminism into "transversal politics," problematizing women's homogeneity and reinforcing feminist solidarity beyond borders and boundaries, as well as transcending a simplistic cosmopolitan approach.

The first part of the chapter discusses this transition in feminist politics from identity politics to transversal politics, including an exploration of the dialogically situated epistemology that underlies such politics. The second part argues that in spite of the great advances made, contemporary transnational feminist politics are ridden with their own inherent problems, partly common to those in feminist identity politics and partly due to tensions in the construction of feminist politics as women's/human rights politics.

Identity Politics versus Transversal Politics

"Sisterhood is powerful," argued a popular feminist slogan in the 1970s (Morgan, 1970), with the rise of what is known as the second wave of feminism. In this construction, all women are sisters, there is no inherent real conflict among any women, and solidarity is, or at least should be, unproblematic.

The argument of 1970s feminism, however, went even further to say not only that all women are sisters, but that they all share the same condition of oppression, and the same situated gaze of the world. One of the most powerful feminist tools of the 1970s was the "consciousness-raising" group (Piercy and Freeman 1972). Within the discourse of consciousness-raising, women who see the world differently, or who argue that they are not as oppressed by men and patriarchy as some other women, are not recognized as having different histories and/or locations, but just as expressing symptoms of their unraised consciousness. Once it is "properly" raised, they would share the same experiential-cum-political world-view as their sisters (Yuval-Davis, 1984, 1994).

It was experiential-cum-political because another foundation slogan of the 1970s feminist movement was "The personal is political" (first used, according to Humm, 1995, by Carol Hanisch in 1969 in a Redstockings pamphlet). One way of understanding this slogan—a way that withstood the test of time—has been to argue (before poststructuralists attributed this insight to Foucault) that power relations and power dynamics exist in all social locations, in the bedroom as well as in the government. Another interpretation of this slogan, however, has been that one can develop political judgments only from one's own standpoint, and personal experi-ence of womanhood was seen as the unifying factor (Smith, 1990). Women and other marginal and disadvantaged elements in the society (the feminist movement was strongly affected by the development of the black movement in the United States and other Western countries but also by Marxist/Hegelian epistemology) have been long excluded from main-stream political interests and mainstream alternative politics in the Left. Therefore, the primary, if not the only, political task they have had is to consider and fight against their own oppression and exclusion, which is often also seen as a lever for a comprehensive social and political transfor-mation.

The combined effect of these hegemonic constructions of feminist pol-itics in the 1970s (the differences among radical, socialist, and liberal fem-inists notwithstanding) was to create what is known as "identity politics" (Moghadam, 1994). In such politics, all the members of the oppressed social category are constructed as homogeneous; all dimensions of social locations are reduced into the primary one. Thus there is no differentia-tion in this approach between categorical locations, social identities, and political values. As a result, identity politics conflates individual and col-lective identities, therefore assuming that any member of any social cate-gory or identity can speak for all the other members of that category, for with their consciousness properly raised, they all share the same voice: "as a woman," "as a black," and so forth.

Even when marginal elements within each of these marginal groupings began to revolt against this so-called representative voice—for example, when black women and lesbian women and working-class women and older women and disabled women and so on started to argue that the hegemonic voice is that of white middle-class heterosexual able-bodied women, the first reaction was toward fragmentation and multiplication of "representative" voices of different small social categories ("as a black woman . . ."; "as a disabled woman . . ."; "as a lesbian Asian disabled woman," etc.), rather than a rejection of that model of identity politics itself. This rejection came later, with the introduction into feminist thinking of intersectional analysis (e.g., Anthias and Yuval-Davis, 1983; Crenshaw, 1989; Harding, 1993), as well as with the growing hegemony of poststructuralist, if not postmodernist, paradigms within feminist theory (e.g., Scott, 1992; Butler, 1992). Homogenizing and reifying women, or even any subcategory of women, were no longer feasible or acceptable.

As a result, standpoint theory, the epistemological approach developed by feminists, was rejected by some, especially postmodernist feminists (see, e.g., the debate in *Signs* 22(2), 1997, and articles by Hartsock, Hekman, and others). Others, who did not want to lose the theoretical insights of this approach, transformed and incorporated into it a recognition of diversity among women and a dialogical approach (Hill-Collins, 1990; Benhabib, 1992; Stoetzler and Yuval-Davis 2002).

While these debates occupied many of the feminists who were engaged in developing women's and gender studies in academia, important developments also took place in other locations in which feminist activists were engaged. One such location was the legal arena, and especially the success of establishing equal opportunities legislation and legal watchdogs in the public spheres of many, especially Western, welfare states. Feminist lobbying was crucial for these developments, but so was the development of a growing body of feminist legal and sociolegal expertise. In such work, although the connections between the plight of individual women and the collective social and political and legal status of women were highlighted, more and more feminist activism became engaged in advocacy work. Women's groups and women's centers became engaged in defending individual cases of abused, oppressed, and discriminated against women, while at the same time continuing to lobby for changes in the collective legal position of women. In many cases campaigns for individual women became an illustration and flagships for general points in law and policy regulations (see, e.g., WING, 1985 and SBS, 1990 in the UK).

While these developments took place in many local settings, there has also been a development in global women's networking that built upon these local achievements but also added to them lobbying of UN agencies and networking across borders and boundaries. The feminist movement has tended to be internationalist since the first wave of feminism. Its cosmopolitan approach was expressed in Virginia Woolf's famous declaration "As a woman I have no country." However, as Kumari Jayawardena (1986) and others have shown, the struggle for women's equality and liberation has just as often, especially in colonial societies, been formulated by many women's groups as part of their people's national and anticolonial liberation struggles. And even Woolf's pacifism was drowned out by "patriotic" women in World War I and World War II.

During the second wave of feminism, the UN came to play a role of growing importance as a transnational location in which women and feminists from different parts of the world would meet. Of crucial importance has been the work since 1946 of the freestanding Commission on the Status of Women (CSW), the development of the Convention on the Elimination of All Forms of Discrimination against Women (CEDAW) in 1979, the 1985–1995 UN Decade for Women, and the international women's conferences that took place at its beginning and end in Nairobi and Beijing. In these conferences, the role of NGOs and the number of women participants has grown significantly. Gradually, and with the help of the new communication technologies that facilitated virtual meetings of feminists also apart from the conferences via international phone calls, faxes, and e-mails, large global networks of women developed, as did the interdependence of local and global feminist activism.

Part of the reason for this focus of feminist activism around the UN is that the UN has become the primary site for the whole arena of human rights since the 1948 Universal Declaration of Human Rights. A major focus of the work of the CSW has been to make the case for the equality of women and men and to apply human rights fully to all women. However, it was at the 1993 conference on human rights in Vienna that the slogan "Women's rights are human rights" was launched as the primary mobilizing slogan (Agosin, 2002) and where issues of violence against women (and later on in the 1994 UN Cairo conference the reproductive and health rights of women; see Petchesky, 2004) became a central part of the human rights agenda. Moreover, if human rights are sometimes defined as "laws without teeth" that are only gradually being incorporated into regional and national legislation (Klug, 2001), feminists active in the campaign to establish the International Criminal Court at the turn of the new millennium have managed successfully to incorporate violence against women into the agenda of the international legislation on war crimes and crimes against humanity (Copelon, 2000).

Feminist activism related to situations of ethnic and national conflicts and wars has been another significant front for the development of an international women's movement (Cockburn, 1998; Zajovic, 1994). Meetings among women from different sides of the conflict often took place in neutral zones and with the support of other international women's groups, as well as in NGO UN forums. Identity politics could not survive in their previous feminist format during these activities. The women who took part in the meetings were conscious all too often that they could not be seen as representing all women, not even all members of their ethnic and national collectivities, because most of the latter often supported the continuing confrontation and conflict. While the membership of these women in the conflicting collectivities was crucial to their participation in the encounter, their shared aspirations to find a common emancipatory solution to the conflict has been just as important. A new kind of feminist politics has been born, called "transversal politics" by the Italian feminists who sponsored many of the initial meetings of feminists from Israel/Palestine and the different components of former Yugoslavia. As the participants of a conference on "transversal politics" in London, organized by Cynthia Cockburn and Lynette Hunter (1999) found out, many other feminist organizations, at both national and international levels, have been engaged, throughout the 1990s in transversal politics, without knowing that they actually were doing so.

So What Is "Transversal Politics"?

Although I first heard about transversal politics in a letter of invitation written by two Italian feminists, Raphaela Lambertini and Elizabetta Dominini, inviting me to a meeting between Palestinian and Israeli (both Jewish and Palestinian) women that took place in Bologna in 1993, I learned later that there has been a whole tradition of autonomous left politics in Bologna under the name of transversalism since the 1970s. The name "transversal politics," however, was first coined in France by Guattari (1974) in a somewhat different context. Both in my own consequent writings on transversal politics (e.g., Yuval-Davis 1994, 1997) and in that of others (e.g., Cockburn 1998; Eschle, 2001), transversal politics are used both descriptively, referring to political activities and organizing that have been taking place in a variety of locations, and normatively, as a model of political activism that is worth following.

Before describing what transversal politics is, it is important to state what it is not. Transversal politics has been developed as an alternative to the assimilationist "universalistic" politics of the Left, on the one hand, and to identity politics, on the other hand. The first has proved to be ethnocentric and exclusionary (Balibar, 1990), assuming a West-centric commonality of interests and viewpoints. Identity politics, as explained earlier, was a result of resisting such politics. However, in their turn, they proved to be essentialist, as they were reifying boundaries between groups. By homogenizing and collapsing individual into collective identities, they were also undemocratic within groups (Cain & Yuval-Davis, 1990). Transversalism, on the other hand, as Guattari (1974) envisioned it, was about the politics of the construction of a radical political group as a collective subject, in which there is a constant flow of communication both horizontally and vertically—hence the name "transversalism," without such processes of reification taking place. The Bologna tradition of transversal politics expanded it beyond the boundaries of the political group and developed it into a more general politics of dialogue and cooperation.

Transversal politics is based, first, on a dialogical standpoint epistemology (Harding, 1991; Stoetzler and Yuval-Davis, 2002), a recognition that from each positioning the world is seen differently, and thus any knowledge based on just one positioning is "unfinished" (to differentiate from "invalid'; Hill-Collins, 1990:236). Thus, the only way to approach "the truth" is by a dialogue between people of differential positionings, and the wider the better. Second, transversal politics follows the principle of the encompassment (Dumont, 1972) of difference by equality (Yuval-Davis and Werbner, 1999). The claim is that, on the one hand, differences are important but, on the other hand, notions of difference should be encompassed by, rather than replace, notions of equality. Such notions of difference are not hierarchical and assume a priori respect for others' positionings, including acknowledgment of their differential social, economic, and political power.

Third, transversal politics differentiates—both conceptually and politically—between positioning, identity, and values. People who identify themselves as belonging to the same collectivity or social category can actually be positioned very differently in relation to a whole range of social locations (e.g., class, gender, ability, sexuality, stage in the life cycle). At the same time, people with similar positionings and/or identities can have very different social and political values (Yuval-Davis, 1994, 1997, 2003).

Several implications can be drawn from this. First, feminists and other community activists cannot (and should not) see themselves as representatives of their constituencies (unless they were democratically elected and are accountable for their actions). Rather, they are advocates, working to promote their cause. However, even as advocates, it is important that the activists should be reflective and conscious of the multiplexity of their specific positionings, both in relation to other members in their constituencies and in relation to other participants in any specific encounter. One of the problems with both identity politics is that such activists and "community leaders" too often become the "authentic voice" of their communities (in their own eyes no less than in the view of others). This is often harmful to women and other marginal elements within these same communities (Sahgal and Yuval-Davis, 1992; Yeatman, 1992).

The second implication of the preceding is that advocates do not necessarily have to always be members of the constituency they advocate for. It is the message, not the messenger, that counts. This avoids the necessity of constructing fixed and reified boundaries for social categories and groups. It does not mean, of course, that it is immaterial who the "messenger" is, but it does avoid (or at least resist) becoming involved in exclusionary politics. The feminists in Bologna introduced the concepts of "rooting" and "shifting" to explain how this could be done (letter of invitation to the conference in Bologna of Israeli and Palestinian feminists, December 1990). The idea is that each such "messenger" and each participant in a political dialogue would bring with them the reflective knowledge of their own positioning and identity. This is the "rooting." At the same time, they should also try to "shift"—to put themselves in the situation of those with whom they are in dialogue and who are different from them.

Transversal politics, nevertheless, does not assume that the dialogue is without boundaries, and that each conflict of interest is reconcilable—although, as Jan Jindi Pettman (1992:157) points out, "There are almost always possibilities for congenial or at least tolerable personal, social and political engagements." Similar, compatible values can cut across differences in positionings and identities. The struggle against oppression and discrimination might (and mostly does) have a specific categorical focus, but it is never confined just to that category. Often, especially since the 1994 UN conference on human rights, the common value system of transversal feminists from different locations is described as that of "women's rights as human rights."

Some Issues in Transversal Politics

For several years after discovering and analyzing transversal politics, I tried to promote it as the model of feminist (and other emancipatory) politics we should all follow. Gradually, however, in the tradition of the Foucauldian "ethics of discomfort" (1997), I have become more and more aware of some of the problems in transversal politics. In this section I want to highlight some of these endemic problems. First, I raise some issues concerning the notions of rooting and shifting; second, I raise issues concerning advocacy and decision-making mechanisms; and third, I raise some issues relating to the discursive framework of "women's rights are human rights" in which transversal political activists often work.

As I mentioned in the introduction to this chapter, I am aware that many of the problems of contemporary global feminist activism are due to the changing political climate, the constraints, pressures, and co-optative strategies of both global neoliberalisms and fundamentalisms inside and outside the UN (Barton, 2004; Imam & Yuval-Davis, 2004). However, this chapter concentrates on what I consider internal problematics that need to be resolved at the same time and codependently with developing strategies to face, confront, and hopefully overcome the external forces.

Rooting and Shifting

The interplay in transversal politics between rooting and shifting assumes that although knowledge and imagination are situated, there is a possibility of transcending the limitations of the specific situatedness of the subject in the shifting. Such transcendence is assumed possible first as a result of a combination of listening to the situated knowledge and fantasy of the other participants in the dialogue and second, via empathetic imaginings in which the subject attempts to position herself in the standpoint of the other participants. However, an active act of imagining is involved already in the act of rooting. While I shall not attempt in this chapter to examine the kinds of active imaginings that are involved in these processes (see Yuval-Davis, forthcoming), I want to problematize here some of assumptions involved. What does it actually mean to "root" in one's identity and positioning? Is it an act of description or creation (Scott, 1992:25)? Is there such a thing as a coherent subject in which one roots (Butler, 1992:9;

Benhabib, 1992:214)? Although transversal politics avoids homogenizing social categories and groupings, it could be argued that it homogenizes and fixates the positioning of the subject in a way that necessarily distorts and/or excludes some dimensions of one's subjectivity and identity.

Nor can we assume that the rooting would be simply relational, in the way Nancy Fraser (1998) and others articulate it in terms of recognizing the self via the relationship with the significant Other. The whole point of transversal politics is to transcend the binary divisions of those who are in different positionings in the dialogue. The aim of the rooting process (or "centering," as others prefer to call it) is *not* to imagine oneself just in relation to the social category of the Other but also in other ways through which different kinds of relationships with the partners in the transversal dialogue may be developed. That is probably one of the most important differences between identity politics and transversal politics. Rooting, or centering, therefore, cannot be an assumed and straightforward or fixed process. It is imperative that the form—and contents—of the constructive processes involved should become dynamic as well as explicit.

If this critique is valid concerning the processes of rooting, it should be even more so concerning those involved in shifting.

If the subject is constituted within its particular situated context, to what extent and how would it be possible for her to "shift," to imagine herself in somebody else's positionings? Wouldn't she necessarily imagine the meaning of the narratives of the other participants in the transversal dialogue in very different ways than those intended by the narrators? Seyla Benhabib (1992:227) and many others who support transversal politics would refute such a claim. Benhabib argues that at least within the hermeneutic horizon of modernity, an "interactive universalism" is possible. As Anna Lowenhaupt Tsing (1993) pointed out, no community is really completely isolated anymore, and therefore all paradigms of knowledge have at least some common points of meaning.

This is especially true in transversal politics because no transversal dialogue is without boundaries, and its participants do not assume that each conflict of interest is reconcilable. Transversal dialogue is possible when the different participants share compatible value systems that can cut across differences in positionings and identities. In other words, transversal politics takes place within what Alison Assiter (1996) calls "epistemological communities" (79) within which knowledge and values are located. Members in such epistemological communities learn their notions of reality—and of right and wrong—within such communities. As in medieval guilds, some members of the communities have more knowledge, and probably more important, hold more authority to determine—or to imagine—such knowledge, than others. However, in principle, such common knowledge and values can also be constructed as a result of egalitarian dialogue.

Assiter emphasizes that while members of epistemological communities share certain fundamental interests and beliefs, "they may additionally be members of diverse other social, cultural and political groupings" (82). In other words, the notion of epistemological communities separates social positionings and social values, and therefore offers a way to imagine the possibility of shifting beyond common material and historical locations. The boundaries of the dialogue are the boundaries of the moral/epistemological communities.

The question is, however, how such transversal epistemological communities are created. "Modernity" is too wide and general a field of reference; notions of "cultural imperialism" are too one-sided. Anyone who has taken part, for example, in the feminist transversal politics around the UN conferences held in Vienna, Cairo, and Beijing would know that often it was feminists from the "South" who were the most organized and innovative in these processes. Anyone who took part in transversal politics of feminists across the borders and boundaries of ethnic and national conflicts would know that the processes of change have radically affected women on both sides and have often created such common epistemological communities.

I have always disliked the notion of "hybridity" (e.g., Bhabha, 1994) because of its mechanical nature as well as its importing essentialism via the back door. Gloria Anzaldua's notion of "living on the border" (1987) also does not resolve the issue, as its construction does not allow for the differential border living of members of different collectivities—it is always imagined from the standpoint of the marginal "Other." At the same time, just to assume that people who are differentially positioned, even if they share roughly similar values, can automatically succeed in the process of shifting, is, I fear, all too often too naive.

This is why I found Donna Haraway's notion of "companion species" (2000), that are changing each other and inventing each other to be able to coexist, such a provocative and seductive form of imagining. At the same time, because the primary engagement of Haraway's discourse is about the relationships between humans and nonhumans and the subject matter of her paper on companion species is dogs, I fear we still have to look for a different suitable name for this process among humans who engage in the preparatory processes toward a transversal dialogue.

What is important, however, more than the name, is the realization that transversal politics is not only a dialogue in which two or more partners are negotiating a common political position, but it is a process in which all the participants are mutually reconstructing themselves and the others engaged with them in it. In such a process, although mutual respect and equal values are assumed in principle, one cannot ignore the dimension of (more often than not unequal) power relations and the mechanisms by which decisions are reached.

Power, Advocacy, and Decision-Making Mechanisms

The issue of decision-making mechanisms has plagued the second wave of feminism since the beginning. The movement's consensual approach to decisions was partly a result of its overall egalitarian antihierarchical perspective. This approach was also a result of the identity politics nature of the movement, as it assumed that all women/sisters needed to speak in one voice. This was never the case, and a classic paper, "The Tyranny of Structurelessness," written by Jo Freeman (1970), highlighted the fact that in reality, those who made the decisions and spoke in the name of "women" typically were the unelected activists in feminist organizations.

The transition from identity politics to transversal politics made clearer the separation between individual and collective voice, between representativeness and advocacy. However, as advocates, the activists have no more mandate—and even less legitimacy—to speak in the name of all women, or all women of the specific groupings addressed by the particular advocacy. In spite of the extent to which activists/advocates are self-selecting and the constitution of the activist group is arbitrary and not representative, the practice of decision making by consensus persists. This is often a learning and enriching experience; it is also not a very efficient process. Moreover, it endows more power to those with more staying power than anyone else, and it may reduce decisions to the lowest common denominator.[3] Above all, this process of decision making raises the issue of accountability. If the advocates do not represent anyone and no one has chosen them to act as advocates, then who is in the position of monitoring their actions and decisions? To whom should they report and justify their actions?

The transition from identity politics to transversal politics took place during the same period that the women's movement underwent the process of NGOization. This enabled activists to obtain resources for their activism and also to establish a space in which to work on a full-time basis. It also established a certain stability and visibility for organizations and enabled them to be credited formally as participants in a variety of national, regional, and transnational events, including the UN forums.

NGOs are accountable. But except for those relatively rare cases where they are mass membership based, those to whom they are accountable are primarily their funders. This means that the alternative that emerged in the 1990s to the feminist "tyranny of structurelessness" has become the "tyranny of funders." While many funders of feminist NGOs share the goals of the advocacy organizations, this is not always the case, and inevitably this kind of accountability affects the priorities and policies of NGOs.[4]

"Women's Rights Are Human Rights"

Problematizing the notion of "women's rights are human rights" does not mean that I do not admire the major work and achievements of feminist work within this field. On the contrary—they have helped with significant breakthroughs relating to women's positions both locally and globally. This does not mean, however, that problems associated with such discursive constructions need to be ignored, or—in the long run—can be ignored, for feminist momentum to be keep going, especially in the face of the growing opposition to women's rights in a variety of political fundamentalist agendas.

I would like to raise here three issues that seem to me problematic in this context. First, the legal and professionalized nature of much of the "rights" work; second, its top-down nature; and third, its concentration on civil and political rights.

I am aware that many of the critiques of "human rights" (Chea, 1997; Grewal, 1999) are preoccupied with other issues—some view human rights as a West-centric notion, others attack their universalistic and individualistic nature. Because I am dealing here with critical constructions of "human rights" that have grown within global feminist transversal politics, I do not believe that these critiques are valid. At the same time, the three problematic issues I am raising, while not invalidating the "women's rights as human rights" feminist approach, suggest issues that need addressing.

"Rights" as a Legal Issue

As can be seen from the sketchy history presented earlier in the chapter, feminist advocacy has emerged from two directions. First, it came from the realization that feminist activists cannot be constructed unproblematically as representative of women—in both meanings of the word: in the first place, they are usually not "typical" of the category of women for whose rights they struggle—they often come from a higher class position, are more educated and more skilled, have been more in touch with women from other collectivities, and so forth. In the second place, nobody elected them to represent these women—nor has any other feminist device developed that would attribute a representative status to these women. In this sense feminist advocacy means working to promote women's rights on behalf of but not necessarily as part of any particular group.

Given the growing body of legislation that emerged to secure the rights of women and other disadvantaged social groupings over the years, such advocacy has gradually come to require more and more legal expertise: in international law, in human rights legislation, in employment law, in domestic violence law, and so forth. This has meant the growing professionalization of feminist advocacy. Even those who are not actually in the legal profession have had to acquire sociolegal expertise. This has gone hand in hand with the NGOization of feminist advocacy, since such work often requires full-time engagement with it. To a large extent feminism has stopped being a mass social movement and has become the full-time business of trained experts.

Feminism in between Human Rights and Democracy

The professionalization of feminist activism has created a certain stratification and top-down quality within it. However, this quality is not limited to the legal and other expertise that is often a requirement of engagement in feminist activism on a regular basis. As important, if not more so, its top-down nature is anchored in its deductive nature as advocacy for predetermined rights. As will become clear a little later, I do not necessarily consider this latter characteristic as something that needs to be, or can be, rejected, but it does need problematization and containment.

Afsane Najmabadi (1995:7; see also Yuval-Davis 1997:124) has argued, in the context of Islamist Iran and the debate on what should constitute an appropriate feminist strategy there, that feminism is a "modern" phenomenon, based on a set of "foundational truths" that are part of the Enlightenment heritage and that, as such, they constitute a competing paradigm to that of Islamism and therefore cannot be effective. She argues in favor of "postmodern" feminism, based on a piecemeal, "pragmatic" issue-based approach. While Najmabadi's approach can prove to be of tactical use in particular historical locations (in which there are not sufficient secular pluralistic spaces within which to promote a feminist agenda in any other way), I do not think that her "postmodern" approach solves the basic issue, which is that feminist values (e.g., women's equality, women's rights over their own bodies, etc.—even if not all those who hold to these values would necessarily call themselves feminists) are part of an epistemological community, that is, a normative community in which values are shared, taught, and learned. In this sense I do not think that there is any escape from the fact that the boundaries of feminist transversal dialogue are limited and that no matter how unpopular feminist values are in a specific location, rejecting them cannot be an effective feminist strategy or tactic, although focusing on only some specific issues rather than on the overall construction of gender relations in that society can be pragmatically effective. As such, feminist values are not inherently democratic, in the sense that their validity does not depend on popular acceptance or rejection of them.

However, within the boundaries of feminist epistemological communities, listening to the differentially situated voices is essential. Transversal feminist politics depend on a decentered, non-West-centric, nonracialized, and as comprehensive as possible dialogical approach. I consider it the highest feminist achievement of the last twenty years that so much of the 1970s inherent ethnocentric, West-centric, and often even racist constructions have been rejected and that such a wide, often Southern-led dialogue has contributed to the determination of global feminist agendas. Not that racism disappeared completely from feminist practice or that separatist identity politics does not undergo seasonal revivals, especially as the overall international political climate is changing for the worse.

Such pitfalls have to be fought against, as should be the elitism of professional NGOs. We should be especially wary of the co-option of supposedly feminist concerns by those with other political (as well as economic and even military) agendas. As Zillah Eisenstein points out (2004), there is a whole constituency of neoliberal feminists who, although using feminist discourse and labeling themselves as feminist, should be seen as outside the boundaries of the feminist epistemological community, as they promote a very different set of political goals.

In practice, it is not always easy to determine where the boundaries of this community pass because they are permeable, shifting, and to a certain extent contentious. A general rule of thumb, however, can be that a wide, heterogeneous, decentered dialogue should always be encouraged, but the core of emancipatory feminist values should not be up for negotiation.

Human Rights Discourse as a Heritage of the Cold War Discourse

The UN Universal Declaration of Human Rights of 1946 has served as the foundation document for the growing human rights international discourse and legislation. Although it was American led, its formulation was also a product of a wide and heterogeneous participation from a variety of UN members. Its construction of "human rights" included both civil and political rights, as well as social, economic, and cultural rights. However, shortly afterward, human rights work and its subsequent international conventions became stamped by the dynamics of the cold war, and as a result, human rights discourse, dominated by the West, came to emphasize almost exclusively civil and political rights. As a result, social, economic, and cultural rights were marginalized at best in the international human rights discourse (unlike much of the Western, especially European, discourse on citizenship rights in which the welfare state and social rights occupied quite central roles). In the post–cold war era, during the 1993 UN Vienna conference on human rights and subsequently, there have been many attempts to correct the balance, but there has also been much resistance to this. For example, Michael Ignatieff (2003), the director of the Carr Center for Human Rights at Harvard University, strongly defends the delineation of human rights in the civil and political arenas and has argued that any attempt to significantly expand the arena of human rights in other directions would lead to their overall decline. However, his voice is becoming to a certain extent a minority one on this issue. With the growing visibility of the impact of hegemonic neoliberal globalization, and with the shrinking of the welfare state in the West as well, more and more international human rights organizations are finding the need to incorporate social, economic, and cultural rights into the heart of the human rights agenda (leading among them has been Amnesty International).

Some would argue, however, that such a correction is not enough. The problem is more basic, depending on the construction of "rights" themselves. This has been the origin of the "capabilities" and "human security" approaches (Nussbaum and Glover, 1995; Sen, 1999) that have shifted the focus from abstract entitlements to the lived realities of people's lives in the intersected positionings of people in general and women in particular in different global locations. Viewed from this perspective, the construction of feminist agendas as a discourse of "rights" can be partial at best. Such an agenda concentrates on normative yardsticks for women's/human lives, and this is one reason legal discourse has been so dominant in recent global feminist activism. Organizations such as Women's International Coalition for Economic Justice, and others, have put emphasis on training and providing resources for women to become more autonomous and more able to fight for their rights within the contexts of their daily lives. The danger in the latter approach is, however, that it might be easily co-opted to neoliberal economistic discourse of distributing microcredit to women as their road to salvation (Eisenstein, 2004).

Conclusion

Global feminist activism has had tremendous achievements in the symbolic and normative field, as well as in the realities of women's lives all over the globe, although the global economic and political climate, the growing hegemony of neoliberalism and its collusions, as well as confrontations with a variety of fundamentalist identity movements have made the consolidation and progression of these feminist struggles more and more difficult during the last few years. In addition to the issues relating to the changing global historical context, there are, however, some inherent issues in the way feminist activism is constructed and operating, and this has been the focus of this chapter. These problems need to be tackled for further progress to be made (and/or backlash resisted). I hope that some of the issues raised here might make some contribution to the transversal dialogue required as a necessary—but not sufficient—condition to bring such changes about.

Notes

1. An alternative global (and by now also regional and national) annual gathering of a variety of groups and individuals who are anti-neoliberal globalization, both from the 'old left' and from various new social movements. It started in 2000 as an alternative forum to the Davos meetings of top political and economic decision makers in Porto Allegre, but the 2003 meeting took place in Mumbai.

2. The Association of Women in Development, an international academic and political feminist forum, has been dealing with issues of women's human rights and development, mainly in the South.

3. I am indebted to Kristen Timothy, who pointed out to me that such a consensual decision-making mechanism operates also within the UN with similar effects.

4. I know of at least two cases in which members of radical international NGOs wanted to carry out a systematic research to find out how priorities of funders have shaped the priorities of the NGOs, but they were forbidden to do so by other members of the NGO board, fearing future repercussions to their fund-raising activities.

Bibliography

Agosin, Marjorie, ed. 2002. *Women, Gender and Human Rights: A Global Perspective.* New Brunswick, N.J.: Rutgers University Press.

Anthias, Floya, and Nira Yuval-Davis. 1983. "Contextualising Feminism: Gender, Ethnic and Class Divisions." *Feminist Review* 15:62–75.

Anzaldua, Gloria. 1987. *Borderlines/La Frontera: The New Mestiza.* San Francisco: Spinsters/Aunt Lute Books.

Assiter, Alison. 1996. *Enlightened Women: Modernist Feminism in a Postmodern Age.* London: Routledge.

Balibar, Etienne. 1990. "Paradoxes of Universality." In D. T. Goldberg, ed., *Anatomy of Racism,* 283–294. Minneapolis: Minnesota University Press.

Barton, Carol. 2004. "Global Women's Movements at a Crossroads: Seeking Definition, New Alliances and Greater Impact." *Socialism and Democracy* 18: 151–184.

Benhabib, Seyla. 1992. *Situating the Self.* Oxford: Polity Press with Blackwell.

Bhabha, Homi. 1994. *The Location of Culture.* London: Routledge.

Bunch, Charlotte. 1990. "Women's Rights as Human Rights: Towards a Re-vision of Human Rights." *Human Rights Quarterly* 12:489–498.

Bunch, Charlotte, with Peggy Antobus, Samantha Frost, and Niamh Reilly. 2001. "International Networking for Women's Human Rights." In Michael Edwards and John Gaventa, eds., *Global Citizen Action,* 217–229. Boulder, Colo.: Lynne Rienner.

Butler, Judith 1992. "Contingent Foundations: Feminism and the Question of 'Postmodernism.'" In J. Butler and J. W. Scott, eds., *Feminists Theorize the Political,* 3–21. London: Routledge.

Cain, Harrie, and Nira Yuval-Davis. 1990. "'The Equal Opportunities Community' and the Anti-racist Struggle." *Critical Social Policy,* no. 29: 5–26.

Chea, Pheng. 1997. "Posit(ion)ing Human Rights in the Current Global Conjecture." *Public Culture* 9:233–266.

Cockburn, Cynthia. 1998. *The Space between Us.* London: Zed Books.

Cockburn, Cynthia, and Lynnete Hunter. 1999. "Introduction: Transversal Politics and Translating Practices" *Soundings,* no. 12: 94–98.

Copelon, Rhonda. 2000. "Gender Crimes as War Crimes: Integrating Crimes against Women into International Criminal Law." *McGill Law Journal* 46:217.

Crenshaw, Kimberle. 1989. *Demarginalizing the Intersection of Race and Sex.* Chicago: University of Chicago Press.

Dumont, Louis. 1972. *Human Hierarchies.* New York: Paladin.

Eisenstein, Zillah. 2004. *Against Empire: Feminisms, Racism and "The" West.* London: Zed Books.

Eschle, Catherine. 2001. *Global Democracy, Social Movements and Feminism.* Boulder, Colo.: Westview Press.

Foucault, Michel. 1997. "For an Ethics of Discomfort." In Foucault, *The Politics of Truth,* 83–145. Cambridge, Mass. MIT Press.

Fraser, Nancy, with Axel Honneth. 1998. *Redistribution or Recognition? A Philosophical Exchange.* London: Verso.

Freeman, Jo. 1970. "The Tyranny of Structurelesness." *Berkeley Journal of Sociology* 17:151–165.

Grewal, Inderpal. 1999. "Women's Rights as Human Rights: Feminist Practices, Global Feminism and Human Rights Regimes in Transnationality." *Citizenship Studies* 3:337–354.

Guattari, Felix. 1974. *Psychoanalyse et Transversalité.* Paris: Maspero.

Haraway, Donna. 1991. *Simians, Cyborgs and Women: The Reinvention of Women.* London: Free Association Press.

———. 2000. "Alpha Bitches Online: The Dog Genome for the Next Generation." Paper presented at the Fourth European Feminist Research Conference, Bologna, September 28–October 1.

Harding, Sandra. 1991. *Whose Science, Whose Knowledge?* London: Open University Press.

———. 1993. "Rethinking Standpoint Epistemology: What Is 'Strong Objectivity'?" In Linda Alcoff and Elizabeth Potter, eds., *Feminist Epistemologies,* 49–82. New York: Routledge.

Hartsock, Nancy C. M. 1997. "Comment on Heckman's 'Truth and Method: Feminist Standpoint Theory Revisited.'" *Signs* 22:367–374.

Hekman, Susan. 1997. "Truth and Method: Feminist Standpoint Theory Revisited." *Signs* 22:341–365.

Hill-Collins, Patricia. 1990. *Black Feminist Thought: Knowledge, Consciousness and the Politics of Empowerment.* London: HarperCollins.

Humm, Maggie. 1995. *The Dictionary of Feminist Theory.* 2nd ed. Columbus: Ohio University Press.

Ignatief, Michael. 2003. *Human Rights as Politics and Idolatry.* Princeton, N.J.: Princeton University Press.

Imam, Ayesha, and Nira Yuval-Davis, eds. 2004. *The Warning Signs of Fundamentalisms.* London: Women Living under Muslim Laws.

Jayawardena, Kumari. 1986. *Feminism and Nationalism in the Third World.* London: Zed Books.

Klug, Francesca. 2001. *The Story of the United Kingdom's New Bill of Rights.* New York: Penguin.

Lowenhaupt Tsing, Anna. 1993. *In the Realms of the Diamond Queen.* Princeton, N.J.: Princeton University Press.

Moghadam, Valentine M., ed. 1994. *Identity Politics and Women.* Boulder, Colo.: Westview Press.

Morgan, Robin, ed. 1970. *Sisterhood Is Powerful.* New York: Vintage.

Najmabadi, Afsaneh. 1995. "Feminisms in an Islamic Republic: Years of Hardship Years of Growth." Paper presented at the School of Oriental and African Studies, University of London, October.

Nussbaum, Martha C., and Jonathan Glover, eds. 1995. *Women, Culture and Development: A Study of Human Capabilities.* Oxford: Clarendon Press.

Passerini, Louisa. 2000. "Discontinuity of History and Diaspora of Languages." *New Left Review,* January/February, 137–144

Petchesky, Ros. 2004. *Global Prescriptions: Gendering Health and Human Rights.* London: Zed Books.

Pettman, Jan Jindi. 1992. *Living in the Margins: Racism, Sexism and Feminism in Australia.* Sydney: Allen and Unwin.

Piercy, Marge, with Jane Freeman. 1972. "Getting Together: How to Start a Women's Liberation Group." New England Free Press.

Sahgal, Gita, and Nira Yuval-Davis. 1992. *Refusing Holy Orders: Women and Fundamentalism in Britain.* London: Virago.

SBS (Southall Black Sisters). 1990. *Against the Grain: A Celebration of Survival and Struggle.* London: SBS.

Scott, Joan W. 1992. "Experience." In J. Butler and J. W. Scott, eds., *Feminists Theorize the Political,* 22–40. London: Routledge.

Sen, Amartya 1999. *Development as Freedom.* New York: Knopf.

Smith, Dorothy. 1990. *The Conceptual Practices of Power: A Feminist Sociology of Knowledge*. Boston: Northeastern University Press.

Stoetzler, Marcel, and Nira Yuval-Davis. 2002. "Standpoint Theory, Situated Knowledge and the Situated Imagination." *Feminist Theory* 3:315–333.

WING (Women, Immigration and Nationality Group). 1985. *Worlds Apart: Women under Immigration and Nationality Laws*. London: Pluto Press.

Yeatman, Anna. 1992. "Minorities and the Politics of Difference." *Political Theory Newsletter* 4:1.

Yuval-Davis, Nira. 1984. "Zionism, Antisemitism and the Struggle against Racism." *Spare Rib*, September, 9–14.

———. 1994. "Women, Ethnicity and Empowerment." *Feminism & Psychology* 4, no. 1: 179–198.

———. 1997. *Gender and Nation*. London: Sage.

———. 2003. "Belonging/s: In between the Indigene and the Diasporic." In Umut Ozkirimli, ed., *Nationalism in the 21st Century*, 127–144. Basingstoke: Macmillan.

———. Forthcoming. "Transversal Politics and the Situated Imagination" *Women's Studies International Forum*.

Yuval-Davis, Nira, and Pnina Werbner, eds. 1999. *Women, Citizenship and Difference*. London: Zed Books.

Zajovic, Stasa, ed. 1994. *Women for Peace*. Belgrade: Women in Black.

12

Challenges in Transnational Feminist Mobilization

Aili Mari Tripp

The expansion and diversification of the international women's movement over the past three decades is a healthy development. The closing of the North-South gap in objectives as described in this book has been critical in building transnational linkages. But one of the biggest constraints on transnational feminism today comes from problems *in the manner in which* issues are treated and discussed, on *how* to best achieve agreed upon goals, and on *how* international support should be rendered. This chapter explores some of the continuing constraints on building and maintaining transnational ties that arise not only from the different agendas, strategies, and priorities of women in different parts of the globe but also from a lack of appreciation of the goals and strategies of others working in different contexts.

There have been many important initiatives from the global North that have exhibited strong transnational cooperation. One example is the "34 Million Friends" campaign started by Lois Abraham and Jane Roberts in 2002 to get people to donate one dollar each to make up the money that President Bush cut from the United Nations Population Fund. The Help Afghan Women campaign of the Feminist Majority is another such initiative. However, one of the major challenges to strengthening international cooperation is the way movements, particularly in the North, identify with and support women's movements in parts of the world other than their own (Snyder 2003). When international support is extended, it is not always offered in ways that reflect an understanding of other women's movements, their local contexts, and their needs.

Keck and Sikkink (1998) describe what they call the boomerang effect, in which nongovernmental organizations bypass their own state and seek out transnational advocacy networks, such as those around human rights, indigenous rights, the environment, and women's rights, in order to pressure their state from the outside to resolve a conflict. Such transnational networks provide local actors access, leverage, information, and resources that they otherwise would not have. The boomerang model assumes that local actors are the ones seeking support from the outside to strengthen their cause vis-à-vis their own state. Yet, often transnational movements engage with local issues from the outside, while remaining detached from the domestic movements involved in these issues. Moreover, not all transnational advocacy movements or interventions are readily welcomed by domestic actors. It is important to understand why some transnational advocacy activities are welcomed and others are spurned.

In this chapter I discuss some examples of how tensions between outsider advocacy networks and local movements manifest themselves and some of the difficulties domestic movements encounter when global advocacy networks are built and organized without adequate consultation and appreciation of local dynamics. Several problems are common to the examples I draw from several parts of the world: northern Nigeria, the former Yugoslavia, Afghanistan, and Africa more generally. The problems of hubris, disregard of local context, a "rescue" mentality, and distancing from the "other" that I discuss here are unfortunately to be found in many other settings as well.

Hubris in Transnational Assistance

Sometimes outsiders do not feel the need to consult with local actors about their facts or strategies because they believe they are providing an unquestionable "good" in taking action on behalf of another group of people. They are so focused on mobilizing and getting their constituents and the broader public to feel good about their involvement that they fail to notice the potential damage that their activism can cause, especially in cases of insufficient collaboration with those on the ground who are the most knowledgeable about their own circumstances.

External attempts to intervene have at their worst included cases where outsiders believed they knew better than those on the ground what strategy should be adopted and thus willfully ignored requests by local activists to desist in their activities. One such case was the transnational response to the introduction of Islamic sharia laws in northern Nigeria in the last few years. These laws have especially serious negative repercussions for women, but international attempts to put pressure on the courts in northern Nigeria have often backfired. One particular case is that of Bariya Magazu, an unmarried teenager convicted of extramarital sex and sentenced to flogging in Zamfara, Nigeria, in 1999. Ms. Magazu's sentence was passed illegally without notice, and she was flogged before she was able to contact anyone. According to Nigerian activists, the extralegal action against her was taken deliberately to defy international pressure surrounding her case. The local activists learned from this that international petition campaigns were not necessarily the best strategy in every situation.

In March 2002, a sharia court in Bakori, Katsina State, sentenced Amina Lawal Kurami to death by stoning, finding her guilty of adultery after she had given birth to a baby out of wedlock. In the Lawal case, thousands of petitions were launched to save her from stoning, and about 33,800 Web sites mentioned her case. When she was finally acquitted, the news media outlets and petition Web sites gave almost full credit to international pressures. They failed to comprehend the reasons for her release or the potential damage their campaigns may have caused.

Based on past experience in such cases,[1] Nigerian activists and lawyers with BAOBAB for Women's Rights (a Nigerian organization that was working most closely with these cases) asked international activists to desist from sending letters of protest about the Lawal case on three occasions in May, August, and September 2003. They were concerned that many of the letters were based on inaccurate information, which resulted in a loss of credibility for them and further setbacks because it was assumed that local activists had provided this inaccurate information to outsiders. One of these inaccurate Internet-circulated petitions alleged that the Nigerian Supreme Court had upheld Lawal's death sentence and claimed that a similar petition had been effective in a previous case. It advised individuals to sign an online Amnesty International petition against death sentences. BAOBAB pleaded in an e-mail sent to various list-servs that outsiders "check the accuracy of the information with local activists, before further circulating petitions or responding to them." BAOBAB pointed out: "If we remember that it is local activists who most facilitate turning rights principles into everyday reality for people, then reducing the ability and potential of local activists to carry out women's and human rights promotion and defense is a counter-productive mode of proceeding" (2003).

BAOBAB's work around the Amina Lawal case was also harmed by international activists who presented Islam and Africa as barbaric and savage in their petition campaigns. To Nigerian activists these letters and petitions simply perpetuated racism and played into the hands of the Islamic political religious extremists. "These kinds of statements arouse hostilities and the sentiments of vigilantes who carry out extra legal acts of violence at the behest of state actors. They are the ones who pose the real danger to the women who have been charged. All the completed appeals processes have been successful in the local state sharia courts," wrote the BAOBAB activists in their pleas to international activists. They feared that such letters and petitions would further endanger Lawal, as well as the activists and lawyers who faced hostile crowds on their way to court.

Not all international organizations ignored BAOBAB's pleas against international petitions. Women Living under Muslim Laws (WLUML) and the International Association of Women Judges (IAWJ), for example, provided important support. WLUML told the Nigerian partners that they needed to provide up-to-date and accurate information to the international community. In cooperation with their Nigerian partners, they helped write and disseminate such information. When asked not to circulate the petitions, IAWJ then asked how it could better support the defense efforts, and instead helped raise funds to cover defense legal costs.

Amnesty International Secretariat and Amnesty's USA chapter similarly issued press releases disassociating themselves from the petitions. These organizations that were responsive to BAOBAB's requests did not simply provide uncritical support. They negotiated with their Nigerian partners when they disagreed with their analysis and approach, and as a result changes in tactics on both sides occurred (Imam 2004). Rather than assuming that international groups already knew what was right to do, a cooperative stance emerged. Nonetheless, many other groups and individuals simply disregarded these requests. That they did not know better was not really an excuse, but rather another manifestation of the problem.

Oversimplifications and Disregard of Context

When outsiders do not take the time to learn about or attend to the particulars of a situation, their efforts can backfire. This is particularly true in conflict situations, where one-sided support to a particular local group can have extremely harmful unintended consequences. As one example, consider the case of the article written by University of Michigan law professor Catharine MacKinnon in *Ms. Magazine* about pornography as the motivator for the rapes of Muslims and Croatians in former Yugoslavia during the war in Bosnia (1992–1995). Women's rights activists in the region claimed that the publicity given to the article contributed to further stirring up ethnic animosities and to polarizing the women's movement in the former Yugoslavia.

Regardless of whether or not one agrees with MacKinnon's position on pornography, the critique of her article by women in the region offers insight into some of the common problems with well-intentioned Western attempts to provide support. By not consulting a variety of local actors, MacKinnon ran the risk of operating with incomplete or one-sided information. Vesna Kesic and other local women's rights activists claim that MacKinnon made numerous unsubstantiated statements that could not be verified by people working with rape survivors in Bosnia. MacKinnon, who provided legal counsel to rape survivors in Bosnia, claimed that pornography had saturated Yugoslavia prior to the conflict. Yet Kesic notes that pornography was not openly permitted in Yugoslavia under socialism, just as in other socialist countries. MacKinnon also took a debate about pornography that came out of the U.S. context and superimposed it on to a dramatically different context in an attempt to persuade a U.S. audience that pornography sexualizes violence against women, being the "theory" behind the practice of rape. For Kesic and others, MacKinnon trivialized the horrors of this genocide by equating its widespread rape and killing with pornography. But the biggest damage inflicted by the article was the way in which its arguments were used by others within Yugoslavia to stir ethnic hatred and promote revenge.

MacKinnon's writings played into an internal conflict between women's rights activists in the former Yugoslavia by emphasizing the ethnic dimensions of the use of rape. In this conflict, some in the former Yugoslavia saw rape as part of a universal problem of violence against women, while others took a "patriotic" approach and saw rape as a product of hatred of the Serbian army for Muslim or Croatian women (Benderly 1997). MacKinnon's ignorance of or disregard for the complexities of women's mobilization meant that the article's focus on Serbian rapes was especially polarizing at a time when women's organizations were fighting hard to bridge ethnic differences. In December 1992 the Zagreb Women's Lobby worked with feminist, pacifist, and nonnationalist organizations in Serbia and Croatia to found the Center for Women War Victims with the goal of offering support for rape victims and refugee women regardless of nationality. These attempts at cooperation were fragile and could be easily disrupted. External interventions that seemed to ratify an ethnic-nationalist interpretation were especially problematic as a result (Batinic 2001, 9).

MacKinnon was not the only one whose interventions exacerbated these tensions. Other external feminist activities, like the International Congress of Women's Solidarity, organized by German feminist groups from Berlin and held in January 1993 in Zagreb, ended up further splitting women's groups (O. Kesic 1999). But MacKinnon's article is emblematic of how transnational activists can be blind to the local dimensions of a problem. Perhaps most important, MacKinnon's article did not take into account the sophisticated and complex arguments feminists on the ground had developed to discuss the rapes. Many Yugoslav feminists felt MacKinnon ended up giving succor to a one-sided nationalist view of the rapes.

Much of feminist discourse in former Yugoslavia deliberately resisted using the language of "destroying Bosnian and Croatian ethnic groups by raping and impregnating them," even though they were well aware that Bosnians had been most victimized by rape. Local feminists regarded the mixing of ethnic and gender representation through symbols and images as inflaming hostilities and generating even greater violence. They had seen how claims of rape had been exaggerated and manipulated by all sides to provoke conflict in this region. The symbolic metanarratives about ethnicity and the victimization of women as symbolic of a disgraced people were being used to incite people to fight and to inspire even greater violence (V. Kesic 2000, 33). Although the gendered nature of rape and military violence was their concern, in this context it was more important to them to reduce hostility than to stir outrage.

Many Yugoslav women activists from all ethnic groups were especially concerned because all the governments involved in these wars manipulated and politicized rape and inflated the numbers of victims. The majority of victims of Serb rapes in Bosnia were Muslim women, and there were allegedly no mass rapes in the war in Croatia. Nevertheless, Croatian nationalist rhetoric focused on Croatian rape victims as representing the rape of Croatia. Women's suffering was being used as a national symbol (V. Kesic 2000, 31). In 1986 and 1987, panic spread in Belgrade as rumors of Albanian rapes of Serbian women proliferated. Yet Kosovo police registered only one rape of a Serb woman by an Albanian man. These rumors fueled ethnic tensions and later conflicts (V. Kesic 2002, 315). In this context, to stress rape as a particular horror, as MacKinnon did, was to undercut efforts by local feminists to reduce the violence and instead play into violent, nationalist hands. While stirring outrage over rape in war was a consciousness-raising tool in the political context of the United States, it did this at the cost of women in the former Yugoslavia who became more, not less, susceptible to victimization. In general, transnational activists who ignore the local context of issues in favor of the way the concern is understood by their own constituents "back home" do more to exploit the issue for their own political gain than to lay a groundwork for real alliance.

Rescue Paradigm

A third problem has to do with the "rescue paradigm" within which some transnational feminist actors operate that seems to legitimate ignoring local actors altogether by stressing their neediness and backwardness. Concern about such ethnocentric attitudes has been raised especially by organizations in Africa that are fighting to abolish the practice of female genital cutting. Western organizations and individuals have often sought to champion this cause in a way that disregards and trivializes local efforts. Seble Dawitt, a Somali lawyer, and filmmaker Salem Mekuria pointed out the following in a 1993 *New York Times* editorial page article regarding Alice Walker's movie *Warrior Marks* and book *Possessing the Secret of Joy:*

> As is common in Western depictions of Africa, Ms. Walker and her collaborator, Prathiba Parmar, portray the continent as a monolith. African women and children are the props, and the village background against which Alice Walker, heroine-savior, comes to articulate their pain and condemn those who inflict it. . . . This film is emblematic of the Western feminist tendency to see female genital mutilation as the gender oppression to end all oppressions. Instead of being an issue worthy of attention in itself, it has become a powerfully emotive lens through which to view personal pain—a gauge by which to measure distance between the West and the rest of humanity. . . . Superior Western attitudes do not enhance dialogue or equal exchange of ideas.

Mekuria (1995) explained further in a longer essay on the same subject:

> Empowering feminist production has the responsibility to expose not just the practices, but the institutions, structures, and systems that embody and perpetuate the oppression of women. . . . They should validate the humanity and dignity of the victims, depicting them as people who possess the potential to change the oppressive conditions that militate against their full realization. . . . The feminists' task, therefore, is to facilitate the empowerment process; not to take it over, or to dominate the victims' struggle. . . . Indeed, the depiction of the victims of this oppressive practice in *Warrior Marks* is so demeaning that the overall effect is one of denigration rather than empowerment. The African women subjects are presented as a collection of helpless bundles of mutilated creatures, stereotypes who are far from being living, dignified human beings. They are pitied and patronized, instead of being cherished, nurtured, and invested with faith as human subjects potentially capable of understanding and changing the conditions that dehumanize them. (2)

Another aspect of this problem in transnational advocacy comes from distancing others and making too much of differences between "us," the privileged, and the "other." This approach refuses to recognize not only the common humanity of women but also the commonality of experiences of gender oppression despite the differences. One sometimes gets the impression that some Northern activists think that women in the North exist above culture and without oppression, whereas women in other parts of the world are steeped in oppressive cultures. This leads not only to fantasies of rescue that exaggerate Northern women's power and freedom but often also to an inability to see local feminists as active, intelligent, competent partners for their efforts.

Homogenizing and Essentializing Partners

Stereotypes further complicate the ability to recognize and cooperate with partners. Outsiders sometimes homogenize and essentialize the other as "all Africans," "all Arabs," "all Asians," or all peoples who are different from "us." "All" of one group or another is reduced to a particular practice or belief, to which the entire society is depicted as mindlessly adhering. A good example of this overgeneralization and flattening out of complexity can be found in reactions to veiling. Identifying this and other practices as particular symbols of female oppression can be problematic, especially when they become totalizing and emblematic of an entire people. This was the case with the focus on veiling amid efforts by Western women to assist Afghani women. In 1996, the Taliban took over Afghanistan and imposed harsh restrictions on women. The Feminist Majority and many celebrities, led by Mavis Leno, took up a well-intentioned petition campaign to "save" the burqa-clad women who were victimized by this regime. The burqa is a "symbol of the total oppression of women," said Norma Gattsek, leader of the Feminist Majority's Campaign to End Gender Apartheid in Afghanistan, a mobilization that was launched in 1997 (Shah 2001). Swatches from the burqa could be purchased from the gift page of the Feminist Majority Web site under an ad that reads: "This swatch of mesh represents the obstructed view of the world for an entire nation of women who were once free." The Feminist Majority has become more careful in the way it talks about the burqa in response to criticism, but initially this passive-victim image was one of the primary ways in which women in Afghanistan were depicted. The burqa swatch, which still could be found prominently displayed on the Feminist Majority Web page in 2004, was eventually removed.

Egyptian journalist Mona Eltahawy, who lives in the United States, wrote in the *Washington Post* of the swatches:

> Using the swatches makes gimmicks of Afghan women. They are too reminiscent of the array of ribbons on sale for various diseases—pink ribbons for breast cancer, red ribbons for AIDS, etc. Also, they beg the question: Where are the swatches that represent the oppression of other women? It smacks of hypocrisy when we highlight the plight of women only when those imposing that plight are our enemies.
>
> I have met women who choose to cover their entire body, including their face. We must support that choice. What kind of freedom do we claim to uphold if it is only the freedom to choose what we choose? Isn't that what it's about for women all over the world, be it the choice to vote, have an abortion, drive a car, wear a miniskirt or wear a scarf? (2002)

The focus on the burqa collapsed women's experiences into a single practice and did not sufficiently allow for Afghan women's own experiences, choices, opinions, and agency to matter.

Starvation, war, militarization, and lack of security loomed as much larger problems in the eyes of women in Afghanistan at the time. In 2000, Dr. Lynn L. Amowitz of Physicians for Human Rights led a three-month study in Afghanistan, interviewing more than 200,000 Afghan women and men, from both rural and urban areas, some under Taliban control and others not. Contrary to the images portrayed in the West, many women in Kabul worked, went to school, and wore Western clothing. In rural areas, the picture was somewhat different, but it was mainly customary ways of thinking, poverty, and war that prevented many women from entering public life and gaining an education even before the Taliban took over. Inability to afford health care was a big concern. More than 85 percent of women in non-Taliban-controlled areas and 75 percent in the Taliban-controlled areas said they wore the *chadari* (a head-to-toe covering for women with a mesh cloth over the face through which a woman may see and breathe) all the time, and the report indicated that this had been the practice prior to the Taliban takeover.

However, the Afghan women also reportedly told humanitarian aid workers that they had more important concerns than the *chadari,* referring to economic destruction, poverty, drought, and war. Afghanistan was and is, as sociologist Valentine Moghadam (2002) has pointed out, "characterized by a strong division of roles, sex segregation, and social controls over women" (1). It was unlikely even after the overthrow of the Taliban that women would stop wearing the *chadari.*

The Feminist Majority's ethnocentric rhetoric to build support for its cause included press releases referring to the United States as the "civilized world" in contrast to "barbaric" Afghanistan. In spite of this rhetoric, the Feminist Majority's campaign was part of an important initiative that helped to internationalize the American feminist movement. This was, as Moghadam (2003) explained, perhaps the first time a women's issue had generated so much interest as to influence U.S. foreign policy. It demonstrated the power of transnational advocacy movements in putting the spotlight on and generating support for Afghan women's access to education, health services, employment, political participation, and legal equality.

Afghani and Pakistani women's activists, coupled with transnational networks of feminist, refugee, human rights, and many other groups worldwide, were able to play a constructive, major role in bringing international attention to the dire situation of women in Afghanistan. Right after the Taliban came to power, the Feminist Majority was instrumental in getting the United States not to recognize this government and to withdraw its support from Unocal, a U.S. oil company, to build an oil pipeline from the Caucasus through Afghanistan. After the Taliban were ousted, the Feminist Majority joined international networks to lobby to guarantee Afghan women's rights and representation in the new political bodies, and to obtain international funding for girls schools, women's hospitals and clinics, and other humanitarian programs (http://www.helpafghanwomen .com/). It continued to press for an expansion of peacekeeping forces, support for the Afghan Ministry for Women's Affairs, the Independent Human Rights Commission, and Afghan women-led nongovernmental organizations.

Conclusions

All four cases considered here—responding to the Islamic courts' punishments for alleged adultery in northern Nigeria, rape in the conflict in former Yugoslavia, female genital cutting in Africa, and women under the Taliban in Afghanistan—share many similarities. In all cases, international support was welcomed, but the way it was being delivered was a problem. Local activists were not empowered by the interventions, and in some cases women were endangered more than helped. If domestic feminist movements are to more effectively engage in global efforts to improve the status of women, there is much to learn from these cases. The most salient implications seem to be the following.

First, international actors should consider that local actors have the most intimate knowledge of issues, other players, conditions, laws, and cultural sensitivities. Domestic actors generally have greater legitimacy than outsiders. Taking action that affects another society requires consulting local organizations properly regarding the advisability of a strategy, its timing, and the way in which the issues are framed in the international arena. Effective feminist action necessitates having accurate, up-to-date information on a situation, including the local dynamics, history of the conflict, past and present struggles of women's and feminist organizations, and an understanding of the different positions taken by various local actors.

Being feminist in an international campaign involves paying attention to what has already been done by local actors and taking cues from them rather than assuming that they do not exist or that they are irrelevant. In the case of *Warrior Marks,* there was an assumption that because outsiders already had all the answers, they had nothing to learn from those involved in the practice of female genital cutting or from those who had been involved in efforts to eradicate the practice. This complacency may have also contributed to the carelessness displayed toward both factual accuracy and local concerns in the transnational campaigns around Amina Lawal.

As Ayesha Imam (2004) put it so aptly:

> Those outside must be both more respectful of the analyses and agency of those activists most closely involved in the issues on the ground and the wishes of the women and men directly suffering rights violations, and, more knowledgeable about the situation. To be informed, activists must answer a number of questions: Would a particular response make things better or worse? For which individuals or groups of people? How? Would another sort of response be more effective? Is what is being requested feasible and legal? What sort of language would be most appropriate? Are the facts presented accurate? Is there enough information that the specifics are not lost in overgeneralization?
>
> Informed and respectful solidarity also means finding out about the groups involved at national and local levels. This is particularly the case when there may be more than one group (of locals or internationals), advocating different things. Who are the groups? What are their past histories? What constituencies do they work with or represent? What areas of rights do they work in? Why are they asking for a given kind of strategy or support? What are their reputations? Respectful solidarity further requires recognizing that while neither locals nor internationals can automatically be assumed to have a monopoly on the best analysis or the most effective strategy, it is locals who have to live with the consequences of any wrong or mistaken decisions.

Not all petition campaigns are harmful. International letter-writing campaigns were very successful in the case of Fatima Yacoub in Chad in the mid-1990s. But the BAOBAB appeal emphasized the need to use local structures that addressed local power struggles that were driving the politicization of religion or ethnicity. Engagement in the local arena demanded accurate knowledge of the situation and moreover afforded greater legitimacy than "outside" pressure. As BAOBAB (2003) put it:

There is an unbecoming arrogance in assuming that international human rights organisations or others always know better than those directly involved, and therefore can take actions that fly in the face of their express wishes. Of course, there is always the possibility that those directly involved are wrong but surely the course of action is to persuade them of the correctness of one's analysis and strategies, rather than ignore their wishes.

Working closely with and learning from the expertise of local activists is not just a matter of respect. Failure to do so can also endanger people on the ground and create unnecessary hostilities. This was the case in both Yugoslavia and Nigeria, where activists appealed for accurate representation of the issues internationally and warned against the dangers of making statements in the international media that could prove inflammatory and exacerbate matters in an already very tense situation.

Second, international actors' selection of issues to highlight should reflect local priorities. They should not use the problems of women in another part of the world to recruit supporters or donors for themselves. One tendency in international campaigns is to select sensational issues that may affect a few instead of issues that are not as likely to grab attention yet may affect millions of women in an even more direct and harmful way. While this may help build the constituency of the international campaign, the question that still needs to be asked is whether it is the most pressing need of those being assisted. Why is it that the issues that tend to capture the Western imagination have to do with female genital cutting, honor killings, stoning as Islamic punishment for adultery, the burqa in Afghanistan, and the like? Why is there an intense focus on the 15 women who die every year in Jordan as a result of honor killings when more than 3,000 women in the United States (about one-third of all women murdered) also die of domestic violence? Widening the gulf between "us" and "them" may make "us" feel powerful and even lead us to open our checkbooks to help a relatively few dramatically victimized women, but the more pressing needs of the majority of women fall into oblivion.

The less dramatically violent issues of starvation, civil war, access to health care, access to water, conditions of refugees and internally displaced persons, and other such concerns that have gender dimensions to them may be every bit as violent, but they do not share the same kind of international spotlight as the aforementioned issues. They are not emotionally riveting because their consequences are not seen immediately, thus they do not grab the headlines. Death of 3.8 million in civil war in the Democratic Republic of Congo, genocide in Sudan, or internal displacement in northern Uganda are not seen as being as important as the persecution of a few women threatened with stoning to death for adultery in Nigeria. Starvation does not grab headlines the way female genital cutting or honor killings do, yet a slow, painful death by starvation is far more common than honor killings.

The selection of issues, I fear, sometimes reflects a fascination with the distant exotic. The Western feminist interest in difference that grew out of transnational conferences such as Beijing, as well as specific experiences in these countries, has created an appreciation for different feminisms and different experiences of women, but it has at times also led to an exoticization of that difference and a sense of superiority. As Vesna Kesic (2002) explains, this may be because we believe women in the West do not suffer the same brutalities that women elsewhere suffer as a result of their cultures:

> Western media reflect (or create) a particular perception of these "distant events" that happen in the non-West (even if it is a part of Europe) . . . on the doom of women in the Arab world, and on raped Kosova women. . . . [They] present the situation of women in these parts of the world as so exceptional, so different, so exotic that nothing like it can be imagined in the West. "Exceptionalizing" is a way of creating cultural differences. . . . Is the situation for women in Kosovo or Bosnia really so different from the one in the United States or in Western Europe? For how many years has a raped woman been able easily to step into a U.S. or Western European court and testify that she was raped without feeling threatened or ashamed? Without fearing that she will be asked how short her skirt was, or why she was out on the streets so late? And without fear that her husband, boyfriend, even family will reject her. . . . A "Western approach," be it by "helpful sisters" or the "well-meaning" media, is not helpful if it fails to address the issue with the same political and theoretical seriousness with which violence against women was discussed in the West itself—nor if it keeps on emphasizing "cultural differences." (317–318)

Charlotte Bunch and Susana Fried (1996) argued that women across the globe were able to unite around the issue of violence against women because it was based on a universality of justice rather than a commonality of experience. I argue that it is the ability to recognize the commonality of experience in the other that makes it possible to conceive of a universality of justice. This is not to say that everyone suffers in the same way or to the same degree. But people have to recognize what they share with others in order to think in terms of common solutions. If feminist activists or their constituents in the global North think other societies are too different and incomprehensible, it becomes all too easy to distance oneself and ignore them, and think of "our" problems only in national terms. Thus the greater recognition of commonalities in these global struggles for women's rights changes not only the approach to the "other" but also the strategies for thinking about and working on problems "at home." Greater transnational engagement by the North would create greater understanding of these commonalities and better bases on which cooperation can be built.

Third, to be taken seriously as global advocates for women's rights, women in the most powerful countries in the world have a particular role to play. They have a unique opportunity to influence the governments and institutions that affect women the world over. Women in the North can and should seek greater influence over their government's policies around foreign affairs, military intervention abroad, foreign aid, immigration, support for the United Nations, and other arenas that affect women globally. They can play more of a role in trying to influence the International Monetary Fund, World Bank, World Trade Organization, and other bodies that have an impact on the daily lives of millions of women around the world. Fighting for international economic justice in these agencies would go a long way toward helping build bridges between the North and South and would give northern feminists more credibility when they engage in international campaigns.

Without a fundamental change in the Northern movements and their reengagement on a new basis into the global women's movements, we are not going to see fundamental changes in the global inequalities that underlie so many of the problems women face worldwide. Although the expansion of the Internet and e-mail and ease of travel have facilitated communications, the weaknesses in transnational dialogue and deep mutual understanding remain a problem of considerable magnitude. While the Internet can be a powerful and useful tool in advocacy, frequent and rapid miscommunication, like the Internet petitions and Web sites that display ethnocentric language and symbols for all the world to see, is part of the problem, not a tool for its solution.

Fourth, movements in the North, in particular, need to be more engaged in transnational issues not just to improve conditions for women around the world but for their own sake. Pointing to international trends and changing norms in the advancement of women to argue for the advancement of women domestically is a powerful tool. It should be used by women not only in the South but also in the industrially advanced countries that are lagging in various areas. Women in the United States, for example, can learn from strategies that have worked elsewhere and profit from international debates and lessons that have been learned in other parts of the world on issues they have not yet fully engaged.

The cautions raised in this chapter are not an excuse to withdraw from transnational engagement for fear of doing more harm than good. Rather, they are an appeal to work across international borders more collaboratively, with higher regard for local actors, and with greater understanding of the complexities of the issues involved. It requires also considering one's own motivations for selecting particular issues over others. Only through greater dialogue can these questions be worked through. Dialogue involves respectful sharing of views and experiences and can inform both transnational and local strategies in productive ways.

NOTE

1. In a less publicized but similar case in 2002, Zafran Bibi was sentenced to be stoned to death under a zina ordinance in the town of Kohat in Pakistan. Zafran Bibi says she was raped by her husband's younger brother and became pregnant as a result, subsequently giving birth to a daughter. Pakistani women activists asked the international community not to intervene and instead to prioritize local pressure and the Pakistani activists' strategy of working through their legal system. Zafran Bibi was released that same year by the Federal Shariat Court (FSC) because she was found to have been coerced into committing zina, and therefore not liable to any punishment. See http://www.wluml.org/english/actionsfulltxt .shtml?cmd%5B156%5D=i-156-3127

BIBLIOGRAPHY

BAOBAB for Women's Rights, Lagos, Nigeria. 2003. "Please Stop the International Amina Lawal Protest Letter Campaigns." Signed Ayesha Imam (Board Member) and Sindi Medar-Gould (Executive Director). May, August, and September 2003.

Batinic, Jelena. 2001. "Feminism, Nationalism and War: The 'Yugoslav Case' in Feminist Texts." *Journal of International Women's Studies* 3, no. 1: 1–23.

Benderly, Jill. 1997. "Rape, Feminism, and Nationalism in the War in Yugoslav

Successor States." In Lois A. West., ed., *Feminist Nationalism*, 59–72. New York: Routledge.

Bunch, Charlotte, and Susana Fried. 1996. "Beijing '95: Moving Women's Human Rights from Margin to Center." *Signs* 22:200–204.

Dawitt, Seble, and Salem Mekuria. 1993. "The West Just Doesn't Get It." *New York Times,* December 7, A27.

Eltahawy, Mona. 2002. "Analysis: When Women Cannot Choose." *Washington Post Opinion,* February 5.

Imam, Ayesha. 2004. "International Solidarity Strategies and Women's Rights under Sharia Law in Nigeria." Paper presented at the conference "Women, Islam and Transnational Feminism," organized by the Women and Citizenship Research Circle, University of Wisconsin–Madison, March 5.

Keck, Margaret E., and Kathryn Sikkink. 1998. *Activists beyond Borders: Advocacy Networks in International Politics.* Ithaca, N.Y.: Cornell University Press.

Kesic, Obrad. 1999. "Women and Gender Imagery in Bosnia: Amazons, Sluts, Victims, Witches, and Wombs." In Sabrina P. Ramet, ed., *Gender and Politics in the Western Balkans: Women and Society in Yugoslavia and the Yugoslav Successor States,* 187–202. University Park: Penn State University Press.

Kesic, Vesna. 2000. "From Reverence to Rape: An Anthropology of Ethnic and Genderized Violence." In Marguerite R. Waller and Jennifer Rycenga, eds., *Frontline Feminisms: Women, War, and Resistance,* 23–39. New York: Garland.

———. 2002. "Muslim Women, Croatian Women, Serbian Women, Albanian Women…" In Dusan I. Bjelic and Obrad Savic, eds., *Balkan as Metaphor: Between Globalization and Fragmentation,* 311–321. Cambridge, Mass.: MIT Press.

MacKinnon, Catharine A. 1993. "Turning Rape into Pornography: Postmodern Genocide" *Ms.* 4, no. 1: 24–31.

Mekuria, Salem. 1995. "Female Genital Mutilation in Africa: Some African Views." *ACAS Bulletin* 44/45:1–5.

Moghadam, Valentine M. 2000. "Transnational Feminist Networks: Collective Action in an Era of Globalization." *International Sociology* 15, no. 1: 57–85.

———. 2002. "Women's Rights in Afghanistan: Progress?" *Perihelion* (European Rim Policy and Investment Council), December.

———. 2003. "Global Feminism and Women's Citizenship in the Muslim World: The Cases of Iran, Algeria, and Afghanistan." Paper presented at the conference "Citizenship, Borders, and Gender: Mobility and Immobility," New Haven, Connecticut, May 8–10.

Shah, Sonia. 2001. "Unveiling the Taleban Dress Codes Are Not the Issue, New Study Finds." http://www.zmag.org/sustainers/content/2001-07/10shah.htm.

Snyder, Margaret C. 2003. "African Contributions to the Global Women's Movement." Paper presented to "National Feminisms, Transnational Arenas, Universal Human Rights," Havens Center Colloquium Series, Madison, Wisconsin, April 14.

About the Contributors

Melinda Adams is an assistant professor of political science at James Madison University. Her research focuses on women's political action in domestic and international arenas. A current research project focuses on gender equity policies in the African Union.

Aida Bagić has been active in the women's scene in Croatia since 1989, when she was a volunteer on the SOS telephone for women and children victims of violence. She was a founding activist in the Autonomous Women's House in Zagreb, the Anti-War Campaign, Croatia, and has been involved in other women's and peace initiatives. She also worked as a coordinator of the Centre for Women's Studies, Zagreb, Croatia. She has just completed a study on the role of international assistance in the development of women's organisations in post-Yugoslav countries that was supported by an International Policy Fellowship from the Open Society Institute, Budapest.

Yakin Ertürk has been on the faculty of the Department of Sociology and the Gender and Women's Studies Programme at the Middle East Technical University, Ankara, Turkey, and in 2002 became the head of the program. She also taught at the Centre for Girls, at King Saud University in Riyadh (1979–1982) and from 1979 to 1981 served as its chair. Between 1997 and 2001 she took leave from her university post and joined the United Nations, serving first as Director of the International Research and Training Institute for the Advancement of Women (INSTRAW) in Santo Domingo, Dominican Republic (October 1997–February 1999), then as Director of the Division for the Advancement of Women (DAW) at UN headquarters in New York (March 1999–October 2001).

Myra Marx Ferree is Professor of Sociology at the University of Wisconsin–Madison, where she is also affiliated with the Women's Studies Program, the Center for German and European Studies, and the European Union Center. Her most recent books include *Shaping Abortion Discourse: Democracy and the Public Sphere in Germany and the United States* (2002), *Controversy and Coalition: The New Feminist Movement* (2000), and *Revisioning Gender: New Directions in the Social Sciences* (1998). Her work has focused both on women's movements in the United States and Europe and on the micropolitics of power in households.

Amy G. Mazur is Associate Professor of Political Science and Criminal Justice at Washington State University and coconvener of the Research Network on Gender Politics and the State. Professor Mazur is the author or editor of four books, including *Gender Bias and the State* and, most recently, *Theorizing Feminist Policy.* She has published articles in *Political Research Quarterly, French Politics and Society, Policy Studies Journal, West European Politics, European Journal of Political Research,* and *Contemporary French Civilization.*

Dorothy E. McBride is Professor of Political Science at Florida Atlantic University and coconvener of the Research Network on Gender Politics and the State. Professor McBride's research interests include women, politics, and policy in advanced industrial states. She is the author or coeditor of several books, including *Abortion: Public Policy in Comparative Perspective, Comparative State Feminism,* and *Women's Rights in the U.S.A.: Policy Debates and Gender Roles.*

Hilkka Pietilä is a Finnish freelance researcher and writer. She is the author or coauthor of eleven books on women and the United Nations, including *United Nations and the Advancement of Women* and *Making Women Matter.* She is the former Secretary General of the Finnish United Nations Association.

Tetyana Pudrovska is a Ph.D. student at the Department of Sociology, University of Wisconsin–Madison. She also has a graduate degree in linguistics from Kharkiv National University, Ukraine. Her current research interests include social demography, sociology of gender, aging, and the life course.

Margaret (Peg) Snyder is the founding director of the United Nations Development Fund for Women (UNIFEM) and was cofounder of the African Centre for Women at UNECA and member of the Committee to Organize Women's World Banking. She is currently Seminar Associate at Columbia University and adviser to the UN's intellectual history project.

Sarah Swider is currently a graduate student in the Department of Sociology at the University of Wisconsin–Madison. She received her master's degree from Cornell University in international and comparative industrial labor relations. Her work focuses on the sociology of development, gender, sociology of work, migrant issues, economic sociology, and East Asia.

Aili Mari Tripp is Associate Dean of International Studies, Director of the Women's Studies Research Center, and Professor of Political Science and Women's Studies at the University of Wisconsin–Madison. She is author of *Women and Politics in Uganda* (2000) and *Changing the Rules: The Politics of Liberalization and the Urban Informal Economy in Tanzania* (1997). She has edited *Women in Africa* (2003) and coedited *The Women's Movement in Uganda: History, Challenges and Prospects* (2002), as well as *What Went Right in Tanzania? People's Responses to Directed Development* (1996). She has also published numerous articles and book chapters on women and politics in Africa; women's responses to economic reform; and the political impact of transformations of associational life in Africa.

Nira Yuval-Davis is Professor of Gender and Ethnic Studies at the University of Greenwich, London, and Visiting Professor at the Department of Cultural Studies at the University of East London. Professor Yuval-Davis has written extensively on theoretical and empirical aspects of women, nationalism, racism, fundamentalism, and citizenship in Europe, Israel, and elsewhere. She is the author or coauthor of ten books, including *Gender and Nation*, which has been translated into six languages.

Index